Hildeb

Words have no wings,
but fly far.

Korean proverb

Publisher
K+G, KARTO+GRAFIK Verlagsgesellschaft mbH
© All rights reserved by
K+G, KARTO+GRAFIK Verlagsgesellschaft mbH
Schönberger Weg 15–17
6000 Frankfurt/Main 90
First Edition 1987
Second Edition 1988
Printed in West Germany
ISBN 3-88989-086-5

Distributed in the United Kingdom by
Harrap Columbus,
19–23 Ludgate Hill,
London EC4M 7PD
Tel: (01) 248 6444

Distributed in the United States by
HUNTER Publishing Inc.,
300 Raritan Center Parkway,
Edison, New Jersey 08818
Tel: (201) 225 1900

Authors
Dr. Dieter Rumpf, Dr. Peter Thiele

Photo Credits
Dr. Dieter Rumpf, Dr. Peter Thiele

Illustrations
Eckart Müller, Peter Rank, Manfred Rup

Maps
K+G, KARTO+GRAFIK Verlagsgesellschaft mbH

Translation
Katherine Inglis-Meyer, M.A.

Lithography
Haußmann-Repro, 6100 Darmstadt

Type Setting
LibroSatz, 6239 Kriftel

Printed by
Schwab Offset KG, 6452 Hainburg/Hess.

A modified McCune-Reischauer transcription is used throughout.

Hildebrand's Travel Guide

Impressions

Photographs p. 6
Travel Experiences and Reflections p. 52

Information

Land and People p. 81
Regions and Places of Interest p. 171
Useful Information p. 239
Contents p. 252

Supplement: Travel Map

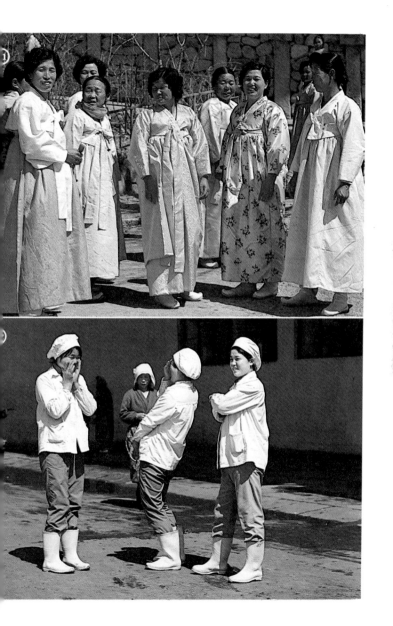

Captions

1. Cherry blossom before a traditional temple gateway.

2. Chahamun (Chaha Gate), the main entrance to the temple, Pulgŭk-sa in Kyŏngju.

3. Stone lantern in front of a subsidiary temple building, Kŭmsan-sa (Gold Mountain Temple) near Chŏnju.

4. Bongsan-sa (Mountain Spirit Temple), Buddhist temple near Seoul.

5. Great temple hall of Pŏpju-sa, Buddhist temple in the Songni (Sogni) National Park near Taejon.

6. Haein-sa, Buddhist temple in the Kaya Mountains. Three-storey pagoda built of stone in 808 A. D. (Silla Period) and the main half of the temple, the Taejokkwangjŏn.

7. The Gate of the King of Heaven in Pŏpju-sa, Buddhist temple near Taejon.

8. Kwanch'ok-sa, Buddhist "Temple of Candlelight" near Nonsan. Lower gate leading to the temple compound.

9. Pulguk-sa, Buddhist temple in Kyŏngju. Entrance to the temple precinct.

10. Kwanch'ok-sa near Nonsan. The 1,000-year old Unjin Miruk is the biggest stone statue of Buddha in Korea. It is built of several huge blocks of stone fitted together.

11. Votive offerings in the form of miniature Shakyamuni Buddhas in Bhumisparsa Mudra; at a Buddhist temple near Seoul.

12. Four guardians of heaven at the entrance to Kwanch'ok-sa, Buddhist temple near Nonsan.

13. Four guardians of heaven at the gate of Tongdo-sa, Buddhist temple near Pusan.

14. Dragon figure with a precious stone in its mouth guards the Yongamsa, the "Dragon Jewel Temple".

15. Statue of a bodhisattva in Kŭmsan-sa, the "Gold Mountain Temple" near Chonju.

16. Maitreya Buddha (Buddha of the Future) in the main hall, the Wontongpojon, of Naksan-sa, a Buddhist temple near Sokch'o.

17. Traditional funeral procession near Seoul. Note the light-coloured clothing traditionally worn by mourners and the decorated coffin on the bamboo stand.

18. Hill country between Taegu and the Buddhist temple, Haein-sa.

19. Landscape in early morning mist. Near Tongdo-sa, a temple northeast of Pusan.

20. Camellia in bloom.

21. Azalea blossoms.

22. Magnificent, flowering magnolia tree.

23. White ginseng (Panax ginseng), called "insam" (= human root) in Korean. Ginseng is valued – not only in Korea – for its curative and restorative properties. Export of ginseng has become an important factor in Korea's economy.

24. Dried, salted fish is sold "by the running metre" in the Chŏnju market.

25. The town of Cheju. View from the KAL Hotel.

26. Namdae-mun, Seoul's South Gate – National Treasure No. 1 with skyscrapers!

27. View over the town of Chŏnju. Houses here are built in the traditional style.

28. Busy shopping street in Seoul, near the Namdae-mun (South Gate).

29. Koreans in traditional, formal dress in front of Kyŏngbok Palace in Seoul.

30. Graduation Day at Seoul National University (SNU).

31. Group of women in traditional dress ("hanbok"), Suwŏn.

32. Young women in the fish market at Pusan harbour.

33. Little girl in festive costume, Suwŏn.

34. Korean girls in Seoul dressed in Western-style clothes.

35. Country girl from Cheju.

36. Little boy in traditional dress, Seoul.

37. Girls in national costume bring flowers to congratulate their elder sisters and brothers on graduating from SNU.

38. Little country boy on Cheju Island.

39. Little girl in kindergarten uniform, Seoul.

40. Fish market in Mokp'o; a Korean woman selling fresh fish.

41. In the Korean Folk Village in Suwŏn you can watch brushwood being treated.

42. Women weeding the grass in the grounds of the National Museum in Kyŏngju.

43. A ginseng seller at the Namdae-mun (South Gate) market in Seoul.

44. Fortune teller at the Korean Folk Village in Suwŏn.

45. A diver from Cheju Island selling fresh shellfish and other seafoods at Sogwipŏ.

46. Market stall with seafoods and spices in the town of Cheju.

47. Group of schoolboys in uniform in front of a burial mound in the Kyŏngju Tumuli Park.

48. Folk dance group in the Korean Folk Village, Suwŏn.

49. Hahoe, an old village on the River Naktong near Andong.

50. Island scene in the Hallyosudo (Hallyo Strait) National Park, southwest of Pusan.

The Olympic Games –
Small Country with Big Plans

Youm Bo-hyum accepted the Olympic flag with a smile. The last competitions of the Los Angeles games completed, the Lord Mayor of Seoul had stepped into the bright lights of the Olympic arena. Now it was his turn. The games of the 23rd Olympiad were over, and the stage was set for the 24th Olympic Games of the modern era, to be held in Seoul, South Korea.

When the Olympic flag was handed over in Los Angeles on 12th August, 1984, six Korean children presented American children, their "hosts", with gifts – the custom in Korea. The colourful dance troupe of the city of Seoul contributed an enchanting fan dance to the festivities. This marked the end of the ceremonial takeover. Since then, all eyes have been turned towards Seoul.

The decision to stage the 24th Olympic Games in Seoul was made by the International Olympic Committee back in 1981. Even before 1981 the Koreans had started planning a new sports compound for the capital, with a view to holding the 1986 Asian Games there. Now they have realized these plans relatively quickly. The Olympic stadium, which can hold 100,000 spectators, was erected at breathtaking speed and inaugurated in a pompous gala in September, 1984.

Situated in the southeast of the city, near the River Han, it takes just 30 minutes by subway from the city centre (Seoul City Hall) to reach the Sports Complex, the subway station serving the Olympic arenas. Connections to the Olympic grounds are so well organized, and are on such a gigantic scale, that 180,000 people per hour can come and go by public transport.

The huge oval of the main stadium is furnished with 75,000 green, yellow, blue and orange permanent seats. The brown railings have no sharp edges where the visitor could hurt himself in the hustle and bustle of such a huge crowd.

Everywhere one has the feeling that ergonomics experts, colour psychologists and computer scientists have collaborated in designing a stadium in accordance with the latest scientific findings.

As well as the main stadium (which covers an area of 132,000 sq. metres and has a total of 52 entrances) there is a stadium for athletics, an indoor swimming pool, and three other arenas. Moreover, there are administrative buildings, several car parks, and various supply and catering facilities in the Olympic Complex.

All the sports facilities are fitted out with the latest electronic equipment. Computerised scoreboards can show competition results in a matter of seconds in neon lettering. The overhead lighting with its 784 metallic halide lamps provides a steady and ideal light for TV broadcasting. Word processors for characters of Chinese origin and Korea's own "han'gŭl" signs can convert the script into Latin letters as quick as lightning. Electronically-controlled measuring instruments will ensure accuracy of up to 1/1,000th of a second at the games. It is simply overwhelming to see all this modern technical apparatus. The computerization of the modern Olympic Games continues in Seoul. What would the ancient Greeks have said to all this? Or even the "modern" Olympic champions of 1896?

Just 3.5 km (2 miles) east of the Seoul Sports Complex, the National Sports Complex (the "Olympic Park") is gradually taking shape. It will have a cycling track, swimming pool, facilities for fencing, weight-lifting and gymnastics. As in the Berlin Olympic Stadium of 1936, a sports college is being built here too. Also part of the National Sports Complex, the Olympic Village will provide accommodation for 12,000 participants, as well as for the 11,000 journalists who are expected and who will thus be able to enjoy closer contact with the Olympic competitors.

In Korea, every effort is being made to live up to the motto of the next Olympic Games: "Harmony, Peace and Progress". A supporting programme of more than fifty cultural and artistic events is being prepared. Over twenty displays of folk dance, concerts of traditional court music, and masked dance dramas will accompany the Games. The foreign visitor is sure to get a lasting impression of Korean culture, music and dance that he can take home with him. As the Games fall in the time of harvest thanksgiving and the full moon, there will be special celebrations for the famous Ch'usok festival which is traditionally held on the 15th day of the 8th lunar month. On this day, offerings of food are made to ancestors, an archery competition takes place, and, in the mountains, people watch the moon rising. This is a day when Koreans don their colourful, traditional dress as a matter of course.

For the foreign visitor, this might mean the chance of being invited to a festive meal of rice cakes, sojo and sweetmeats. One thing is sure, Hodori the tiger, official mascot of the Games, will welcome guests from all over the world.   (Thiele)

**Divided country –
Multiple suffering**
It all began when disastrous flooding in September 1984 devastated large areas of South Korea. North Korea sent the South an offer of help and this was accepted by Seoul, probably to the great astonishment of the North. Shortly afterwards, columns of North Korean lorries moved southwards, crossing the border at the 38th parallel for the first time in 40 years. At the same time, freighters unloaded cement at the port of Inch'ŏn, west of Seoul. Six weeks later, delegates from North and South Korea met for preliminary talks in P'anmunjŏm, the truce village in the demilitarized zone (DMZ). Seoul had not really needed North Korean aid, it was stressed later, but

Five Rings for the Tiger

His name is Hodori; he has a friendly smile and bristling whiskers; and he wears a "sang mo", a traditional black Korean hat, at a cheeky angle on his head. Hodori is a tiger, a cuddly Korean tiger cub. He was chosen as mascot for the 1988 Olympic Games out of thousands of designs. In 58 variations, this dancing tiger will spread cheerfulness, and even a touch of cosmopolitanism, into homes all round the world – thanks to television. In all the Olympic disciplines, be it football, tennis, wrestling, weight-lifting, cycling or swimming, Hodori will smile playfully when the champions are presented with medals or new records set up! The actual competitors and organizers probably won't feel quite so relaxed!

But Hodori will not only act as a mascot for the 23 disciplines of the 24th Olympic Games. He will also act as representative of Korean folklore seven times, and will twirl the ribbon of his hat into a number or a letter nineteen times. His other nine appearances will be to publicize the Olympic Games in advance.

As well as Hodori the Korean tiger, there is another official, more serious emblem which was chosen to represent the Seoul Olympics. It is taken from the ancient Korean decorative motif, "taeguk", the three colours of which symbolized heaven, earth and humanity. For the Olympics this has been modified to signify harmony, peace and progress.

Professor Yang Seung, who designed this emblem for the Games, wanted to give visual expression to the modern slogan: "The world comes to Seoul; Seoul goes out to the world" through the medium of this traditional, symbolic motif.   *(Rumpf)*

had accepted it for tactical reasons: South Korea wanted to resume contact with North Korea. The plan had worked.

Since then things have begun to move a little in the rigid fronts between the estranged brother countries. In the forty years since partition there have never been talks on so many different levels. On the list of priorities is a trade agreement and the creation of a committee for economic co-operation, as well as the re-establishment of a railway connection and the opening of two ports on each side of the border for domestic trade between the two Koreas.

On the other side of the 38th parallel, in the North, people even started worrying about how to prevent an East bloc boycott of the Olympic Games in Seoul. The North Korean vice premier, Chong Jun-gi, came up with an extraordinary suggestion to save the Games – North and South Korea should both be hosts to the 1988 Games. For, if the North Korean capital, P'yong'yang, were the second host, then the participation of those countries for whom the Olympic Games in Seoul alone would be a thorn in the flesh could also be ensured. Seoul, however, reacted with irritation and annoyance to this offer of help.

The idea of partnership is new to the two nations. In 1972, when Red Cross delegations from North and South Korea met for the first time to discuss the subject of reuniting families, there was still deep distrust on both sides. Quite justifiably so, as it turned out, for the Communist brothers in the north had made use of the apparent thaw in relations to dig more tunnels into South Korea under the demarcation line.

Events in Burma in 1983 did not further the cause either. During an official visit to Burma of a South Korean government delegation, North Korean agents ignited a bomb at the Martyrs' Shrine, the shrine dedicated to Burma's national hero, Aung San, in Rangoon. Twenty-one people were killed in the attack, including four cabinet ministers and other members of the delegation, and all hopes of a swift reconciliation between the hostile brothers died. So it was quite amazing that people were prepared to sit down at the negotiating table only one year later. The results of the North-South dialogue, published a year later, were really dramatic: the first exchange of visits was to take place. Koreans, followed by a whole retinue of journalists and cultural groups, looked for relatives in the other half of the divided country, and embraced them in front of the TV cameras of the world.

Humanitarian questions were always high on Seoul's list of priorities when it came to negotiations. The brutal partition of the country had torn millions of families apart and brought immense suffering. It has not yet been possible to ease that suffering. In 1983, when South Korean television started a campaign to trace missing persons, 200,000 people phoned the television studios. It soon became clear just how emotionally-charged the issue was. In the end, 7,000 families could be re-united.

Times would seem to be favourable for a cautious rapprochement. At the 1988 Olympic Games South Korea wants to be admired as a country which has brought about an economic miracle, as a country that has managed to leap into the modern age of industry. It wants to follow Japan's example and achieve respectability by organizing the Games as perfectly as Japan did in 1964. And it wants to come to the fore as an economic power. Tokyo has become the yardstick for Seoul on this point too. Quarrels with the brothers in the North, even if they are only verbal ones, do not fit into this kind of scenario . . . .

It is now certain that the Olympic Games will not be hosted jointly by North and South. It is also certain that progress made so far on the path towards complete reconciliation could easily be reversed in a very short space of time. A first step has been made – after forty years in which no-one was allowed to write letters to, or even telephone, his relations in the other zone – but this is still no reason for euphoria.

(Rumpf)

Where is the King?

They ruled the Korean peninsula for 2,000 years. Some of them had to pay tribute to their powerful neighbour in the west, China; some of them ruled their kingdom wisely, absorbing cultural trends and innovations from abroad; others were set on military conquest, and ruled with an iron hand. Paekche, Koguryŏ, Ancient Shilla, Unified Shilla, Koryŏ and finally Yi (or Choson) – those were the names of the kingdoms and dynasties that left their mark on the peninsula.

It was King Kojong, the 27th ruler of the Yi dynasty, who tried in vain to check the decline of the monarchy by proclaiming himself Emperor of Taehan in 1897. Only 8 years later he abdicated in favour of his son, Sunjong, who remained king by the grace of the Japanese for another 5 years. Then, in 1910, came the absolute end of the Korean monarchy: Korea was annexed to Japan.

But, if you happen to meet a slim, bespectacled, elderly gentleman in Seoul, and if he just happens to have studied architecture in America, it might be Prince Kyu Lee. He would have been the 29th King of Korea if his uncle, King Sunjong, had not succumbed to the superior force of the Japanese. Kyu Lee was born and brought up in Japan, but left in 1950 to go to America to study. His wife is American and he has an American passport.

Fate did not always treat the descendants of the last Korean kings very graciously. In 1970 Crown Prince Yi Un, the father of Kyu Lee and the younger half-brother of the last King Sunjong, died. He had always liked being photographed in the uniform of commander-in-chief of the army, although he looked a little effeminate and wore glasses. He was not allowed to return officially to Korea with his Japanese

Crown Prince Yi Un

wife and his son, Kyu Lee, until seven years before his death. Shortly before he died he was taken to the villa of "Joy and Kindness" (Nakson-jae), an annexe of Ch'angdok Palace, where the dynastic history of Korea had ended a few decades before.

The 84-year-old Princess Yi Pangja, who has described the fate of the Korean Royal Family in her autobiography "The World is One", still lives in this villa. She was born in Japan, and, before her marriage to Yi Un, was considered a possible match for the Crown Prince of Japan. She was involved in the education of handicapped children well on into her old age, and in 1971 was distinguished for her services in this field by the Korean government.

Princess Tokhye too found a peaceful refuge in the palace of "Joy and Kindness", where she spent the last years of her life. She was born in 1912 and, as the daughter of King Kojong's seventh wife, is the only living child of a Korean king. At the end of the twenties she was married to a Japanese aristocrat; the daughter of this marriage died in the period of confusion at the end of World War II.

2,000 years of royal history finally came to an end in 1910. If, as you walk through modern Seoul, you chance to meet a slim, bespectacled, elderly gentleman who studied architecture in America, you might be looking at the 29th King of Korea – if history had taken a different turn...

(Rumpf)

Seoul – Young Moloch with an Ancient Face

This is a city you can smell. It is not like many other metropolises which are enveloped in the standard smell of anonymity and have nothing individual about them. You may not be able to smell Seoul immediately at Kimpo Airport, for the latter has been built far outside the city, in the middle of rather uninteresting scenery. Perhaps not even when you are driving along the four-lane highway that runs along the River Han, following it like a faithful dog, and gradually approach the still distant silhouette of the city. But after about 15 kilometres, you will cross one of the many bridges over the Han (the

"Korean Rhine") and find yourself on the north bank. Here, the first hoardings with Korea's curious, graphic "han'gŭl" script appear, hesitatingly at first, then bigger and bigger, more and more obtrusive. You will get off the bus, and then, for the first time, your sense of smell will be aroused. It will take a while before you know what the smell is if this is your first visit to the country; old Korea hands recognize it more quickly.

The smell is garlic. And it permeates the whole city. In restaurants, of course, where it is an ingredient of almost every Korean dish. There you are served marinated cloves of garlic in little bowls which the inexperienced and unsuspecting tourist takes a good bite of. But you can smell garlic in the cinema too, and even in the theatre where it has to compete for the leading role with expensive perfumes. You notice it in parks too, because many men meet there. But it is quite astonishing that you also smell it in places where there are no people – the smell seems to have become entrenched even in the smooth facades of buildings. But one thing is very important: garlic is to the Korean what pasta is to the Italian – till death do them part. Garlic and the Koreans' love of it thus form one of those traditional, old lines on the seemingly modern face of Seoul, lines which have not been camouflaged with up-to-date make-up. The city is a young moloch with 10 million people and an ancient face. Unlike many Asian cities, Seoul has not become uniform; garlic is an aspect of its independence and individuality.

However, there is something else about this city: it is grey. The colour grey and garlic are equally important aspects of Seoul. The mountains with their sparse growth are grey; like fierce guardians they stand over the town threateningly, especially in the north, sending their heralds right into the centre of the city in the form of more gentle hills. These hills divide Seoul, the modern parts too, into districts that crawl higher and higher up the wooded slopes as they run out of space down below. A pointed needle in the shape of a TV tower has been planted on top of one of them, Namsan (South Mountain). From here you have a wonderful panorama, it is true, but you are not allowed to photograph it for the family album. The reason for this temporary, but compulsory abstinence from photography is that the Korean Secret Service, which has the reputation of being a rather ruthless security organization, has built its headquarters on one side of the hill.

Only in the south of the city, on the other side of the River Han, is Seoul flat and open. Here, the city can breathe and stretch, and it is here that typical satellite towns have been built, towns with high-rise flats that are the dream of many Koreans. These blocks, which are often like grey, concrete silos, are not characterized by any particularly imaginative style of building. But what is unusual about them is that the unlucky number 4 does not appear as a house number. Indeed, the fourth floor never seems to exist in Korea, not even in luxury hotels.

Here in the south of the city Korean industriousness has also conjured up the modern Olympic Complex from nowhere. It includes a stadium for 100,000 people, the shape and colours of which are supposed to echo those of ancient porcelain.

But the roofs and walls of the small traditional houses are grey. They huddle together like frightened children below the menacing skyscrapers that reach into the greyish-blue sky and seem to rob the little ones of air to breathe. The old houses spread their wide curved roofs like wings, as if they could take off at any moment and fly right back into the past – taking with them the old men living inside, whose clothes are mainly grey too, with the trousers fastened at the ankle.

Yet this grey is not boring, and it is certainly not unattractive. It is rather a deliberately-chosen contrast to the yellow of the forsythia, the pink of the azaleas, and the green of the trees that are planted in the tiniest free spaces: it reveals a fine sense of colour.

Garlic and grey – those are my first associations when I think of Seoul. They help to make this huge city unmistakable, typically Korean in fact, not anonymous and nondescript.

These age-old qualities defy, as it were, all the modern things that Seoul has to offer. Everyone is obviously very proud of the latter, however, since Seoul can now compete with Tokyo: the highest building in East Asia with more than 60 floors, higher even than Namsan; an underground railway (since 1974) below raised highways where rush-hour traffic looks into the third-floor windows of apartment blocks; nightclubs such as "Walker Hill" where revue girls are generous with their charms; and extensive public parks, where a children's paradise has been created in the playgrounds. Many a new housing development reminds the visitor of Manhattan, although the flats stand on ground once ruled by the precepts of Confucius.

Traditional and modern rub shoulders in Seoul, and yet the one does not exclude the other – even though the metropolis is bursting at the seams. 150,000 people lived here at the end of the last century; in 1950 the population was already 500,000; and in a few years time it will be 12 or even 14 million. Hardly imaginable? For Koreans, a matter of course, and not at all claustrophobic.

But one thing modern Seoul definitely is <u>not</u> is a symbol of the "Land of Morning Calm", a symbol that ingenious advertisers use enthusiastically to "sell" Korea. The "Morning Calm" has been lost in the din of the traffic, crushed by crowds of people, disfigured by billboards. You have to look around very carefully in certain districts to catch a glimpse of what it must have been like before 1910, when the rulers of the Yi dynasty were in power and still propagating the teachings of Confucius. You can still find such districts (it is better to take a Korean along with you as a guide), places where the street is a workshop for many people: there are markets where broad-faced country women with shrewd smiles that make their eyes disappear almost completely offer everything for sale that the Korean soil and sea produce; there are snack bars where housewives who always seem to be in a hurry can enjoy some indefinable dish – no doubt there'll be garlic in it anyway! In houses edging the street there are innumerable shops selling good quality silk, and not just the usual grey: no, brilliant colours predominate, and harmonize with the lively scene around.

But near here you also encounter the admittedly brief history of the city (Seoul bore the royal crown for only five centuries, whereas in other parts of the peninsula mighty potentates paid tribute to China 1,400 years earlier). Here stands one of the original nine city gates, and although it is much smaller, it looks more powerful than the high buildings that surround it. Just as if it were aware of how important it was under the Yi kings: a symbol of the power of those who resided behind the 16-kilometre-long town wall encompassing the square city, a symbol of their strength in face of enemies. The East and South Gates (Namdae-mun and Tongdae-mun) are especially popular as motifs for photographs when visitors do a tour of the city. Sadly, the endless flow of traffic around these historical monuments prevents a close inspection of the gates and the Taoist symbols of "ŭm" and "yang" which can still be found on them. But the clay animals led by a monk that protected the city from all evil spirits for five centuries still ride on the curved roofs.

In those days Seoul had a different name: Hanyang. This village on the north bank of the Han was to rise to the status of capital of the Yi dynasty. Taejo, the founder of the dynasty, actually wanted to build his palace in 1392 near the present-day town of Taejon, at the foot of the Kyeryong Mountains, but the famous priest Muhak, a convinced geomancer, suggested Hanyang, which already looked back on 1,300 years of eventful history. Taejo named the new centre of government Hanyang. The name Seoul probably came from the old Shilla word for capital, "sorabul"; it could not be written in Chinese characters. The town wall was built, the nine

gates (five remain), proud palaces . . . .
In 1910 a new name was forced on the royal city: the Japanese occupiers called the capital of their colony Keijo. After 1945, and especially after the end of the Korean War in 1953, the city rose again as Seoul, like a phoenix from the ashes.

Only a few steps away from the big luxury hotels in the town centre stands Tŏksu Palace. It was in the throne room at Tŏksu that the King used to demonstrate the splendour of the Korean Court to foreign ambassadors. That aspect of Korea is now historical, but it comes alive again in the National Museum.

The museum's architecture is an odd mixture of traditional and modern building styles. Inside, you can admire 5,000 years of the finest Korean art, from the celadons of the Koryŏ Period to the world-famous Maitreya Buddha who sits half cross-legged, his head resting on the fingertips of his right hand and his elbow resting on his raised knee, staring meditatively – almost a little sceptically – at the ground. Outside, in front of the museum, the halls and pavilions of Kyŏngbok Palace spread out against a background of skyscrapers: an island of peace in the midst of a bustling city, a city that now makes it clear that she is essential to East Asia.

Then there is Changdŏk Palace with its "Secret Gardens" which haven't been such a secret for a few years now. You have to like military drill if you want to visit this palace, which was destroyed in 1592 and rebuilt in 1611. The "drill" begins at the entrance gate, the Tonhwamun.

The times of the guided tours (conducted in Korean, Japanese and English) are written there on boards, and stewards make sure they begin on the dot! Nobody is allowed into the grounds without a guide – yellow cap, flag in hand, orders barked into the megaphone. You have to follow along obediently behind the guide for a whole hour, through halls, pavilions and residential quarters (King Sojong was the last to enjoy the good life here, back in 1867). Then, at last, you enter the "Secret Gardens" at an easy marching pace, where the strict guide allows you a 15-minute rest by the pond. Then it's up and away again; the only thing that is missing is a whistle! Yes, this is also Seoul.

Ultramodern things that harmonize with traditional ones (if possible, all painted grey and smelling of garlic!) – this capital of Korea is an original mixture, as individual as the Koreans themselves. Visitors from the West often like it for one particular reason: everything is impeccably clean. And you do not always need to march – left, right, left, right. Thank goodness! That would spoil this otherwise so likeable city.

(Rumpf)

Kyŏngju –
The Pearl Still Shines

In 1979 Kyŏngju was listed by UNESCO as one of the ten most important places of cultural interest in the world. Since then the town has worn this distinction like a medal, a medal which she polishes every day till it shines. For, if the whole of Korea is clean, Kyŏngju is immaculate. Even cigarette ends are not allowed to lie around long in this "museum without walls" – in Kyŏngju, Korea proudly admires the reflection of its own great history. People have become so attached to this history that even new buildings (with the exception of luxury hotels such as Kolon, Kyŏngju Tokyu or Kyŏngju Chosun) must now be built in traditional style. Kyŏngju has not always been treated with such circumspection.

Visitors to Kyŏngju come by motorway, either from Pusan in the south or from Taegu which lies west of Kyŏngju. It takes about two hours by car from Pusan, one from Taegu. This gives you time to get into the right mood for this great cultural experience, heralded by the statue of a rider in Shillan style which stands right beside the toll gates on the motorway. But where are the town and all the sights?

According to the statistics, 120,000 people live in Kyŏngju, in the valley where rulers of the Kingdom of Shilla built splendid memorials to Buddhism, their new religion, and monuments of immortality to themselves in the form of majestic tumuli. There is no sign at all of burial mounds or temples, however,

61

if you drive straight from the motor-way to the luxury hotels. You look in vain too for a city with 120,000 inhabitants; they cannot possibly all live in the few small houses that make up the so-called centre of Kyŏngju. It becomes clear now, if not before, that you will have a long way to drive if you want to visit the sights.

For a long period, history was at home in this sunny valley surround-ed by the five mythical mountains which were supposed to protect Kyŏngju from all foreign aggression. This hoped-for protection was not always enough. Still, for about a thousand years, from 57 B.C. to 935 A.D., the valley was the capital of a kingdom whose fame reached as far as distant China. In the days of the Shillan rulers, Kyŏngju was called Sorabul, which means capital; almost a million people are said to have lived here in its heyday. Ara-bian merchants came and brought science and learning with them. Some people say that there was a community of Nestorian Christians from China in Kyŏngju. Art in the form of painting, jewellery, pottery and sculpture matched progress in mathematics, astronomy and techni-cal sciences. Glazed roof and wall tiles ornamented with talismans decorated the houses of the nobility. The whole of Sorabul shone with a splendour that was in fact essentially an imitation of the Tang style in China. Certain groups from this dynasty had helped the founders of the second Shilla Kingdom to power and had made sure they stayed there, their militay intervention being tempered by their cultural influence, however.

This splendour perished as a result of corruption and conflicts within the aristocracy. The Koryŏ Kingdom rose from the ruins of Shilla (918), and seventeen years later the last Shillan king abdicated. Songdo (Kaesong) became the new capital, while Kyŏngju declined to the status of a small country town, preserving, however, its dreams of past glory – in spite of all the plun-dering by Japanese, Mongolian and Manchurian invaders.

But the dreams were disturbed some fifty years ago. Japanese schol-ars were the first to come, followed by others who probed Kyŏngju's ancient mysteries with modern tech-nological aids. Burial mounds were excavated, temples restored, and treasures removed to the new Na-tional Museum (built in 1975). Tour-ism started to develop around 1965 and it is now everyone's main con-cern. Kyŏngju's days of dreaming are well and truly over. In the luxury hotels, a Philippine singer serves up American pop songs to accompany juicy steaks; buses swarm like ants along the new roads, taking hurry-ing tourists from highlight to high-light; hordes of schoolchildren fool around in front of 1,500-year-old monuments with an irreverence that is quite restful. Kyŏngju is definitely an important place again – in foot-ball too... the local eleven is said to be not bad at all!

The kings, princesses and gener-als who have been lying in their tombs under earth and stones for more than a thousand years, surrounded by magnificent gifts, presumably had quite different plans for their Sorabul. At a time when, in distant Europe, Rome was in its death throes, perhaps they dreamed of a great East Asian Empire. They certainly saw themselves as defenders of the Buddhist faith, the religion that Chinese and Indian missionaries had brought over the borders of a kingdom which was soon to stretch to P'yŏng'yang and Wonsan in present-day North Korea. And no doubt they puzzled over which form their reincarnation would take.

*Ornamental gold
crown (Paekche, 6th century)*

But they probably did not give much thought to the mass of peasants and workers in their service, people who enjoyed no rights at all but who created a wealth of precious objects for the nobility. Slavery and serfdom carved ugly lines on the face of Kyŏngju. The people were not even allowed to retain their own names. The thousands of Kims and Kangs, Lees and Paks to be found in telephone directories today – along with a few hundred other family names and no more – bear witness to this uglier aspect of Kyŏngju's history. These names are in no way comparable with Smith or Jones: they are the names of powerful families, names that were forced upon the serfs of these families – the only "gift" these underprivileged people ever received from their masters.

The unpaid labour of peasants and craftsmen was transformed into the gold of Shilla. It filled the tombs, and today it is displayed in the museums: crowns and belts, dangling earrings and magnificent necklaces. These items bear witness to the great cultural achievements of the period, as do objects to be found outside the museums.

There is the "Place near the Stars", as Ch'omsongdae, the astronomical observatory was called. Built of stone, it is almost ten metres (thirty feet) high and is the oldest observatory in East Asia. There is Pulguk-sa, a temple full of legends, where marble bridges and stone pagodas form a fascinating contrast to the wooden temple buildings. There is the Sŏkkuram Grotto, where the rosy light of dawn used to raise the granite Buddha from the "Region of Passions" to the "Region of Pure Forms"; and the pagoda of Punhwang-sa, built of stone hewn to look like bricks. And there is the pond of Anapji, where the last Shillan king sealed the fate of his dynasty.

But nowadays it is from a much bigger lake, from the luxury hotels of the Pomun Lake Resort northeast of Kyŏngju city, that tourists from all over the world start out on their excursions into one of the most exciting chapters of Korean history. The glory that was Kyŏngju has not died.   *(Rumpf)*

Race to the
Buddha in the Grotto

I seem to remember that everything was different before, about a decade ago, and better. At 5 a.m., when it was still dark outside, the telephone would ring in the hotel room, and shortly afterwards tea or coffee would be served in the empty lobby – the hotel had not yet awakened, and there were only a few people around, their faces showing signs of weariness after a long night shift. After this simple breakfast, the group would board the cold bus, and no one would be offended if the driver yawned a little. The engine always sounded far too loud in the stillness as it started off into the darkness.

As the bus laboriously wound its way up Mount Toham, the black night sky would gradually pale. Everyone looked out of the windows in suspense, for the drive had now become a race against the dawn. With the brightening of the sky, with every disappearance of a star, we would wish anxiously that we were already at our destination.

Then – at last! – the whole tour group could sprint away from the car park. It was a question of minutes. To everyone the path through the woods to the cave, the goal of this early morning keep-fit exercise, seemed endless.

But we always arrived in time. As the sun rose over the distant sea in the east, sending its first rays from Japan to awaken the Korean peninsula, it bathed the white, granite Buddha in the grotto in a rosy light, transfiguring the tall stone statue into a being from another sphere.

That must have been the intention of the man who built the grotto, moreover. A minister of state in the Shilla Kingdom, he designed both grotto and Buddha as an everlasting memorial to his parents. From the earthly region of the passions ("kamadhatu") the Buddha rises, wrapped in the rays of the rising sun, to the higher region of the pure spheres of heaven ("rupadhatu"). This beautiful sight always compensated for the early morning exertion and the rumbling stomach.

From yesterday to today.... The group now has an elaborate breakfast – another apple here, a delicate Danish pastry there. Everyone, including the bus driver, is wide awake and in a good mood as our bus gradually climbs Mount Toham, under no pressure of time. It does not matter whether we arrive early or late. The distance from the car park to the grotto seems very short, for we stroll along in the shadow of the trees hardly noticing the sun which is already high in the sky.

Of course the Buddha in Sokkuram Grotto is no longer wrapped in that rosy veil of morning light which made him so mysterious, almost supernatural. The rays of the sun rising over the sea are no longer caught in the holy sign on his forehead: whereas the golden "urna", the curl between Buddha's eyebrows, used to glow in the morning light, the lighting in the grotto today only brings a weak gleam. In order to protect them from tourists, the Buddha and the grotto have been violated. For Korean art experts it must have become very important to protect both of them a few years ago: the grotto was cut off from visitors by a glass wall. Photography forbidden.

Without doubt, it is now much easier to visit Sŏkkuram Grotto on Mount Toham near Kyŏngju. But there's also no doubt that the atmosphere of the place has been destroyed. The real attraction has gone....

All over the Buddhist world, from India's Gandhara and along the Silk Road to the Far East, believers built cave temples again and again. For two basic principles of Buddhist architecture – mountain and cave – could be realized in such creations. The mountain symbolizes the image and axis of the cosmos, pointing upwards to the highest of all cosmic regions, the realm of no form ("arupadhatu"); the cave, on the other hand, is seen as an image of the womb, out of which the two regions of forms develop. In cave temples, therefore, the essential elements of Buddhist cosmology could be expressed visually, in an architectural metaphor.

The Koreans, however, had problems with caves. Their homeland did not exactly abound in caves suitable for such a purpose and, in any case, the Koreans themselves preferred to build with wood. And so they created the magnificent artificial grotto of Sokkuram, the goal of inumerable races against the rising sun – until the recent alterations, that is.

Kim Taesong must have been a fascinating person. The son of poor peasants in the village of Moryang (west of Kyŏngju), he lived during the reign of the 35th Shillan king, Kyŏngdok. After the death of his father, the boy – who had an unusually big head and a broad, flat forehead ("taesong" means "great castle") – stayed at home with his mother. A pious Buddhist, he died young, but was to be reborn as the child of the Prime Minister, Kim Mun-yang. This was announced by a mysterious voice from heaven. When he was born again, his (new) parents discovered the golden character for "taesong" on the palm of his hand.

In honour of his first parents, Kim Taesong later had the famous Buddhist temple, Pulguk-sa, built at Kyŏngju. It was to his second parents that he dedicated Sŏkkuram Grotto.

If we stay in the realm of legend, we learn that at this time (around the middle of the 8th century) five sacred peaks were supposed to protect the splendid capital, Kyŏngju. Mount Toham was one of these, and that is why Kim chose it for his temple grotto. The mouth of the cave and the Buddha on his throne within faced east – towards Japan. But twice this failed to protect Korea.

During the Yi dynasty, when Neo-Confucianism gained ground, the grotto gradually fell into decay, and it was not rediscovered and restored until a few decades ago. The glass wall and air conditioning are part of this restoration.

Without reservation, the 3.5 m (11 ft)-high granite Buddha in the lotus position ("padma asana"), a representation of Amitabha, is one of the loveliest creations of Mahayana Buddhism. Korean tradition combined here harmoniously with Chinese art of the T'ang period: the figure remained massive, earth-bound, and yet seemed to rise above all earthly constraints. The Buddha's right hand is touching the earth as a sign of his victory over passion in the mirror of Mara, the Tempter.

Amitabha sits on his throne in a rotunda which opens onto a square antechamber and a short corridor. Two octagonal pillars on lotus pedestals link the corridor with the round interior chamber which is built of precisely-hewn granite blocks.

There are rows of beautiful reliefs. Buddhist saints and finally the ten Great Disciples follow the ancient Indian gods, Indra and Brahma, carved out of stone near the entrance. In arched niches little bodhisattva statues symbolize the attendants of Buddha, who sits on a lotus throne in the middle of the rotunda. Eight Generals guard the antechamber, while two half-naked gate guardians, fierce and powerful, are depicted in relief at the beginning of the passageway. Some scholars believe that they are in typical "taekwŏn-do" fighting postures. In the corridor itself the Four Deva Kings (Lokapala), Guardians of the World who rule the mystical world in every quarter, can be seen dressed in the magnificent armour of the T'ang period, crushing little demons under their dancing feet.

It doesn't really matter: even today, even without the special atmosphere at sunrise, even with the glass wall that prevents your entering the grotto and seeing many of the reliefs, the visit to Sŏkkuram Grotto on Mount Toham near Kyŏngju is still a highlight of a journey to the "Land of the Morning Calm". Even at midday, or even later . . . .   *(Rumpf)*

Butterflies in the Rice Field

A poet expressed it this way: when you travel through the Korean countryside, you see women in traditional clothes walking along the paths between the green rice fields. Their pastel-coloured dresses sway in the gentle breeze, and the women float like butterflies over the ground....

Very poetical, it's true. But the traditional clothing of Korean women does indeed inspire such images. "Hanbok" is the general name for traditional clothes, for men and women, and you can still see this style of dress today, even in the streets of the big cities. Of course, standardized European clothing predominates there now, and one sees everything from jeans to ties.... In the country, however, and especially at celebrations or festivals of any kind, it is "hanbok" that sets the tone.

And this has been the case for centuries. In the 13th century Chinese culture was highly favoured by the Koreans, as happened often in their history. Among other things, Chinese clothing was adopted, and this is where the blouse ("chogori") and skirt ("chima") of the Korean women, as well as the wide trousers ("paji") and shirt ("chogori") of the men came from. Nowadays a good combination of colours is considered important in traditional dress, whereas originally plain white was preferred. White was the colour of mourning and had to be worn for three years after the death of any member of the royal court. And since there were many deaths at court, especially during the Yi dynasty, the Koreans had to keep to this impractical white clothing. It was a good time for laundresses!

Women whose proportions no longer correspond exactly to ideal female measurements are very thankful for "chimachogori". The long wide skirt, which falls from the bust-line, covers up all physical shortcomings, while the long-sleeved blouse tied with a big bow gives the finishing touch. The men's wide trousers not only allow them to wear several pairs of underpants during the cold winter months, but also conceal bandy legs, which are not exactly rare here.

For men's dress, however, the hat was always especially important. The elegant version of the "kat" was made of woven horse-hair, and is now very popular as a souvenir for tourists. Everyday hats were made of woven bamboo. Moreover, the social status of the wearer could be deduced from the shape of his hat.

According to Confucian rules, only a married man was allowed to wear his hair in a top-knot under a hat. An unmarried man had to wear his hair hanging loose, and a hat was not set on his head till his wedding day, a kind of wedding ring as it were. Broad brims were meant to prevent the men from seeing the sky during a period of mourning.

In the villages today you can still see worthy old gentlemen in white or pale blue clothes called "turumagi" – jacket, trousers and wide coat. Their wispy, silvery beards show they are Confucian scholars.

Butterflies and Confucius for "chimachogori" and "turumagi" – this traditional form of dress known by the common name of "hanbok" adds an exotic splash of colour to the Korean experience, and it is to be hoped that this colour does not fade too soon. Even if the modern secretary in the big city does prefer tight-fitting jeans. *(Rumpf)*

Spring Breeze Serves Tea – Kisaeng: More Than Just Beauty

Hwang Chin-i came from Songdo, modern Kaesŏng, which was in those days the capital of the mighty Koryŏ dynasty. She was of noble birth, she was young and beautiful – and she was an exceptionally gifted poetess. The artistic expressiveness of her "sijo" poems surpassed even that of very famous poets. She had, therefore, all the prerequisites for a life of wealth and happiness. But Hwang Chin-i was a "kisaeng", a creature of pleasure for the nobility. The only difference between her and all the other kisaeng in the country was her aristocratic birth.

It was an unhappy love affair that led this lovely girl along the path to the position of kisaeng. The son of a neighbour had fallen in love with Hwang Chin-i, and had died of a broken heart far from home when he realized that his feelings were not reciprocated. As the funeral procession with the bier passed her house, the hearse stopped as if under a spell and could not be brought into motion again. Only then did Hwang Chin-i notice the funeral party. She spread her dress over the coffin, thus breaking the spell, but because she did this, she was considered the widow of the dead man, and her family could no longer arrange a marriage for her. And so Hwang Chin-i became a kisaeng.

She soon gained a reputation as a perfect calligraphist as well as a gifted poet. She was surrounded by admirers, some of whom became her lovers; it is said that there were Buddhist monks among them. She only seldom lost her heart to someone, but when she did, she remained devoted to him. At the end of her life Hwang Chin-i wanted her body to be laid out at the East Gate of Songdo and not buried, as a warning to all women. But her family would not respect this last wish, and when she died, they built a tomb at the side of the road leading to the East Gate. This last resting-place of Bright Moon, as Hwang Chin-i was called, soon became famous as a place of pilgrimage, frequented especially by unsuccessful poets. A kisaeng had become a saint...

You should also read the following tale so that you do not make a mistake if you happen to meet Miss Spring Breeze in Korea.

The girl lived in Chinju, in the south of Korea, and was called Non'gae. She was the kisaeng of the commander of the local garrison when the Japanese invaders descended on the country in 1592. Her patron was killed by the enemy swords. When the Japanese began to celebrate their victory with lots of women and strong drink, Non'gae went along with them. The victorious general too noticed how beautiful the young Korean girl was, and so he willingly followed her on a moonlit stroll to the river gorge. The moon was the only witness when Non'gae jumped to her death in the gorge, the drunken general clasped tightly in her arms. That was one general less in the Japanese army...

A shrine was built in honour of this kisaeng, and her patriotic deed is commemorated to this day.

There is also the story of Ch'un-p'ung from Pyŏngyang, which was the kisaeng capital at that time. Ch'un-p'ung means Spring Breeze and, according to an old legend, it was a Buddhist monk on a pilgrimage who gave life to this charming breeze – Ch'un-p'ung turned down even a minister of state.

So when you meet a kisaeng in Korea, remember that this profession was created for the pleasure of the aristocracy. The kisaeng had to be not just beautiful, but intelligent, too. But perhaps you belong to the large number of tourists who know about as much or as little about the kisaeng when they go home as they did when they arrived. That would be a pity, however, as an essential aspect of Korean culture, one which has a long history, would remain unexplored. It costs a great many won to find out about this aspect of culture, though, for a visit to a kisaeng house today is always expensive.

Traditionally, kisaeng came from the lower classes; someone of aristocratic birth like Hwang Chin-i was the exception. They were, however, the only women who were allowed to move freely between classes in traditional society – and they were the only women who had access to education. For, according to the precepts of the Chinese sage, Confucius (precepts which were strictly adhered to, especially in the Yi dynasty), education only poisoned a woman's soul. This meant that the female population of the Land of the Morning Calm was uneducated right up to the beginning of modern times. They were not even allowed to leave the house in the daylight, and there was always some man they had to obey: first their father, then their husband, and after the death of their husband, their son. Some satirists maintain that Korean men have managed to "preserve" some of this code up to the present day. But one thing Confucius and the other Korean lords of creation must have overlooked: the educated man needed an educated female partner to talk to at home, too. They could talk to their loved ones about many things, but not about those subjects that demanded education, insight and understanding. The educated kisaeng, to get back to our subject, were the only women who could serve this purpose. And this is why they were able to rise to such influential positions – as mistresses, it is true, not wives. It is said that many a royal ruler of Korea was the offspring of a kisaeng.

It's thought that the profession of kisaeng originated in the 6th century, during the period of the Three Kingdoms, though it did not then have the later cultural connotations. During the reign of the 24th Shillan king, Chinhŭng, there was a movement called "wonhwa" (the true flowers), where pretty young girls represented model Korean womanhood. Because of various disputes leading even to murder (not very exemplary conduct!) King Chinhŭng abolished the organization. In its

place "hwarang" (flower youth) was founded, a movement to educate young men for leading positions. This military, political, religious, social and cultural elite formed the backbone of the later "Unified Shilla". The word "kisaeng" is not documented in this period.

With one exception: Ch'ong-wang, the kisaeng of the famous General Kim Yu-shin who rose to become a war hero in the struggles leading up to the foundation of "Unified Shilla". It is presumed there was a son from this liaison.

There is no mention of the kisaeng in the historical documents of the Koryŏ period which was culturally so important, but the word appears several times in the annals of the Yi dynasty. This suggests that the kisaeng system was in fact known to, and thought highly of, by historians before the Yi period, who nevertheless passed over the phenomenon in silence out of a sense of false modesty perhaps. In the Yi dyansty, however, the whole business was institutionalized. Both a kisaeng's ability and her sphere of activity were clearly defined, and it was laid down by law whether she had to appear at the palace, and only at the palace, as a dancer and singer or as an acupuncturist. Moreover, kisaeng were not allowed to marry. It was not till the reign of Injo, the 16th King of the Yi dynasty, that the kisaeng were freed from this golden cage and allowed to stay in the homes of the "yangban", the nobility. At the same time the ban on marriage was lifted.

The kisaeng's training ("sojae") lasted three years, with the emphasis on writing poetry. Dancing, singing, acupuncture and etiquette were also taught. At the age of about 15 the great moment arrived when the "tonggi" (the young kisaeng) became a "full woman". At this ceremony the young girl was led by an older kisaeng to a carefully selected aristocrat to spend the night with him. Every kisaeng remained proud of this "man of the first night" for the rest of her life. For some of them, however, the ritual that took place when they were thirty must have been less pleasurable, for at that age the kisaeng was forced to retire. She became a "twegi" and had to seek other employment. The more fortunate kisaeng rose to become the concubines of noble masters.

Looking through historical sources, it appears that particular regions produced special abilities. The girls from the north, for example, were supposed to be more beautiful than those from the south; people still believe today that the ideal match is a man from the south and a woman from the north. Kangnŭng on the east coast was well-known for the lovely voices of its kisaeng; the best poetesses were said to come from the Andong area; and the girls from Cheju Island were famed for their riding skills. Uiju in the far north produced the best sword-dancers, whereas the best interpreters of all courtly dances came from Hamhung and Pyŏngyang.

The end of the Yi dynasty (and the simultaneous seizure of power by the Japanese) brought the long history of the Korean kisaeng to a close. The Japanese occupiers did actually try to keep the kisaeng system alive, but the only educated women of the Yi period who had been taught the courtly arts, an inherent part of Korean culture, were soon reduced to mere entertainers. This decline has continued unchecked.

Nevertheless, a visit to one of the kisaeng houses in Seoul, Kyŏngju or Pusan, while expensive, is still a great experience. The restaurants are built in the traditional style and divided into several small rooms with polished floors and underfloor heating. Shoes have to be removed before sitting on brightly embroidered cushions on the floor (perhaps a little uncomfortable!) at a table which groans under the weight of all the culinary delicacies of Korea. While young girls perform ancient dances, others dressed in traditional silk costumes kneel devotedly beside the guest, anticipating his every wish for food and drink. Many a mature gentleman feels transported back to the period of early childhood, without forgetting that a kisaeng's duties are not limited to just feeding him.

But not all the traditional rules that were laid down in the Yi dynasty are adhered to strictly today. There are several kisaeng, for example, who are well over thirty.

(Rumpf)

Pusan – Window to Japan

I must admit I like this city. It is true that it is neither particularly beautiful nor very interesting from an historical point of view. It is an economic giant and a cultural dwarf. It is Korea's second biggest metropolis, but in many districts it is like a village. It looks back on a past that was not very impressive, and forward to a great future. And it is a port. This was not considered important in old Korea where they traditionally concentrated on the land. But when the Yi dynasty closed off its kingdom from the rest of the world, this city remained open, a window to Japan. It was the Japanese then who, from the end of the nineteenth century to 1945, laid the foundations for the present importance of Pusan.

The town now has almost 4 million inhabitants. It lies on the southeast tip of the Korean peninsula,

only 120 sea miles from Japan's main island, Honshu. (The locals say that on a clear day you can see Honshu with the naked eye as a fine line on the horizon.)

Its economic muscles hardened by industry, Pusan is expanding rapidly from year to year, and already frightens Seoul, the big sister in the north. The city symbolizes the Korea of the past few decades, the swift economic rise of a country which is getting ready to march in the front line of the industrial giants in East Asia.

The port has huge shipyards where already almost 20% of the world's production of ocean-going ships are welded and hammered – only in Japan is more gross tonnage launched than here. Ulsan and Inch'ŏn have now overtaken Pusan as far as imports are concerned; but the huge container port proves that exports are a different matter, and here Pusan has maintained its leading role.

In 1876 it was decreed in distant Seoul that Pusan should be opened as a Japanese trading post; in no time at all 2,000 Japanese tradesmen were convinced of the potential for financial success of the venture. In 1905, a good 25 years later, Japanese workers were sweating in the mild, southern climate as they built a railway line to carry the Tenno's soldiers as quickly as possible north to the battle line of the Tsarist troops. The decisive battle, however, was fought not far from Pusan, when the Russian fleet sank in the gunsmoke of the Japanese cannons off the island of Tsushima (1905).

And the Japanese Emperor stayed on in Pusan; in the following decades the Japanese built shipyards and modernized the eastern port which the island of Yong-do separates from the southern port. A 215 m (700 ft)-long drawbridge which has not been used for years was then considered a masterpiece of East Asian engineering; and it linked Pusan to this hilly, wooded island which obstructs the view of the town completely when you approach by sea.

The view from T'aejongdae Park on Yong-do Island out to sea is all the more beautiful: distant islets merge with the milky horizon, and, together with the cargo boats lying at anchor, form a delicate ink painting like those on ancient Chinese

scrolls. And the waves of the Sea of Japan break here against steep cliffs. King Muyŏl, the Shillan ruler, must have been fascinated by this scenery too, for he spent all his spare time here.

The mild climate and the small difference in tidal levels (only a metre) have made Pusan into the main Korean bathing resort. More than 8 million sun worshippers and water sports fans populate the sandy beaches of Haeundae and Songdo. Beautifully-bronzed Koreans are the delight of the luxury hotels which have profited in the last few years from this longing for the sea and the sun – and probably also from the fishermen chugging out for the night's fishing by torchlight, providing onlookers with a picturesque scene on a clear evening.

Let us return to the sights of the city itself: the hill near the town centre is called Yongdusan Park, and the city fathers have planted a television transmission tower, 120 m (nearly 400 ft) high, on top of it. Perhaps the shape of the hill does really look like a dragon's head, as the name "Yongdu" suggests. But it is Hong Kong you think of when you look down from the observation platform of the tower over the sea of houses around the harbour.

Right below the notice which says you may enjoy the view but on no account take photographs, the foreign tourist finds himself standing next to a Korean soldier. No matter how these two individuals may differ, they have one thing in common: the clicking of their cameras – with apologies to South Korea's Secret Service!

In the park below, however, the statue of the great naval hero, Admiral Yi Sun-shin, stands on guard. Yi Sun-shin was the man who rapped Japan rather painfully on its greedy knuckles almost 400 years ago, when he used his iron-clad ships against it in the waters off Pusan, interrupting the lines of supply of the invading army.

Nowadays, however, shopkeepers welcome the Japanese with open arms and are so obliging that they even write out the prices in "yen" instead of "won". And the bronze admiral does not even blink an eyelid. Perhaps he is hoping for help from the four-clawed dragon nearby who, in an almost playful manner, spouts fire in the direction of the aquarium at the foot of the TV tower. Classes of schoolchildren, who used to be dressed in standardized black uniforms that recalled old Prussia, sit on the edge of the terrace, doing what is obviously a "must" on Korean school outings: they are painting the whole scene on large sheets of paper.

It is, however, a strange fascination that emanates from the United Nations Cemetery. It was laid out in 1955 as a memorial to the clash of ideologies on the Korean peninsula. Here are the graves of 2,286 soldiers who fought under the United Nations flag in the savage civil war that lasted three years. Origi-

nally 11,000 dead from 16 nations lay here, but many have been transferred to their native countries in the last few years. More than 37,000 men from distant countries and continents, most of them young, lay down their lives in this war. It took an especially heavy toll of the Turkish soldiers who fought. The cemetery with its well-tended lawns and colourful flags fluttering against the clear blue sky, gives an illusion of sense to the inferno of war. At least the men who survived the war must have believed this when they stipulated in their wills that they wished to be buried here – some 35 years after the bloody struggle.

The Chagalch'i Fish Market, on a lighter note, proves to be more a battle of smells. Forget your nose, but not your camera! Along the docks serving the fishing fleet the struggle for shark, octopus, sardines, mussels and anything else that has been caught in the fishermen's nets breaks out daily, and lasts well into the afternoon. The clever housewife makes sure she gets there before the men who buy in bulk, for then she can be sure that the prices are still low.

Yes, and there actually are a few historical things in Pusan too, though on a rather small scale, of course, compared to the rest of Korea. There is Unsu Temple on the way to the airport; and Anjong Temple which guards the approach to Haeundae beach. But the old Shillan temple, Pomo-sa, not far from the entry to the Seoul-Pusan motorway, is of particular interest. Set in the midst of pine woods, this Buddhist temple is one of the three most famous temples in this southern province of Korea, the others being Haein-sa and the nearby Tongdo-sa. The famous monk, Wonhyo Taesa, is said to have meditated here once upon a time.

I discovered my liking for Pusan when I went for a stroll through Kwangbok-dong. This district, behind the fish market and separated from it only by a four-lane highway, is the pulsating heart of this great city. Garish posters advertise the latest celluloid products of film studios in Hong Kong and Hollywood; next to them is a billboard showing a man and a woman standing at attention to advertise some body-building institute. And it is here in Kwangbok-dong, in the narrow lanes with shops selling everything the average Korean might need, that you will find the teahouses. They are usually on the first floor and are accessible via a stairway.

For the price of a few "won" you find yourself in the middle of a circle of men whose conversation centres round Pusan and its world. Someone inevitably asks you if you like the city, with the suggestion that you could not possibly do otherwise. I can answer quite honestly that I do. *(Rumpf)*

The Admiral and the Turtle Ships

The man was as extraordinary as the ships he commanded. He rose to become the greatest naval hero of the end of the sixteenth century, and today, even in Europe, he is considered on a par with Nelson and Drake, the two great British admirals. He defeated the enemies of his country – and was himself demoted. When he died of a bullet wound, a shrine was erected in his honour, and in 1932 this shrine was renovated as a symbolic protest against Japanese occupation. He still stands in a commanding position in the middle of Seoul – as a bronze statue on a concrete pedestal, towering over the traffic for all to see, rather like a giant policeman ready to penalize severely every offender. Admiral Yi Sun-shin: if Korea ever had an outstanding strategist, then it was he.

A Japanese admiral must have realized this many years ago. He sank the Russian Tsarist fleet at the naval battle of Tsushima (1905) and, after his victory, his comment is said to have been, "You may compare me to Nelson, but never to the Korean Yi Sun-shin. He was brilliant!" And that is true. When Yi Sun-shin, after some great successes followed by a period in disgrace caused by factional intrigues at court, was asked to resume command of the Korean fleet, he only had twelve ships left at his disposal. With this remnant of a navy he defeated an armada of 133 Japanese ships, more than 30 of which sank. His great victory was recorded as having taken place on 16th September, 1597.

In the village of Asan, near the hot springs of Onyang about one and a half hour's drive from Seoul, stands the shrine of Hyŏngch'ung-sa which is dedicated to the great admiral. The monument is said to have been built about 1706, and there is now a little museum attached to it containing a replica of the type of ship that helped the admiral to his military triumphs. Renovation of the whole precinct was begun in 1932, sponsored by one of Korea's daily newspapers.

Yi Sun-shin was born in Seoul in 1545, but in fact grew up in Asan. He was not career-minded. Although he studied the writings of Confucius, he had no ambition for public office. However, he took up a military career when he was 31 year old, and soon rose from the ranks. Fifteen years later the Korean East Coast fleet was under his command.

In 1592, a year later, the bloody seven-year struggle with the invading Japanese army under Shogun Hideyoshi began. In the very first year of the war the Japanese army advanced far into what is now North Korea, for they had set their sights on the Chinese Empire. It seemed merely a matter of time till the victory of this army was assured as it burned and plundered its way north.

At this time Yi Sun-shin was developing an idea for a new type of ship that would make it possible for the Koreans to cut the Japanese lines of communication and supply, and so turn the war in their favour. His idea was to build iron-clad ships, turtle ships. And it was this idea that turned Yi into a hero; it's an idea that still inspires respect and awe 400 years on.

In secret harbours near Ch'ungmu, Yosu and on Namhae Island, Korean sailors were soon working hard on the new ships which were to stand up brilliantly to the test of their first action in the naval battle of Hansan. Only 14 out of 73 Japanese warships escaped the inferno caused by the turtle ships with their dragon prows and ramming irons in their bows. The next battle took place outside Pusan harbour, when 500 Japanese ships were sent into action with the aim of annihilating the Korean fleet. But instead, 130 Japanese ships were sunk and the rest fled home to their own harbours.

The success of the admiral's ships – which were, by the way, propelled by oarsmen – made the favourites at the Seoul Court feel insecure. Intrigues brought about the downfall of the upstart admiral – and robbed the navy of its leading tactician. However, this proved costly for the Yi rulers. When Yi Sun-shin was rehabilitated in 1597, there were only 12 ships of his great navy left. The rest had been destroyed by the Japanese.

But Yi was obviously a man who did not give up so easily. In the last great battle of the war the Koreans managed to sink more than 200 enemy ships, although the admiral on the bridge was already seriously wounded. The Tenno's soldiers at last retreated to their own islands for good.

Admiral Yi Sun-shin did not live long after this military victory. He died on the 19th November 1598, aged 53, from his fatal bullet wound and was buried on Kogum Island near his last base. Sixteen years later his mortal remains were removed to Hyŏng-ch'ung-sa near Asan (where he had grown up) by order of the highest authority. Nearby is the Yi family home, which is now also a museum, and the grave of his son who fell in the first year of the war against Japan. You can still see the ancient gingko tree below which the great admiral used to practise the art of archery.

His turtle ships, however, were never used again.   *(Rumpf)*

Cards are Trumps

I have met Mr. Kang once more. We have known each other for at least 15 years. When we met for the first time, Mr. Kang was a little tourist agent in the provinces, an insignificant cog in the great tourist machine. Now he is general manager of a large Korean tourist agency. Mr. Kang has made it.

But what I noticed about his rise to this managerial position was that he handed me a new visiting card every time he climbed a new step of the career ladder, even if it was a very small step. One side of his visiting card was printed in Roman letters, the other in "han'gul". Handing over the card with the new title and rank on it became a ritual, during which Mr. Kang insisted that I hand over a new card, too – unfortunately with no new title on it. As we have met often over the years, each of us now has a whole pile of the other's cards. Now, as general manager, Mr. Kang has even gone so far as to let me call him by his second personal name, thus breaking with the conventions of the society in which he grew up. And this after 15 years of sharing the ups and downs of tourism in Korea.

As far as visiting cards go, Mr. Kang is no exception: a visiting card is vital for the Korean businessman. With his card he tells the outsider what rank and influence he has; and he will want to know the same things about his partner. Therefore, under no circumstances should you forget your visiting cards when you go to Korea! Make sure your most important title is printed below your name. "Manager", for example, seems to be used for higher ranks of clerks and positions upwards of this. You are a nobody if you have no card; and without some kind of impressive title you are not a business partner who can be taken seriously.

Koreans are very proud of their family names, some of which go back as far as 1,500 years. The place is teeming with Kangs, Kims and Lees. This abundance of certain names has come about as a result of the fact that serfs in the old days had to assume the name of their masters as an outward sign of their subjugation. Unfortunately that is why there are dozens of employees with the same surname in every larger firm, and this makes it especially difficult to find the person you are looking for. It is not sufficient to simply ask for Mr. Kang. That is why it is important to know his rank and title.

Every Korean has three names: first comes his surname, followed by two personal names. Whereas the first personal name is connected with the line of family ancestors, the second one functions as a pleasant-sounding symbol of good luck. "Shining Hero" or "Long-living" would be possible names for boys, while parents would choose something like "Jade Beauty" or "Sweet-scented Flower" for their daughters. At any rate, the second personal name is the one that presents the parents with a difficult decision. All three names may be written in Korean letters or in Chinese characters.

Women keep their own name even when they marry. The daughter of the Lee family who marries a son from the Chun clan remains a Lee. So you cannot tell by her name if a Korean woman is married or not. Certain forms of polite address, however, should be employed when talking to the wife of a business partner who has a son. You do not simply say her own name, but you ask after the mother of Mr. X. Only in this way can you pay respect to the position of this woman within the family, which is high because she has borne a son.

This politeness is carried to another extreme: the word for Mrs., Miss or Mr. is "ssi", and this syllable is placed after the surname (Kang-ssi). Yet no Korean would dare to call Mrs. Kim "Kim-ssi" to her face or Mr. Kang "Kang-ssi". It is only used if you are talking about Mr. Kang to a third person, and is then used for everyone whether old or young, rich or poor.

Everyone has the right to be addressed correctly – and this means not by his surname, and definitely not by his personal names. These are avoided, and instead general forms of address are used that sound more respectful. Elderly people, for example, are often addressed as "sonsaeng", which actually means teacher: teachers were always held in high respect in the Confucianist tradition.

With his visiting card, therefore, my friend Mr. Kang keeps me up-to-date with his career. And I can only congratulate James on his success. James is his second personal name, and from now on I may use it.

(Rumpf)

Shoes off in Korea House

When tourists in Seoul go up the South Mountain (Namsan), they drive through the Taegye-ro district, passing on their left, just as the road begins to climb, a very large building constructed completely in the traditional palace style. This building was opened in 1956 by the Minister of Culture, and is called Korea House. Now, thirty years later, it is still the largest traditional Korean building in the whole country. The style and furnishings are exact replicas of a building in Kyŏngbok Palace which served as the residence for the queens of the Yi dynasty.

Korea House, which was completely renovated in 1981, is run by a "Society for the Preservation of Culture and Tradition", and is a restaurant, theatre and shopping centre all in one. Many tourist groups, especially Japanese and European ones, not only get a whiff of Korean cuisine here, but also develop a feeling for the splendour of past ages.

In order to enjoy culinary delicacies from many different parts of the country – served on plates and bowls that are copies of ancient ceramics and works by famous potters – you do have to be fairly supple, for you have to sit on cushions on the floor. It's not only the architecture of the house which is in the traditional style, but the furniture and fittings, too. For elderly people who have problems with this Korean way of sitting, however, there are now some tables with a recess below them where you can put your legs. But without shoes! These must be taken off before you enter the house.

For many people the main reason for visiting Korea House is to see performances of folk music and dancing, which take place in the little theatre there daily at 8.30 p.m. except on Sundays. There is nothing comparable in the city to be recorded or filmed. Among so much tradition it is clear that a pragmatic sense of business must also play a part. In the so-called "exhibition" of arts and crafts, products wait for purchasers of varying degrees of wealth.

If you are lucky, you will not only find a bargain at Korea House, but perhaps see a traditional wedding, too. Well-to-do Koreans are willing to pay a high price for the privilege of celebrating a marriage in these princely quarters.

But even if you are not one of these lucky ones, the evening in Korea House will be unforgettable – in spite of aching limbs (you are not used to sitting this way!) and embarrassment (that hole in your sock!). It is lovely and cosy anyway, even in the cold season – thanks to "ondol", the traditional type of underfloor heating.   *(Rumpf)*

And to close, a fairy tale...

In a tiny village in the country there once lived an honest man and a miser. In the honest man's garden there grew a plum tree and this the honest man tended with loving care. Every morning and every evening the honest man watered and manured the soil in which the tree stood. And the tree flourished and grew to be taller and broader than any other plum tree; and it was always the first to carry fruit. This encouraged the honest man and he devoted more and more time to the care of the tree. The plums grew and grew; eventually the magnificent fruits were bigger even than watermelons. All the villagers were amazed at their size, and when autumn came the man carefully picked the plums one after the other and filled many, many baskets with them.

It was against the honest man's nature to eat all the fruit alone. He shared the plums with his neighbours and even sent some to the king, who was amazed at how magnificent they were. "Never have I seen such plums! I'm going to give this hardworking farmer a gift which is as splendid as these plums. What of all the gifts I have recently received could I give to the farmer?" he asked. "There's only one thing", answered the king's secretary meekly, "a bar of solid gold."

So the good man received an ingot of gold. It was not so much the value of the gold which pleased him as the fact that the king had thought to bestow a gift upon him at all.

News of the king's generous gift soon spread throughout the village. The miser heard about it too. "If it is so", he thought to himself, "I'll send the king a gift which is bigger than the plums and then I'll receive an even bigger piece of gold." And he began to think about what he could give the king. Finally he came upon the idea of a buffalo and already he saw himself standing in front of a huge pile of gold. And so he traded all his property, his house and his fields for a buffalo. And this he brought to the court.

"Tell me, my secretary", said the king as he regarded his newest gift, "what can I give in return for this buffalo which has patiently ploughed the farmer's fields? Of all the presents which I have received of late, what can I give to the farmer in return for his gift?" "There are the plums as big as watermelons which you received a few days ago", answered the secretary. "That's a good idea", exclaimed the king, "give the farmer one of those plums!"

And so it came to pass that the farmer received a huge plum in return for his buffalo instead of a pile of gold. Since this was a royal gift, he couldn't complain or demand the return of his buffalo. And so the miser, who had squandered all his property on the purchase of the buffalo, lived the rest of his days as a poor man.

(Adapted from an article in "Morning Calm", Korean Airways Magazine.) *(Rumpf)*

History

The documented history of Korea begins in the period between the 3rd and 1st millenium B. C. – but this does not tell us anything specific about Korean culture. Archaeological finds allow parallels to be drawn between the inhabitants of Korea at this time and the peoples of Central and North Asia. From these early pieces of broken pottery with their incised comb and herringbone patterns the archaeologist and historian can deduce that the roots of the Korean people lay in North and Central Asia. Further evidence is provided by cult objects connected with shamanist and pantheistic beliefs, phenomena which may still be observed in Korea today.

In the Bronze, and then in the Iron Age, the ancient kingdom of **Chosŏn** stretched from the River Liao in South Manchuria to the River Taedong in Northern Korea. The Chosŏn kingdom lasted from the 4th century B. C. to 313 A. D. and played an important role as cultural intermediary for the tribes who lived to the south of it.

Three main kingdoms gradually developed out of these southern tribes:
– **Koguryŏ** (37 B. C.–668 A. D.)
– **Paekche** (18 B. C.–660 A. D.)
– **Shilla** (57 B. C.–660 A. D.)
Alongside these kingdoms there also existed the small principality of **Kaya** in the south (42–562 A.D.), and the principality of **Nangnang**

(108 B.C.–313 A.D.) in the north; Nangnang paid tribute to China.

The fact that the Three Kingdoms (Koguryŏ, Paekche and Shilla) were established at about the same time and lasted equally long brought the peninsula seven centuries of relative political stability and a period of cultural development which laid the foundations for all following cultures. All three kingdoms were hereditary monarchies, and this too ensured continuity. The basis of social order at this time was a strictly-structured hierarchical system.

Buddhism, a new form of religion, was introduced to Korea from China, and with it came Chinese methods of administration as well as new skills. The difference between China and Korea was, however, that any gifted Chinese could attain high office, whereas in Korea this was limited to members of the established clan aristocracy. The Koreans then did not adopt the Chinese practice of allowing upward mobility within their social structure. The Korean king was the head of the army, and his close advisors, members of the nobility, were his generals.

Shilla grew to be the most powerful of the Three Kingdoms, its superiority resulting from excellent organization within the kingdom. In accordance with ancient tribal customs, for example, leaders gathered together on important occasions (in the event of war or a natural catastrophe, when a political decision had to be made, etc.) and decided mat-

81

ters unanimously. These assemblies were called **"hwabaek"**; they took place in **Kumsong, present-day Kyŏngju.** Another successful feature of Shilla was the **"bu" system** which was introduced to allow for the division of the administration into different ministries, the "chipsabu" being the highest executive office in the Shilla state.

Such effective organization meant that the Shilla kingdom was able to consolidate its power considerably and, in 668 A.D., to integrate the other two southern kingdoms to form the new **"Kingdom of Unified Shilla"** (668–935).

The **Hwarang** organization, the so-called **"Flower Youth Movement"**, played an important role in the advance of Shilla. The Hwarang was a society of knights who had attended an academy where they had been instructed in the art of government, administration and warfare. They thus formed a political elite which supported the whole system. They were often taught by Buddhist monks, and had to keep the following commandments: 1. Serve the king loyally; 2. Treat parents with filial piety; 3. Be honest and sincere to friends; 4. Do not yield in battle; 5. Do not kill indiscriminately.

The reign of **King Kyŏngdok** (742–764) marked the culmination of all that made the kingdom of Shilla great. There followed an irreversible decline, a period when internal intrigues, assassinations, peasant revolts, maladministration and corruption plagued the kingdom. The hundred and seventy years between the death of Kyŏngdok and the end of Shillan rule in the year 935 saw no less than twenty monarchs attempt to follow him.

Shilla was replaced by the **Koryŏ dynasty** which had been founded by Wang Kon, a member of a rich merchant's family.

During the Koryŏ period (936–1392) **Buddhism** became an important power factor, the number and influence of Buddhist monks in Korea increasing considerably. It was in Buddhism – and, quite literally, in Buddhist temples – that the Koreans sought refuge as they faced the threat of a **Mongol invasion** in the 13th century.

The history of Korea had always been closely linked to the history of

THE EARLY THREE KINGDOMS
(5th CENTURY)

KOGURYO

Liaorung-song
Kungnae-song
(Hwando-song)

Ansi-song
Soanp'-yong
Maullyong
Hwangch'oryong

P'yongyang

Yellow
Sea of
Han-song
Japan

Mich'uhol
Mt. Pukhan

Unjin
Kwansan-song
Sabi
SHILLA
Ch'angnyong
Kumsong
(Kyŏngju)
Sea
PAEKCHE

PRINCIPALITY
OF KAYA

0   100miles
T'amna

China. When political storms broke out there, the Korean peninsula suffered too. In the 10th century the Khitan, and later the Jurchen, had devastated the Middle Kingdom in the north and northeast of China. Korea had not been spared but had managed to defend itself with some success. However, when the Mongols pushed forward into the peninsula, the Korean kings could not stand up to them for long. The Korean court fell under the control of the Mongols, who had meanwhile established the foreign dynasty of Yüan in China.

It was, however, during these centuries of threatened and perpetrated invasion that the Koreana Tripitaka, surely one of the greatest Korean achievements of all time, was conceived and created. A collection of 81,258 wooden printing blocks featuring Buddhist texts, the Tripitaka Koreana was a form of supplication to Buddha. With them the Koreans hoped to obtain Buddha's protection against first the Khitan and later the Mongol aggressors. The first set of sacred sutra texts was destroyed in a fire at the hands of the Mongols. The blocks were re-carved between 1237 and 1252, however, and these same blocks can be seen today in Haien Temple (see p. 200). They are stored there in rooms with windows covered only by a wooden lattice – this means that air can circulate freely through the shelves and prevents damage to the wood.

Although the Mongols ruled harshly and rigidly, they were nevertheless receptive to all foreign cultural and scientific acquisitions –

unlike the ethnocentric Chinese who believed their culture to be superior to all others. In Korea the Mongols even came forward as teachers of art, arithmetic, astronomy and medicine, knowledge of all of which they had brought from the Near East.

The most important spiritual development of the Koryŏ period was the adoption of **Neo-Confucianism** as taught by the Chinese scholar Chu Hsi (1130–1200). His interpretation of the ancient Confucian principles disapproved, for example, of Buddhist families sending their sons to become monks. Any young man sent to be a monk would, by virtue of the celibacy required of him, be placed outside the normal system of social relationships as seen by the Confucianists. Devotion to the family being one of the precepts of Confucianism, it was above all familial relationships and the continued survival of the family which mattered to them. The stage was therefore set for a clear conflict between Buddhists and Confucianists. That Yi Song-gye, an ardent admirer of Chu Hsi and his teachings, later came to power in Korea (see below) is a clear indication of the impact that Confucianism had.

In the field of art the Koryŏ dynasty adopted the **celadon pottery** techniques of the Sung period in China, and brought this form of ceramics to perfection.

In the field of **historical documentation** two important works were written at this time. In 1145 the Confucianist **Kim Pu-sik** wrote the renowned **"Samguksagi"** (History of the Three Kingdoms) modelled on the work of Confucius who, as well as being a philosopher and teacher, must also be given credit for his documentation of social and historical events. A century later a second important historical chronicle, the **Samgukyusa** (Memories of the Three Kingdoms), was written by the Buddhist monk **Iryŏn.** This is more of a collection of traditional Korean legends, anecdotes and stories, and so it cannot be compared to the scholarly work of Kim Pu-sik.

1392 marked the beginning of the **Chosŏn dynasty** (also called **Yi dynasty** after **Yi Sŏng-gye,** the general who seized power). Later Yi Sŏng-gye was given the title **T'aejo,** which means "great ancestor". Yi reformed the state in many ways. For example, he reorganized the army and created, among other things, a royal bodyguard. The most decisive social change was the official adoption of Neo-Confucianism, a move which above all served to strengthen the position of the hereditary aristocracy, the **"yangban".**

King T'aejo sent a delegation to the court of the Ming emperors in China and asked their advice in choosing a new name for his dynasty. Chosŏn, a familiar name in Korean history, and Hwaryŏng, the king's own place of birth, were suggested. The Emperor of China decided on Chosŏn. So this was the beginning of the Chosŏn Dynasty. T'aejo's action made it clear that Korea recognized the supremacy of China. An important aspect of the relationship between the two countries was the exchange of legations, which represented a kind of foreign trade.

Three years after his accession to power King T'aejo moved his capital from Kaesong to **Hanyang,** now the capital of modern Korea but renamed Seoul.

The greatest ruler of the Yi dynasty was T'aejo's son, **Sejong (1418–1450).** During his reign **"han'gŭl",** an independent Korean alphabet, was introduced. A great cultural and scientific achievment of Sejong's was the establishment of the **"Chiphyŏngjŏn",** a kind of "Academy of Science", a royal research institute where geography and medicine were studied as well as Confucianism. It was in this institute that "han'gŭl" was developed.

In the further course of the history of the Yi dynasty violent disputes broke out within the **"yangban" aristocracy** as the latter became more and more powerful. And there were conflicts between the aristocrats and the court. Because of tax advantages and exemption from certain land taxes (nong jang), the yangban had been constantly extending their estates and had increased the number of their serfs. The yangban class had also procured certain privileges in the field of education through private institutes, "sowon", run on Confucianist lines. They had been clever enough to build up a strong position in the provinces to counterbalance the central government in Seoul.

The power structure, therefore, was not too stable when the Japanese asked permission to march through Korea in order to invade and conquer China. As Korea had close ties with China she could not comply with Japanese demands, but she was in no position to stop the Japanese advance. Conflict was inevitable and in 1592 **Hideyoshi** invaded an ill-prepared Korea with an army of 150,000 and advanced through the country, plundering and murdering all the way. China came to Korea's aid, however, and Japan, realizing that victory was no longer possible, declared itself ready to negotiate. These negotiations between Japan and China dragged on for years; Korea had to suffer the aftermath of the invasion for centuries. Korean antipathy to all things Japanese dates back in part to this period, as does the admiration and worship of **Admiral Yi Sun-shin.**

In the middle of the negotiations Hideyoshi's troops invaded Korea a second time. This time, however, the Koreans were victorious, thanks to Admiral Yi. With his "turtle ships", iron-clad galleys, he fought and defeated the Japanese. The Japanese troops retreated after the death of Hideyoshi.

When a Manchurian army of 30,000 men invaded Korea from the north in 1627, the whole drama was to a certain extent repeated. But in this struggle the Koreans had soon to yield to the Manchus and swear allegiance to them. Korean allegiance to Manchuria lasted up to the end of the Yi dynasty in 1910.

Korea's first contacts with Europeans took place in the 17th and 18th centuries, but they remained strictly limited because of the chauvinistic attitude of the Korean court and the relative isolation of the country. The first European books were brought into Korea from China by the Italian missionary, Ricci, in the seventeenth century.

The wretched state of the country at the end of the 18th century had prepared the ground perfectly for the new faith. In 1795 the first Chinese ordained priest, **Chou Wen-mo,** came to Korea. Catholicism had gained a firm foothold in the peninsula.

The 17th and 18th centuries also saw the rise of the **Sirhak Movement** in Korea, the school of "practical learning". "Sirhak" followers rejected a hierarchical social structure. For them all men were equal. They were of the opinion too that the king could not exist without his people, but that, on the other hand, the people certainly could exist without a king. **Yi Ik** (1681–1763) and **Chŏng Yag-yŏng** (1762–1836) were two well-known representatives of this reform movement; they laid the foundations of democratic thought in Korea. Chŏng Yag-yŏng also had a positive attitude towards Western technology and advocated the acceptance of Western ideas. The followers of this movement did not have much political influence, however, and in any case, as their ideas were directed against the rulers, they could only encourage a new way of thinking but were

Lucius H. Foote was the first American ambassador to Korea at the end of the 19th century.

unable to carry out any of their proposed reforms successfully.

In 1860 **Ch'oe Che-u** (1824–1864), a descendant of an impoverished noble family, founded the **Tonghak Sect** ("Tonghak" = Eastern learning) in Kyŏngju as a counterweight to "sohak" (Western learning, i. e. Catholicism). In particular the impoverished aristocracy and the peasants all over the country became devotees of this new promise of a better life.

Anti-Catholicism was still to be found in the following period too. From 1866 on the King, who was a convinced Confucianist, ordered the merciless persecution of Catholics. Twelve French priests were arrested and executed. More than 8,000

Korean Catholics lost their lives. Peking's political storms had reached into Korea once more.

As of 1860 European warships appeared more and more frequently off the coast of Korea. Pro-Chinese and nationalist groups were locked in internal struggles for power. At the end of the nineteenth century Korea seemed to be experiencing its death throes. The so-called "unequal" treaties, the sole aim of which was to open Korea's ports and conquer new markets, were concluded with America, Russia, Italy and Germany. Paul Georg von Moellendorf was sent from the Imperial court in China as adviser to the Korean king. China wanted to preserve its ancient rights over the vassal state. Korea's Queen Min gave her unconditional support to the Chinese plans.

The Japanese gained influence in Korea during the Sino-Japanese war of 1895 (in which the Chinese were defeated). They built railways and a telegraph network; all ports had to be opened to Japanese ships; the Chinese were forced to leave Korea. Several revolts against the Japanese led by the Tonghak movement were brutally suppressed. Japan was now in the position to lead new military attacks against China from Korea, taking one province after another. In 1895 the **Treaty of Shimonoseki** was signed. Korea became officially independent, but the representation of Japanese interests on the peninsula was increased.

At the end of the century certain reforms were introduced under

Japanese influence: members of the yangban class were allowed to take part in business; child marriages were forbidden (that's to say, the earliest age for marriage was fixed at 20 years for men and 16 years for girls); widows were allowed to remarry; collective liability of a family for a political crime was abolished; the old rules of dress were abolished; girls were allowed to visit public schools. All these reforms carried through under the direction or influence of the Japanese were aimed at strengthening the position of the Japanese "advisers".

These measures were not introduced without resistance: the followers of Queen Min opposed them. In the end the clash of interests took the form of open conflict, and on 8th October, 1895 the Japanese had the Korean queen assassinated. Just two years later the Empire of Korea was proclaimed. The official name was **Taehan Cheguk** which brought back the idea of Han which the Koreans had used for centuries. Korea seemed to be gradually recovering when the Russo-Japanese War broke out. It ended in 1905 with a victory for the Japanese. The **Treaty of Portsmouth** allowed Japan political, military and economic interests in Korea, and this paved the way for the final annexation. An especially important point was that Korean sovereignty was from that time on not to be mentioned in any international treaty. In Korea itself the law was changed so that the Japanese could also buy land there: by 1907 there were already 7,745 Japanese landowners in the penin-

sula. Korea became in fact a Japanese colony, the status of which was finally settled in 1910 with the end of the Yi dynasty.

When the **Treaty of Annexation** was signed on 22nd August 1910, the Japanese took full power in Korea. Secret negotiations between the Japanese General Masatake and Yi Wanyong, a member of the Korean government, preceded its signing. An immediate consequence of the treaty was that Japanese generals were appointed provincial governors in Korea. This takeover and foreign rule at the hands of the Japanese led to violent riots nine years later (1st March to August 1919). The rebellion was brutally suppressed. Yet out of this **March First Movement**, as it was officially called, grew a very strong sense of national identity. During the following years Korean groups were formed abroad to work against Japan. In China there was even an exile Korean government of which **Syngman Rhee,** who was later to become the first premier of the Republic of Korea, was a member.

After the outbreak of war with China in 1937, Korea served the Japanese as a supply base. Moreover, Korea had to act as rice bowl, not only for the Japanese army, but also for a large part of the Japanese population. Towards the end of the Second World War, some 300,000 Japanese soldiers were being fed in Korea alone.

The end of the **Second World War** brought Korea independence from Japan at last, but it also set the stage for another war, a war which was to be the worst which Korea had ever experienced.

Russia had declared war on Japan on 8th August, 1945 and its troops had advanced as far as the 38th parallel (a position which would be most significant later). After the capitulation of Japan less than a month later, Russian and American troops occupied the area north of the 38th parallel and the area south of it respectively. This was considered a provisional solution until a government for all Korea could be established. A joint **U.S./ U.S.S.R. commission** met several times in 1946 and 1947, but was unable to reach any agreement on the Korea question. The U.S. called on the United Nations to supervise elections; on May 10th, 1948 elections were held in South Korea under the auspices of UNCURK (United Nations Commission for the Unification and Rehabilitation of Korea) but the Commission was refused entry into North Korea. In the National Assembly 100 of the 298 seats remained reserved for the deputies who were to have taken them after elections in the north. South Korea was given the name of **Taehan Min'guk** (= Republic of Korea). A constitution was drafted, and from 15th August 1948 Dr. Syngman Rhee could act as the first freely elected president. One month later the **People's Republic of Korea** (North) was proclaimed. American and Soviet troops withdrew and the political and military disputes between the two republics began, first of all in the form of guerilla raids from the north.

The **Korean War** broke out on June 25th, 1950 after North Korean troops attacked the South. T-34 tanks advanced as far as Taegu and South Korea called on the United Nations for support. U.S. troops were the first to come to South Korea's aid, other contingents followed. (Indirect aid to North Korea from the U.S.S.R. was indicative of the Cold War which had by this time broken out between capitalist and communist camps.) The U.N. Cemetery in Pusan bears witness to the tragedy of war. The disastrous dispute came to an end on July 27th, 1953.

Years of privation commenced for the Koreans – years, moreover, which were characterized by rigid political attitudes. General social discontent was given expression in the students' demonstrations of 19th April 1960. The economy stagnated; there was no state provision for the thousands of war widows, 100,000 orphans and 279,000 unemployed who were therefore a burden for already hard-hit families. Economic recovery came only slowly, and even then was not always coupled with political stability.

It is only in the last fifteen years that the Korean "economic miracle" has brought relative stability to the political sphere. There have even been negotiations between North and South Korea recently – perhaps a hopeful step towards a possible reunification of the Korean people. *(Thiele)*

History at a Glance

3000–1000 B.C.: Archaeological finds suggest Central and North Asian influences among the early population; nomadic economy in part.

2333 B.C.: Legendary foundation of the capital Pyŏngyang. For Koreans this date marks the beginning of their history and culture.

4th century B.C.–131 A.D.: Ancient Chosŏn Empire in South Manchuria acts as an important intermediary between North and Central Asia and Korea.

37 B.C.–668 A.D.: Koguryŏ.

18 B.C.–660 A.D.: Paekche.

57 B.C.–660 A.D.: Shilla.
These Three Kingdoms establish themselves under the influence of China. They develop independent political structures, and a Han consciousness grows. Constant interaction of Chinese and Korean history.

618–907: When the Tang dynasty takes over in China, Korea comes under the political influence of China once more.

668–936: "Unified Shilla" established with Chinese help. Kyŏngju becomes the capital.

936–1392: Shilla replaced by Koryŏ dynasty. Buddhism becomes state religion. Great influence of religions on politics and administration.

13th century: Mongolian invasions.

1270: Peace treaty with the Mongols.

1392–1910: Yi or Chosŏn dynasty. Complete organization of state and society on Neo-Confucianist prin-

ciples. Elimination of Buddhist influence to a large extent.

1418–1450: King Sejong. During his reign the independent, native "han'gŭl" alphabet is invented.

1592: Japanese invasion.

1627 and 1636: Manchu invasions from the north. After this, Korea shuts itself off from the rest of the world.

17th century: First contacts are Dutch sailors of the East India Company. Influence of Jesuits via China.

From 1864: Further consolidation of rigid form of government.

1876: Opening of Korean ports to Japanese ships. Increasing Japanese influence until, in

1910: Korea is annexed by Japan.

Until 1945: Korea is a Japanese colony.

1919: Korean revolt against the Japanese occupation is brutally crushed.

1945: After Japanese capitulation, US and Soviet troops occupy Korea. The 38th parallel becomes the line of demarcation.

15th August 1948: Proclamation of the Republic of Korea (South).

9th September 1948: Democratic Republic of Korea (North) proclaimed.

25th June 1950: North Korea attacks South Korea. Beginning of Korean War.

27th Juni 1953: End of Korean War.

1972 to the present day: Negotiations between North and South Korea on the subject of a possible reunification. *(Thiele)*

Geography and Regional Divisions

The name "Korea" stems from the historical **Koryŏ** Kingdom (918–1392). The Koreans themselves call their country **Taehan Minguk** or, in the abbreviated form, **Hanguk**, which is the equivalent of the Chinese Hanguo (= Land of the Han). The more poetical name, "Land of the Morning Calm", **Chosŏn** in Korean, was coined by the Koreans themselves in the olden days. It comes especially from the romanticized descriptions of scenery in the east of the country (e. g. in the Sorak Mountains), where you can indeed experience an atmosphere at sunrise which does engender the much-praised "morning calm".

The Korean peninsula, which was politically divided into the **Democratic People's Republic of Korea** (North Korea) and the **Republic of Korea** (South Korea) after the Second World War, lies between 124 ° and 131 ° longitude east, and between 33 ° and 43 ° latitude north. The peninsula is about 1,000 km (620 miles) long, and 216 km (134 miles) wide at the narrowest point; Korea also comprises some 3,300 offshore islands. These figures, of course, refer to Korea as a whole.

Fom the point of view of political boundaries, Korea (as a whole) borders on the **People's Republic of China** in the north (it shares a border with Tongbei, the "Northeast", formerly Manchuria) and, in a little corner in the extreme north, on the **Soviet Union.** Topographically-speaking, the rivers Yalu and Tumen and the Paektu Mountains form a natural boundary in the north and northeast. East of Korea, and separating it from Japan, lies the **Eastern Sea,** which is usually known as the **Sea of Japan.** The **Yellow Sea,** also known as the **Chinese Sea,** forms a natural barrier in the west. In the south, Korea is separated from **Japan** by the **Taehan Strait,** known in Japan as the **Tsushima Strait.** Korea's coastline (including that of the offshore islands) and inland border are a total 17,371 km (10,800 miles) in length – an indication of the abundance of islands, and of the irregularity of the coastline (the peninsula itself accounts for 8,600 km/5,340 miles).

The whole of Korea has an **area of 221,184 sq. km (85,400 sq. miles).** The peninsula is thus just slightly smaller than Great Britain which covers 229,523 sq. km/ 88,619 sq. miles).

The Democratic People's Republic (North Korea) covers 122,370 sq. km (47,250 sq. miles) while the Republic of South Korea has an area of 98,824 sq. km (38,156 sq. miles). South Korea therefore represents a very compact country, being smaller in fact than England.

Its geographical position has meant that, from an historical point of view, Korea has always played the part of intermediary between the great cultures of China and Japan. Not only different religions, but also other cultural influences from the East Asian and Central Asian mainland, were passed on to Japan via the peninsula. The other side of the coin was that this situation led in the course of history to struggles between the great powers for influence in Korea – usually to the detriment of the Korean people. Even today these conflicts of interest have not yet disappeared or been resolved.

The peninsula's topography is indicative of Korea's position at the edge of mountain chains running from north to south on the Asian mainland. There are **mountains and hills** almost everywhere in Korea. The highest peak in South Korea is **Halla-san** (Mount Halla, 1,950 m/6,400 ft) on Cheju Island; in North Korea it is **Paektu-san** (Mount Paektu, 2,744 m/9,000 ft) on the border with China. Both mountains play an important part in Korean history and mythology.

On the one hand, the presence of mountains and hills tends to give the scenery a certain monotony. But on the other, the short swift-flowing rivers, the plains and the mountains towering above them – in short, the fact that the mountains break up the landscape into small units – produces scenes of unbelievable natural beauty (e.g. in the Sorak mountains).

The **east coast** is very sheer and quite regular compared to the rugged coastline of the south and west with its many inlets. Because there are few bays along the east coast there are few ports of any significance. The most important ones are Wŏnsan (N. Korea), Sokcho'o, Samch'ŏk, Ulchin, P'ohang and Ulsan.

The largest of the few islands lying off the east coast are the volcanic islands of Ullung and Tokto, farming and fishing communities with a population of 22,000. Tokto Island is still a bone of contention between Japan and Korea, for the former considers it part of its Shimane Prefecture.

Unlike the east coast, the **west coast** is very irregular and has many offshore islands of various sizes. The main west coast ports are, starting in the north, Tasado (N. Korea), Nampo (N. Korea), Inch'ŏn (S. Korea) and Kunsan (S. Korea). **Tasado** functions as trading port for the northwest town of Sinuiju; **Nampo** used to be the traditional port for trade with China. **Inch'ŏn** serves Seoul, which lies not far inland, and has relatively deep shipping channels. It is one of the busiest ports in Korea and primarily handles goods produced in the capital. During the Japanese occupation **Kunsan** was the port from which Korean rice was exported from this colonial "rice bowl" to Japan.

The **south coast** is even more indented than the west. The most important ports along the south coast are Pusan, Chinhae, Masan, Yŏsu and Mokp'o. Along with Wonsan, Ulsan and Inch'on, **Pusan** is one of Korea's most important ports – and has been since 1883. Today Pusan handles more volume of goods than any other Korean port. Approximately 80% of South Korea's commercial transactions pass through this harbour. **Chinhae** is now a naval base, **Masan** no more than a fishing port. **Mokp'o** has an intermediate position, being a fishing, naval and commercial port all in one.

Korea at a Glance

Extent of the whole Korean peninsula – 1,000 km (620 miles) from north to south. Narrowest point between the Sea of Japan (East Sea) and the Yellow Sea: 216 km (134 miles). Shortest distance between Korea and Japan: 216 km (134 miles).

Area of the whole Korean peninsula – 221,184 sq. km (85,400 sq. miles), i. e. slightly less than that of Great Britain.
North Korea: 122,370 sq. km (47,250 sq. miles)
South Korea: 98,824 sq. km (38,156 sq. miles).

Geographical position – between 33 ° and 43 ° latitude north, and between 124 ° and 131 ° longitude east.

Coastline – in the east: rocky and rugged, few bays, tidal range = 60 cm (2 ft); in the west: flat, a great many inlets, tidal range = 6–10 m (20–30 ft), one of the biggest in the world.

Islands – over 3,000, 650 of them inhabited. Cheju-do, 96 km (approx. 60 miles) off the south coast, is the largest.

Woodland and forest – cover 70% of the land.

Arable land – covers approx. 22%, mainly in the west of the peninsula.

Mountains – Halla-san on Cheju Island 1,950 m (6,400 ft); Chiri-san 1,915 m (6,280 ft); Sorak-san (Mount Seolag) 1,708 m (5,600 ft).

Rivers – Naktong 525 km (325 miles); Han 514 km (320 miles); Kum 401 km (250 miles).

Climate – temperate climate, four distinct seasons. Considerable differences in summer and winter temperatures. July and August are the hottest months of the year, December and January the coldest. Characteristic sequence of weather in winter: four warm days followed by three cold days. Average annual temperatures – in the south: 12–14 °C (54–57 °F); inland 10–12 °C (50–54 °F); in the north: 8–10 °C (46–50 °F). Rainfall varies between 500 mm (20 ins) and 1,500 mm (60 ins); average annual precipitation is 960 mm (38 ins). The rainy season is from June to August, with 50% of annual rainfall occurring then.

Administration – 9 provinces, plus Seoul which has special status. Pusan, Taegu, Inch'ŏn are under direct government control. The provinces ("do") are divided into 139 districts ("gun") and 46 cities ("shi"). The districts are subdivided into 187 towns ("up") and 1,266 villages ("myon").

Population – estimated to have passed the 40 million mark in 1984. Annual growth of population in the years 1970–82: 1.7% (the figure in the years 1966–70 was 2.3%; 1.7% is nevertheless a fast rate of growth when compared with that of other industrialized nations).

Size of families – 1966: 5.6 people per household; 1970: 5.4 people per household; 1983: 4.5 people per household.

Population density – 403.2 people per sq. km (1983).
Population structure – in 1980: children under 14 years, 33.8%; people of 15–64 years of age, 62.3%; those over 65, 3.9%.
Population distribution – percentage of population living in centres with more than 50,000 inhabitants: in 1970, 41.1%; in 1975, 48.4%; in 1980, 57.3%. Of the urban population of South Korea, 66.3% live in Seoul, Pusan, Taegu and Inch'ŏn.
Gross national product – in 1983: US$ 75.3 billion.
Per capita income – in 1983: US$ 1,884.

(Thiele)

There are several large **islands** off the south coast: Koje-do in the east, Namhae-do moving farther westwards, then Haegak-do and Chin-do in the west. **Cheju-do,** Korea's most important offshore island, also lies off the southwest coast.

Cheju occupies a special position in Korea in many respects – from the point of view of culture, history and the economy, and with respect to flora, fauna and geology. Cheju-do (do = island) covers an area of 1,862 sq. km (720 sq. miles) and has a population of 350,000. The island consists entirely of volcanic rock, and in the middle of it Mount Halla rises to a height of 1,950 m - (6,400 ft).

Generally speaking, Korea rises from west to east in an even sweep. Consequently, most of the rivers, following this incline, flow into the Yellow Sea and Korea Bay. The Nakton River is one exception: it enters the Japan Sea near Pusan on the east coast.

The rivers **Yalu** (Amnok Kang in Korean) and **Tumen** (Tuman Kang in Korean) are the longest rivers in North Korea and form the border with China. They are 790 km (490 miles) and 520 km (320 miles) in length respectively. The longest rivers in South Korea are the **Naktong** (525 km/325 miles) and the **Han** (514 km/320 miles); the Han flows through the South Korean capital, Seoul.

The rivers are not all equally navigable all year round. Because of the heavy rainfall in the monsoon season, the rivers carry much more water in summer than during the dry winter.

As was the case all over the world, the rivers were an important precondition for the settlement and cultivation of the country. 70% of the arable land in Korea is watered by its rivers. Dams have now been built on many rivers to ensure a regular distribution and allocation of water as well as to produce electricity.

The River Han, on which the Korean capital, Seoul, stands, flows into Kangwha Bay, and its banks boast the largest area under cultivation of all Korean rivers. This was probably the most important reason for the foundation of the capital on its banks. *(Thiele)*

Climate

Korea has a cooler climate, especially in winter, than do countries in corresponding latitudes in Europe, for example. This is why we often have the impression that it lies farther north than is in fact the case. Seoul is farther south than Madrid and Rome; it lies on roughly the same latitude as Athens. Korea forms a transitional zone between the continental climate of Central Asia and the maritime, subtropical climate of the monsoon regions.

In winter, temperatures recorded in the south and the north differ greatly. Temperatures can sink to −40°C in the north, while in the south and southeast they can be as high as a few degrees above freezing point. The temperatures in the south and southeast are moderated by "warm" ocean currents. Moreover, winds coming from the north cross over the chain of mountains before reaching the coastal areas, and have the same warm, drying effect as foehn winds.

In the months from November to March winds from the continent, that is, north or northwesterly winds (the northwest monsoon) predominate. these are usually dry and cold. Only the winds blowing in across the Yellow Sea bring rain.

Winter in Korea is characterized by a particular sequence of weather: four warm days are followed by three colder ones. This phenomenon is caused by cold, dry winds from the continental landmass which gradually warm the air over Korea, resulting in differences in temperature between the latter and Siberia. These differences in temperature in turn bring about changes in atmospheric pressure so that cold winds from Siberia can again enter Korea. Because of this phenomenon, the Korean winter does not seem so severe.

In spring (April and May) the weather is changeable. In summer (June to August) conditions are more stable, with winds from the southeast bringing tropical, humid air to the whole country. In autumn (end of September and October) there are usually quite long periods with clear, blue skies and cool air.

The summer monsoon brings the highest levels of rainfall, precipitation occurring primarily in the southeast and east. The area around Taegu, being enclosed by the Sobaek and Taebaek mountains, registers lower levels of rainfall. Precipitation from year to year varies greatly.

From the middle of July to the beginning of September, Korea is occasionally affected by typhoons. The damage that is then caused comes less from the high speeds of the winds than from the violent rains. River embankments and dykes along the paddy fields are often destroyed; carefully-built rice terraces are washed away.   *(Thiele)*

Climatic Table

Seoul

	Jan.	Feb.	Mar.	Apr.	May	June	July	Aug.	Sep.	Oct.	Nov.	Dec.
Average temperature (°C)	-4.9	-1.9	3.6	10.5	16.3	20.8	24.5	25.4	20.3	13.4	6.3	-1.2
Average maximum temperature (°C)	zero	2.8	8.3	16.7	22.2	26.7	28.9	30.6	25.6	19.4	10.6	2.8
Average minimum temperature (°C)	-9.4	-6.7	-1.7	5.0	10.6	16.1	21.1	21.7	15.0	7.2	zero	-6.7
Absolute maximum temperature (°C)	12.2	15.6	22.2	28.3	32.2	36.7	36.6	37.2	32.8	30.0	23.3	14.4
Absolute minimum temperature (°C)	-22.2	-19.4	-15.0	-3.9	2.2	9.4	12.8	14.4	3.3	-3.9	-11.7	-24.4
Average relative humidity (%)	64	64	64	63	66	73	81	78	73	68	68	66
Average rainfall (mm)	17	21	56	68	86	169	358	224	142	49	36	32
No. of days with more than 1 mm rainfall	3	3	6	6	7	9	14	10	7	5	5	5
Hours of sunshine	180	182	207	228	257	214	179	202	206	231	180	161

Pusan

	Jan.	Feb.	Mar.	Apr.	May	June	July	Aug.	Sep.	Oct.	Nov.	Dec.
Average temperature (°C)	1.8	3.5	7.3	12.5	16.7	19.8	23.7	25.4	21.6	16.6	11.1	5.0
Average maximum temperature (°C)	6.1	7.2	11.7	16.7	20.6	23.9	27.2	29.4	25.6	21.1	15.0	8.9
Average minimum temperature (°C)	-1.7	-0.6	-2.8	8.3	12.8	16.7	21.7	22.8	18.3	12.2	6.1	-0.6
Absolute maximum temperature (°C)	18.3	18.8	20.6	25.6	28.9	33.3	34.4	35.6	32.2	26.7	23.9	19.4
Absolute minimum temperature (°C)	-13.9	-11.7	-7.2	-1.7	5.6	9.4	13.9	15.6	9.4	2.2	-3.3	-12.2
Average relative humidity (%)	49	52	59	66	71	80	85	80	74	64	59	53
Average rainfall (mm)	25	44	89	114	139	198	248	165	205	73	44	39
No. of days with more than 1 mm rainfall	3	4	6	7	8	9	11	8	9	4	4	4
Hours of sunshine	205	190	213	219	241	196	183	232	182	218	196	198

Fauna and Flora

Fauna

In the north, Korean fauna is very similar to that of Siberia and Manchuria. In the south of the country, the influence of Chinese and Japanese fauna is clear.

The fauna of the north includes **red deer,** the **Manchurian weasel, brown bear, lynx, water shrew, muskrat, the Manchurian pheasant, black grouse,** the **hawk owl,** the **hawfinch** and the **woodpecker.**

In the south, including the islands of Cheju and Ullung, **black Korean bears,** the **mandarin field vole, deer, Tristram's woodpecker** and various kinds of **pheasant** are indiginous. However, the tourist will seldom catch a glimpse of these animals for they live in remote parts of the country.

Since 1968 many animals have been protected species as they are in danger of dying out. Among these are, for example, the **white-bellied black woodpecker,** the **ibis,** the **white stork** and the **black stork,** different kinds of **swans,** the **Manchurian crane,** the **great bustard,** the **black vulture,** all species of **bear,** and the **Chindo dog.**

In **South Korea, 370 species of birds** have been registered, 266 of them birds of passage. There are also **25 types of reptiles** and **130 different fish.**

One of the most beautiful birds is undoubtedly the **Manchurian crane** (Grus japonensis), with its red feather cap and black secondaries

trimming the wings. This crane almost died out. An American ornithologist, Dr. George Archibald, has been a vigorous champion for its conservation and protection since 1977. As the head of the International Crane Foundation, he started a breeding programme for Manchurian cranes at Baraboo, Wisconsin (USA), in order to secure the survival of the species. In the same year, however, he discovered that a colony of Manchurian cranes had settled in the peacefulness of the Demilitarized Zone of all places, at the 38th Parallel. In winter you can sometimes watch these majestic birds perform their fascinating courtship dances there.

A Korean farmer is reported to have killed a **bear** in 1984. Since bears are protected, as we just mentioned, the man was fined, and the bear meat, including the gall bladder, was sold at a public auction: this brought in about £ 10,000. It seems, therefore, that many people still believe in the magical properties of the gall bladder of a bear. The paws of the bear, and some of the offal, are considered delicacies by Korean gourmets.

The Korean **tiger** (this is, in fact, the Siberian tiger – Panthera tigris altaica – five specimens of which were sighted in the province of North Hangyong in 1935) lives on today only in paintings and legends of the origin of the Korean people, where he appears with a female bear to form a mythical couple, the ancestors of the Korean race.

In the old days tiger bones were ground down to a powder and mixed with alcohol to make the drink "hogolju". This was said to have aphrodisiac properties and was therefore a popular drink among men. Tiger meat, fat, hair, teeth, skin and other parts of the animals used to be used by the Koreans for medicinal purposes. Traditionally-minded pharmacists would give a fortune today for a good tiger claw or other parts of the tiger, if they could only get them.

The most famous of all Korean dogs is the **Chindo-kae** (kae = dog) from the island off Korea's southwest coast called Chindo. This dog is popular as a watchdog because of its faithfulness, strength and reliability. It would have died out if the Korean government had not made it a protected animal on 10th July 1973, and forbidden people to take the dog away from its native island. This special breed – medium-sized, short-haired, with a pointed snout and raised tail, and a colouring that varies from light cream beige to almost brown – is a little like a Chinese chow. The species has survived for so long because of the isolated position of the island. It is regarded by dog experts as an early connecting link to the wolf, from whom our tame dogs are of course descended.

Flora

The great latitudinal range from north to south in Korea (1,000 km/620 miles) and the geographical position of the peninsula between the Sea of Japan (Eastern Sea) and the Yellow Sea give rise to differences in annual average temperatures of between 8 and 14° Centigrade. Average rainfall differs greatly too. In the north there is a precipitation of approx. 500 mm (20 ins); in the south as much as 1,500 mm (60 ins). These two factors – temperature and rainfall – occasion a rich flora. So there are 201 families of plants endemic to Korea, with 3,347 species. More than 4,500 vascular plants find ideal conditions for growth here.

When considering Korea's flora, the country is best divided into three separate botanical regions: north, centre and south.

In the **northern regions** bordering on Tongbei in China, extensive **alpine flora** is to be found; here the influence of Manchurian species is marked. In these areas (where the average annual temperature is about 5° Centigrade) e. g. in the Sorak and Chiri Mountains, **conifers** such as **fir** and many kinds of **pine** grow. **Oak, beech, cedar, larch** and **birch** also thrive in these cooler climes.

In the northern botanical region you also find different kinds of **bamboo,** that is, grasses which you might expect to find further south. **Rhubarb** (Rheum) comes from the East Asian mountains, and one type, Rheum coreanum Nakai, is even endemic to the Changbaek Mountains in Korea. Subspecies of rhubarb are used by Koreans as food and for medicinal purposes. Many types of **rhododendron** are native to Korea, and in particular to the north. **Bilberries** (Vaccinium myrtillus) grow there too, and one particularly tasty variety – Vaccinium ulginosum Linné var. krusianum Herd.

– can be found in the Sorak Mountains as well as in the south, on Mount Halla on the island of Cheju. It is regarded as a relic of the Tertiary period which survived in these remote areas because of the change of climate.

The second botanical region is **Central Korea** – roughly-speaking, the area between the Demilitarized Zone (DMZ) at the 38th Parallel and a line from Yongil Bay (Japan Sea) to Taean Peninsula on the Yellow Sea. Here thrives a wealth of **pines** and **deciduous trees** such as **beech, oak and chestnut.** Roasted chestnuts are sold as a delicacy all over the country. **Hazel trees** and **yoke elm** supply nuts that are very popular with Koreans, too. **Rowan trees, ash, catkin, linden trees and plane trees, forsythia** and **rhododendron** transform the landscape again and again with their blossom and foliage. Every year the countryside becomes a sea of colour that attracts thousands of visitors from all over the world.

The variety of grasses too, such as **horsetail** (equisetum) and **foxtail grass,** the **mosses, cushion plants** and **herbs, shrubs** and **subshrubs** fill every tourist who is at all interested in botany with enthusiasm. Many plants are endemic to this area, and are therefore of particular interest to botanists.

In the south of this central botanical region, in the province of Ch'ungch'ongpukdo, stands the oldest and largest **gingko tree** in the whole of East Asia, in Sogni National Park. The gingko is one of the oldest types of tree in the world. It is known that it existed in the Permian

period, but all types have died out except the "Gingko biloba", which is obviously a very hardy species. This deciduous tree, which can reach a height of 30 m (almost 100 ft), is native to Korea as well as to China and Japan. It has been ascertained that it came originally from the Chinese provinces Anhui and Zhejiang, where it was endemic to the mountain areas, spreading out from there. Gingko trees prefer mountainous

Korea's national flower, the rose of Sharon – "moo kung hwa" – is a kind of hibiscus.

country. As they can reach an age of several hundred years, they were often chosen for temple grounds. Gingkos were brought to Europe by the Dutch in 1754 as a garden tree, and since then have been found there in parks and large gardens. The tree has a pyramid-like shape at first, but it spreads out later in a wide crown. It is this kind of gingko that we can still see in Korean temple precincts. Its golden foliage in autumn casts a spell on the countryside. The leaves are bilabiate and look like little fans, and this is why the gingko is sometimes called the "fan-leaf tree". The ripe seed or nut of the gingko looks like a big, olive-green cherry. The shell consists of two sections: the outside is pulpy and greenish yellow. This pulp tastes sweetish. If you keep it a while, it smells and tastes rancid, while the inside goes hard. The latter has a high fat content and is eaten as a delicacy, as well as being made into oil.

The third botanical region, the **south,** has an average annual temperature of 14° Centigrade and boasts a profusion of subtropical plants. Of particular interest is the island of Cheju, which is within this botanical region and where over 70 kinds of evergreen dicotyledonous plants grow, including tea plants (Camellia sinensis or japonica). Altogether the flora is closely related to that of South Japan, and is characterized by a variety of **camellias, azaleas, aralias** and **gingko trees.** Four-petalled blossoms, such as those of **forsythia** and **privet** (Oleaceae family), can be found on Cheju as well as almost all kinds of **citrus plants,** which thrive splendidly in large plantations on volcanic rock.

The south of Korea is also rich in **heathers** and **medicinal herbs.** On the mainland the number of evergreen plants goes down to 20 different species. Particularly in the vicinity of the two ports, Mokp'o and Pusan, fewer species grow than on the archipelagoes off the coast.

On the whole, the flora of Korea has been specially well preserved in the country's huge national parks and in old Buddhist temple pre-cincts, both of which are nowadays accessible to the public. The Koreans are great walkers and great nature lovers. They look after their plants with loving care, and keep a careful eye on the conservation of the various species in the national parks. Korean gardeners, like the Chinese, are famous all over the world and are greatly admired as experts in many Asian countries. A particular feature of every Korean house is its show of greenery – shrubs, little trees and flowers that are carefully tended.

Many plants in Korea are now protected: 256 types of pine, for example, one of which is the "Pinus bungeana" with its unusual bark; another 158 species of pine which grow in the coastal regions; 11 kinds of willow; 9 types of paulownia; 57 species of oak; and one date palm.

Food crops, etc. are cultivated just as intensively. Apart from Japan, there is probably no other Asian country in which one sees so many fields covered in polythene. Because of the mountainous nature of Korea's terrain, only 20% of the land can be used for agriculture. But agricultural exploitation of the soil available can be increased nowadays by harvesting more often from these polythene-covered fields. This is especially the case with **market gardening.** A great variety of vegetables, including radish, ginger, turnip, taro, potatoes, aubergines and zucchini, garlic, tomatoes, leeks, soya beans, green peppers, sesame, pepper, mint, mushrooms, onions and many kinds of fruit are all grown here. **Rice** is mainly cultivated in the south and west. *(Thiele)*

Hanyak –
Traditional Medicine

As in China, there are two different types of medicine in Korea: western medicine which spread after its introduction in 1884, and the traditional "medicine of the ancients" which goes back more than 4,000 years and is still widely practised today.

Hanyak is the name given by Koreans to this traditional form of medicine. Like so many other things in Korea it originated in China. Confucius is always quoted whenever it is a question of patterns of behaviour that have been handed down and, after all, diagnosis and therapy belong to this category. And traditional medicine does indeed contain many ideas taken from Confucianist philosophy.

First of all, the doctor always visits the patient, and not the other way round. Every symptom of the illness is considered in connection with the living conditions of the patient, the strains in the family and the psychological pressure of his environment, and is then alleviated or even eliminated, depending on the skill of the particular doctor. A diagnosis in the Western sense is unknown, as is preventive medicine. As Dr. Paul S. Crane, a doctor who practised (Western) medicine in Korea for decades, reported, there are said to be 20 million doctors of traditional medicine in Korea – that is, people who consider themselves doctors in the traditional sense.

Traditional Korean medicine is based on **yin** and **yang**, or, as the Koreans say, **ŭm** and **yang.** A human being is healthy when both these forces are in harmony. If one component is out of balance, then he is ill. The "yang" force is aggressive, wild, hot and dry; it symbolizes the south. The "ŭm" force is receptive, repressive, calm, gentle, damp and swollen; it symbolizes the north. If one force destroys the balance (by way of an excess or shortage), then the traditional doctor must stimulate or repress it. In order to do this he must know that the human body, like the cosmos, consists of five basic elements: fire, earth, metal, water and wood. One human organ corresponds to each of these elements. Fire = heart, the seat of reason (the heart comes from the sun, from heaven, it is the vital spark of life). Earth = blood. Metal = lung, the precious breath of life. Water = kidneys. Wood = liver. All these elements are in correlation to each other, as are the human organs and substances. It is only logical then that if there is any disturbance among these elements, the nearest ones will intervene in the system of correlations. The five basic elements or main organs are subdivided into sub-elements or sub-organs. There is a system of vertical correlations as well as horizontal ones.

Twelve lines of force or nerves carry impulses from 360 points on the skin of the human body to the different organs. Thus the thumb stands in correlation to the lung, the index finger to the intestines, the middle finger to the spleen, and the ring finger to the sexual organs.

There are two main systems of blood circulation which correspond yet again to the "ŭm" and "yang" forces. If acupuncture is applied at particular points, then "yin" or "ŭm" force is added and "yang" drawn off, or vice versa. The traditional Korean doctor must be perfectly familiar with these 360 points on the skin in order to be able to treat the patient correctly. It does happen that a doctor applies acupuncture at the wrong spot and this can cause complications. Infections often result in such cases.

As every substance contains "ŭm" and "yang" forces, it follows that the traditional doctor must be able to assess the corresponding medicines, i. e. know about their ŭm/yang content and how to apply them properly.

As well as the Korean ŭm/yang treatment there are another four methods of treatment. These are called **maeng** (= observing the facial expression of the patient), **mun** (= listening to the voice of the patient), **second mun** (= asking the patient about the symptoms and course of the illness), and finally **chŏl** (= taking the pulse and feeling the stomach).

According to the traditional view of medicine, there are three areas of the body where illnesses can originate: firstly, the outer skin of the body; secondly, the internal organs;

and thirdly, the parts that lie between the two. Internal and external treatment of the illness are equally important.

The tongue plays an important part in diagnosis. In ancient Korean medicine, there are eight symptoms, most of them changes of colour on the tongue, from which illness can be deduced.

In addition, the pulse is considered an important indicator of illness. It is felt with three fingers, each of which catches the beat independently. The "doctor" of traditional medicine is familiar with seventeen types of pulse belonging to seventeen different syndromes.

As in Imperial China, a doctor was not allowed to see or touch an undressed woman in Korea. He felt her pulse, for example, through a silk thread that was laid around the woman's wrist. The pulse beats were transmitted to the silk thread. How sensitive a Korean doctor must have been!

Surgical operations were once forbidden for 1,500 years, after an incident involving the famous doctor, Hwat'a, who wanted to perform an operation on the king's head. The king saw this as an attempt on his life, and not only forbade all operations, but also ordered the destruction of all surgical instruments and books on the subject, as well as the execution of the doctor.

A great variety of herbs and grasses are used for making medicines. The Koreans have an immense store of knowledge about "ŭm" and "yang" forces and how much of them is in each grass and herb.

Ginseng is the most important plant used in traditional medicine. This panacea would probably have been called "devil's root" in the olden days in Europe, for it is said to have healing powers for every ache and pain.

Animal ingredients feature too. The gall bladder of the bear, the paw of the tiger, snake meat and dried millipedes are only a small sample of the wide variety of traditional medications.

And if none of this helps, you can still go to the shaman or to the mudang (shamaness) and have devilishly infected "ŭms" and "yangs" exorcised.

Traditional medicine in Korea covers a wide spectrum. Much of it seems logical and sensible, some of it hair-raising and charlatanistic.

In spite of the high standard of "hanyak", however, the year 1884 arrived and Western medicine was introduced to Korea. Dr. H. N. Allen, an American doctor, saved the life of a high-ranking Korean statesman who had been seriously injured during an attempt on his life. After this incident, the Koreans confidence in the doctor's skills, and at the same time in Western medicine, grew.

(Thiele)

Ginseng –
the Anthropomorphic Root

Ginseng – or "insam" as it is called in Korean – occupies a unique position among Korean plants. According to Korean sources, this medicinal root, with all its healing properties and "miracle cures", was already well-known 5,000 years ago. It has been considered a "divine remedy" since ancient times, and respected accordingly. The name ginseng comes from the Chinese word "renshen" (= "human-shaped root"). The plant grows wild in Northeast China, Korea and East Siberia. In Korea it was cultivated very early on in history. Nowadays a whole branch of industry lives from the systematic cultivation of ginseng.

Botanically speaking, ginseng is a perennial radix plant of the Araliaceae family, woody plants with feather-shaped, finger-like or lobate leaves. It grows best in mountainous regions. It gets its botanical name, Panax schinseng, from the Greek term "panacea", a universal remedy. According to pharmaceutical laboratory tests, ginseng contains glycocides, saccharides, fatty substances, B-vitamins, enzymes and phytosterol.

These ingredients, which are well-known in modern pharmacy, were considered responsible in ancient Chinese herbal medicine for keeping the yin/yang forces in the human constitution in equilibrium. According to the traditional idea of dualism (male-female, positive-negative, light-dark, etc.), ginseng is supposed to contain a high concentration of "yang" components and so have a balancing effect in cases of ill health where there is a preponderance of "yin". Such cases include:
– physical decline or loss of strength, which is why the root is taken in all its medical forms (pills, juice, mixtures) as an aphrodisiac
– symptoms of poisoning
– excessive consumption of alcohol
– colds
– menopause and insufficient hormonal production by endocrine glands
– mild diabetes
– weakness before and after childbirth
– metabolic disorders
– declining vitality
– protein deficiency, undernourishment and anaemia
– low blood pressure
– malfunction of the liver.

When the wild plant, which seemed to thrive on particular mineral components in the Korean soil, could no longer meet with demands for ginseng, and when it was being weighed in gold at imperial courts in East Asia, people began to grow it systematically in plantations. During the Yi dynasty, the Koreans made their tributary payments to the Chinese Emperor partly in the form of ginseng – another reason for the regular cultivation of the root.

The Koreans have to take extreme care in nurturing the ginseng root. First of all the ground is prepared with a special mulch of fermented chestnut leaves, a process known to every Korean as "yakt'o". In order to protect the young ginseng plants from direct sunlight, hand-thatched roofs are set up at a specific angle roughly 3 ft above them. The plant is then allowed to grow for four to six years. During this time the roots can be cut off and processed. When the plant does not yield any more, the ginseng farmer must wait ten or fifteen years before the ground can be farmed again – this araliaceae utterly exhausts the soil.

After the plant has flowered in May, the seeds develop. The largest are selected about the middle of July and used for sowing. Sowing and harvesting are done in October. After being cleaned, peeled and steamed the roots are laid out to dry, and then they are made into the different forms of ginseng medicine.

Profits from the export of Korean ginseng root amount nowadays to well over US$ 150 million per year – a very important branch of industry indeed! *(Thiele)*

Industrial Expansion

Although Korea is still considered to be a country which is making the transition from agricultural land to industrialized nation, the threshold between the two has in fact almost been crossed.

Since the first five-year plan was introduced in 1962 the country's economy has taken an unprecedented step forward, a step which could well be an example to all Third World countries. For years Korea has registered a rise of 10% in its gross national product. The crucial factor in this economic development has been the ready availability of cheap labour.

After the disastrous Korean War, the country experienced economic development similar to that of postwar West Germany, but with one major difference: Germany was already fully industrialized. South Korea, on the other hand, was still a predominantly agricultural nation. As in Germany, support came from the USA: from American industry and from the US government, for they knew full well that the Koreans were a hard-working, highly disciplined people. After 1960 commercial loans and investments from abroad increased. This development shows clearly why Korea still has large debts abroad, and why she must spend part of the proceeds from exports to pay off these debts.

Hong Yong-sik was one of the eleven members of the first Korean delegation to visit the U.S.A. and several European countries in 1883.

It also reveals how dependent Korea is on foreign countries, since the availability of credit from abroad depends on foreign confidence in the Korean government.

Gerschenkron's theory that the more backward a country is in the process of industrialization, the more it must take over modern technology from industrialized nations in order to make progress, was put into practice in Korea. This resulted in a complete restructuring of the whole economy.

From 1962 to 1976 the industrial sector expanded four times as rapidly as the agricultural one. In the

More and more...

...tourists are travelling to Korea. In 1985, more than 1.4 million foreign visitors came to the Land of the Morning Calm, an increase of 8% on 1984. As one might expect, the Japanese headed the list of tourists in 1985 with a figure of 640,000; U.S. citizens followed up with 240,000; the British headed the league of European nations with just over 120,000.

Figures for the first half of 1986 were very promising. By the end of June, 570,000 foreigners had already visited Korea (the number of U.S. visitors had increased by 18%, that of British visitors by almost 10%).

With the 1988 Olympics focusing the attention of the world on Korea, an even greater increase in tourism is expected in the coming years.

same period the proportion of the gross national product represented by agricultural production sank from 44.1% to 20.4%, while that of the industrial sector rose from 11.9% to 36%.

After the normalization of Korean-Japanese relations in 1965, Korea's eastern neighbour took over a large share of further investment programmes. In 1959 Japan's share had been 19.1%, but this leapt to 63% in 1975, thus outstripping the private American loans almost threefold. The former archenemy, Japan, has now bought itself back into Korea through the financial side door.

With annual exports of an average 37%, Korea has put Gerschenkron's theory into practice from the very beginning of the first five-year plan in a really breathtaking fashion. The North American market has played a decisive role in this development. Almost 40% of South Korea's exports go to the USA, 20% to Japan, 17% to the European Community, and 13.4% to the Middle East (1977).

Korea's most important exports are textiles, electronic goods, shoes, steel products, plywood, ships, synthetics, cars, petro-chemical products and machinery. In 1976 the Export-Import Bank of Korea was founded, one of its aims being to export complete industrial plants, following the example of other industrialized countries. Big firms such as Hyundai, Daewoo and Samsung, conglomerates on the Japanese model, are among the economic giants of the country, and are some of the best customers of the Export-Import Bank.

Korea's imports consist primarily of raw materials (they accounted for 59.4% of all imports in 1983), and here oil is at the top of the list.

In 1983 Korea had a negative balance of trade amounting to US$ 1.7 billion. This was, however, US$ 1 billion less than in 1982. Lower oil prices, the rise in exports to the USA and a drastic reduction in debts abroad (this policy will be continued in the future) were the main reasons for this improvement. Here too, Korea's economy is expanding.

(Thiele)

Saemaul Undong –
Korea's Green Revolution

Three photographs which probably every visitor to Korea takes home with him: ginseng plantations laid out in the shade of little thatched roofs; beds of vegetables or tobacco carefully covered with long strips of plastic which glitter in the sunshine like newly fallen snow; and – very important – the colourful roofs of the farmhouses in a Korean village. Of these three photographs, however, you could not have taken the last two till later than the sixties.

At that time agriculture was not flourishing at all, and farmers had more to worry about than what the roofs of their little farms looked like. Even worse: many villages were dying, economically speaking. The returns were low and the resulting migration of the rural population to the towns paralyzed whole country areas. After two quite successful five-year plans (1962–1966/1967–1971), where the emphasis had been on economic development through industrialization, on rationalization and increasing exports, the economic difference between town and country sharpened dramatically. The result of the first five-year plan was a growth rate of 8.3%; but in the agricultural sector it was only 5.3%. In the second phase a proud 11% growth rate signalized a continuous upwards trend, while agriculture had to be content with a very slight growth rate of 2.5%. The living standard of industrial workers and employees improved steadily,

whereas the opposite was the case for farmers, who received little support or encouragement from the state.

Statistics show the result of this development: 70% of the whole rural population was employed in agriculture at the beginning of the sixties; in 1971 it was only 46%, and this has now sunk to 25%. Labour was urgently needed and there was a shortage of it; so young people in particular tried their luck in the towns. It was a vicious circle, one which had been set in motion by economic experts as a result of their one-sided encouragement of industry – and one which Park Chung-hee, himself from a farmer's family, wanted to break. His idea: help through self-help. Perhaps Park had got the idea from the Chinese People's Communes which were thriving at that time. The president gave the name **Saemaul Undong ("New Community")** to the movement with which he intended to restructure agriculture.

In 1971 Saemaul Undong was initiated with élan, the encouragement of agricultural development being given priority in the subsequent five-year plan (1972–76). Hard work, self-help and co-operation in conjunction with state support formed the foundation of these efforts to bring greater prosperity to the farming population. In this five-year period the state made more than

US$ 13 billion available to rural communities, each of which had its own particular needs and individual demands at the beginning. In this way differing needs were first satisfied in order to create a basis for economic expansion in the country.

But from the very beginning there was a **four-phase plan** underlying all these efforts. The first goal was the **redevelopment of the rural environment:** houses were renovated, wells were dug, plantations laid out, and sanitary installations completed. The second aim was the **improvement of the rural infrastructure:** roads, bridges and irrigation systems were built. The third phase was then to include the **setting-up of co-operatives** for field work, cattle breeding or the sale of agricultural produce. This was intended to raise the farmers' standard of living directly. With the establishment of small workshops a modest income was secured for the farmers in times of stagnation on the agricultural market. The fourth and final phase was concerned with the **improvement of medical welfare** in the countryside.

The whole project has met with success, even though the structure of Saemaul Undong has changed in the meantime. Nowadays, village committees express their wishes, which are then approved by regional councils. Finally, an advisory "central commission", responsible to the Minister of Home Affairs (who pulls all the strings in the enterprise), gives the go-ahead for the projects in question.

The system has proved so successful that other developing countries have shown interest: 16,000 foreign experts so far have sought on-the-spot information. In spite of the assassination of Park Chung-hee on 26th October 1979 the movement spread to the towns, where the population could also be motivated by the slogan, "hard work, self-help and co-operation". According to the latest official reports, working morale, law-abidingness and co-operation have all improved among the urban population. *(Rumpf)*

Transport

At the beginning of the seventies the aim of Korean traffic planners was to make Seoul accessible within a day from every corner of the country, using one form of transport or another. The result of this was that the communications network was developed systematically; the motorway network in particular was extended, and it is still undergoing further development. In addition to this enlargement of the motorway system, the electrification of the railways, the expansion of the shipyards and the improvement of air travel services were carried out.

Since 1970, passenger traffic has been moving from rail to road. In the Seoul subway too, passenger traffic has increased greatly. This is, of course, due to the extension and completion of this practical and economic means of transport. The subway system was inaugurated in 1974.

The first of Korea's motorways, or **"expressways"** was built in 1968 from Seoul to Inch'ŏn. This was followed by the Seoul-Pusan Expressway (the Kyongbu), the Taejon-Sunch'ŏn Expressway to the southwest, the Pusan-Sunch'ŏn Expressway, the Pusan-Masan route (the Namhae), the Kangnung Expressway between Seoul and the east coast, and the Olympic Expressway between Taegu and Kwangju. The Ulsan-Onjang Expressway in the eastern part of the country is a relatively small section. In 1983 alone more than ten million people passed over Korea's expressways. The number of motor vehicles increased from about 40,000 in 1965 to twenty times that figure in 1983.

The first **railway** line was built in 1899 in order to link the capital with the port of Inch'ŏn on the west coast. It was just over 33 km (20 miles) long. Now, almost a century later, the railway network has been extended to 6,129 km (3,800 miles). The Korean National Railway now owns 539 locomotives, 2,132 passenger carriages and 16,038 goods waggons.

Korea makes a distinction between ocean-going and coastal **shipping.** In a country with 3,000 islands, coastal shipping plays an important part in transport planning. As 580 of these islands are inhabited, an extensive passenger service must be provided. In 1983, 28,600 coasters transported goods and passengers, or were used for coastal fishing.

As is the case all over the world, civil air traffic has increased rapidly over the last fifteen years. Whereas in 1970 only 201,000 people arrived in Korea by international airlines, this figure had already risen to over 1.8 million in 1983.   *(Thiele)*

On Korea's Expressways

If roads are a measure of the industrial standard of a country, then Korea has made great progress in the last ten years. Korea's twelfth expressway was inaugurated in April 1985 and further plans for an extension of the network will soon be realized. About ten years ago, only the stretch between Seoul and Pusan (430 km/267 miles) had been built as an expressway, and was at that time the pride of the experts who were planning the improvement of Korea's infrastructure. Nowadays its broad, straight sections (which could, of course, be used as runways for military aircraft), although not exactly old-fashioned, have been complemented by other expressways which open up less developed regions of the country.

But it is not just the rapid expansion of the road network which amazes the visitor. No, it's also the way the Korean motorways are kept that would bring joy to the hearts of experts anywhere in the world. The central reserve is tended like a miniature Japanese garden, the bushes trimmed artistically into rounds balls. Markings on the road are always impeccable. The side verges look as if they were tended in the same careful way as the green central reserve, and in addition they are planted with decorative shrubs such as forsythia.

The main attraction on any Korean expressway, however, is the slope edging the road! Some have been planted to prevent landslides; many have been completely drained: concrete gutters ensure the smooth runoff of rain water.

The service areas with their restaurants, souvenir shops and sanitary installations (which really deserve their name) are exemplary. Some offer even more than these "essentials": besides modern monuments or statues (such as one for road workers who died during the building of a motorway, or one for the Korean War, or one simply to mark the middle of the Seoul-Pusan section) there are large information signs pointing out places of interest in the neighbourhood and written in Korean and English. An example that could be followed in other countries.

On the other hand, the Korean car driver is not so happy when he has to pay at the petrol station. Petrol prices are high in relation to

the average Korean income; and in addition, toll has to be paid for even short distances on the expressway – toll gates become a very familiar sight when you tour Korea by car.

You cannot race along the expressways either, for there are strict speed limits: 100 km (62 miles) per hour for cars, 80 km (50 miles) per hour for buses and 70 km (43 miles) per hour for lorries. These thwart the ambitions of potential racing drivers from the very beginning, although few drivers seem to stick to them.

But everyone does pay attention to the white or red flags that appear every now and then along the route. These flags draw attention to the danger of possible forest fires. The result is that hardly anyone throws a burning cigarette out of the car window.

When you drive along Korean roads the types of vehicle you meet are also unusual for an Asian country. Whereas Japanese makes predominate elsewhere, they hardly seem to exist in Korea. High import duties and car taxes prevent Honda, Mitsubishi, Mazda and other Japanese firms from doing good business in Korea. Western cars, too, are rarely to be seen. Instead, domestic products predominate. Many of these, however, are licence models of Japanese makes. "Pony" is the Korean Volkswagen; the luxury car is called "Royal Granada". Asia, Hyundai and Taewoo are the firms that share the Korean car market without stepping painfully on each other's toes. While one specializes in the production of buses, the other tries his hand at heavy commercial vehicles, and the third concentrates on the manufacture of private cars. More than 160,000 vehicles left the assembly lines in 1982 (100,000 cars, 21,000 buses and about 40,000 lorries were produced). In the same year there were just over a million vehicles on Korea's roads, the majority of them made in Korea. The size of the road network had af-ter all grown by then to 20,000 km (almost 12,500 miles).

The Korean car industry is now, however, switching to the offensive. The European and American markets are to be supplied with cheap models. If the success of Japan's car industry can be taken as a yardstick, then foreign car manufacturers will no longer enjoy their ride along Korea's excellent expressways as much as the tourist. *(Rumpf)*

The Korean Town

The ancient capitals of the Three Kingdoms – the Shilla capital, Kyŏngju; the Paekche capital, Puyo; and the Koguryŏ capital, Pyŏngyang (now in North Korea) – all had more than a million inhabitants in their heyday. When a new capital was founded, the other larger settlements were neglected.

Even at the beginning of our century, 90% of the Korean population were farmers, and so the urban population was correspondingly small. It was not till the beginning of the thirties that the process of indus-trialization gradually got underway in Korea, and this resulted in a change in the population structure. Nowadays only about 35% of the population work in agriculture. Although a sharp reduction in a relatively short period of time, this is still a fairly large proportion of the population if we consider industri-alized nations of the Western world (3% of the U. S. and U. K. population and around 5% of the Canadian and West German are employed in agriculture).

Korea's first industrial complexes were a power station on the River Pujon (North Korea) and a nitrog-enous fertilizer factory on the River Hungnam (North Korea). This indus-trialization progressed quicker in the north than in the south. Up to the partition of Korea the south was seen as the agricultural area. The population of the capital, Seoul, grew from 200,000 in 1920 to 1.1 million in 1943, and to 10 million in 1985! While there were only 12 towns in Korea in 1920, in 1944 there were already 22; nowadays the figure is 27. The growth of towns began with a vengeance after the Japanese retreat in 1945. The partition of the country in 1953 brought about a second period of rapid urban development. One rea-son for this was the number of refu-gees from North Korea, another was the expansion of industry.

The Koreans categorize towns and cities according to their dominant function.

– Political and administrative centres: Seoul, Ch'ŏngju, Chŏnju, Kwangju, Kangnung, Taegu, Ch'unch'ŏn. Cheju, Haeju, Hamhung.
– Commercial centres: Pusan, Masan, Mokp'o, Kunsan, Inch'ŏn, Kimch'ŏn, Kangnung, Najin, Wonsan, Chinnampo.
– Industrial centres: Hungnam, Songjin, Chongjin, Sinuiji, Pyŏngyang.
– Mining centres: Pukchin, Musan.
– Fishing centres: Sinpo, Sokch'o, Pohang, Chungmu, Samch'on'po, Yŏsu.
– Agricultural centres: Iri, Suwon, Sariwon.
– Centres of transport and communications: Taejon, Chonan, Seoul, Pyŏngyang, Iri.
– Tourist centres: Kyŏngju, Seoul, Pyŏngyang, Kaesong.
– Military centres: Chinhae, Wonju, Kwangju.

There was no town planning in Korea; towns were built within square town walls without any overall plan. Houses were erected according to the calculations of a geomancer, not according to urban needs or suitability. That is why almost all Korean towns give the impression of utter confusion. The streets were narrow and not laid out regularly. The first planning law was passed in 1921 (it proved completely ineffective); it was followed by a second one in 1934. Both were passed by the Japanese in the period of occupation. They aimed at straightening and broadening the streets to make them more suitable for the increased traffic load.

It has only been in the last few years that streets have been given names, and signs put up. But, on the whole, Koreans still orientate themselves by salient features, such as "near the South Gate", "at the fish market", "east of the temple" or "north of the bell tower".

It is only recently that new industrial centres, commercial towns and modern housing developments have been planned in accordance with town planning criteria, but often without taking social and, even more importantly, psychological considerations into account.

Many old town districts which have grown up organically, for example, are now being demolished and replaced by new housing developments – the latter are usually unimaginative and monotonous. Skyscrapers have also become a regular feature of Korean inner cities, for land has become astronomically expensive. Nevertheless, cities are expanding over wide areas because Koreans are used to having their own houses and do not like living in flats. This means that in Seoul, for example, the area south of the River Han has become fantastically built-up in the last few years, and little houses are springing up everywhere there.

Koreans are very mobile. For those who do not own their house, moving is nothing out of the ordinary. Permanent addresses and firmly established homes as in Europe are not the rule here. *(Thiele)*

The Korean Village

As all over East Asia, villages, settlements and houses were originally erected according to the instructions of geomancers or soothsayers. The geomancers worked out the appropriate position of the settlement from old cosmological calculations and with the aid of geomantic compasses. The function of the geomancer is very similar to that of the shaman; often they are one and the same person.

Settlements always stand alongside rivers, on lakes, or beside other watering places. This ensures an abundant supply of water for irrigation – essential for agriculture and, in particular, for the cultivation of rice (wet field culture here). Korea is an agricultural country and therefore consists mainly of small villages and relatively few big towns. Farmers in coastal areas are also usually fishermen. There are few true mountain villages.

Korean villages seem chaotic to the Western visitor. They can often be described as closely-packed, nucleate villages which are still frequently surrounded by loam or stone walls. If the agricultural acreage is small, the settlements are no bigger than hamlets. The houses of the different farms stand close together in an unsystematic arrangement. In each farmhouse lives an extended family whose daily life is shielded from the outside world by walls. You may only enter a house or farm when you are personally invited to do so. It is considered extremely rude if you enter without being expressly requested to.

This type of village, where the houses are crowded together, had the advantage in the old days, of course, of providing better protection. The closer people lived together, the better they could defend themselves against attacks and enemies. People also felt safer from natural catastrophes such as earthquakes, floods, thunder and lightning when they lived close to their neighbours rather than in scattered settlements. In any case, in a densely-populated country like Korea one cannot afford to build spaciously. Every available piece of land is needed for agriculture.

Another reason for the density of populated settlements is the fact that watering places are for common use. Then there is the Korean preference for living in a community. The smallest social unit is not the individual, but the family. This fact leads to particular forms of behaviour in personal relations, and is also revealed in the way villages are built, as described above.

In every village there are a number of public wells from which the farmers' wives draw drinking water every morning before carrying it home in big jars on their heads. So that there are no long distances to be covered between the well and home, the houses are built closely around such a village well. Usually eight to ten families depend on a well like this for their water supply.

The acceleration of industrialization since the fifties has caused a growing social gap between the urban and the rural population in South Korea. In an attempt to close this gap, President Park Chung-hee founded the Saemaul Movement in 1970. Saemaul means "new village" or "new community". As part of this movement rivers are being regulated, river banks stabilized, the power supply increased, central water mains laid and telephone communications established. The coloured corrugated iron or tiled roofs that have replaced the old thatch can be seen from far off. All these measures are aimed at raising the standard of living in the country.

The size of a village is reckoned according to the number of families living there. In Korea there are:
– 150 villages with more than 150 families
– 251 villages with 100–150 families
– 498 villages with 60–100 families
– 595 villages with 30–60 families
– 191 villages with fewer than 30 families.

The third and fourth groups make up 65% of all Korean villages. These figures are from the year 1970. Since then there have been considerable shifts of population because

The traditional dress of government officials and scholars, "turumagi", is still worn by elderly men in the country.

of increased industrialization, urbanization and the improvement of the infrastructure. The largest villages in South Korea are to be found in the provinces of Chŏlla and Kyŏngsang, the smallest on the Kaema Plateau and in the Taebaek Mountains.

(Thiele)

Man and Society

As is the case with many other peoples, the Koreans trace their origin to a legend. According to this legend, the Divine Creator had a son, Hwanung, who wanted to live on earth. In order to make this possible, he breathed on a tiger and a bear who mated and produced a human being, Tangun. Tangun was the leader of nine clans, encompassing three thousand tribes. These made up the first Korean society, the Korean people. Tangun founded his capital in Chonp'yŏng at the foot of Mount Paektu, on the River Yalu. The kingdom expanded from here, and later Pyŏngyang was founded as the new capital further south. The country now covered the area between the Amur and the Ch'ungch'ŏng region. The Koreans call this period the Kingdom of Paedal and it is said to have lasted 1,200 years.

Korean ethnologists trace their own people to **Tungusic** and **Mongolian** tribes. Linguistically they belong to the **Ural-Altaic** group. The Tungus lived, and still live, in the area which used to be called Manchuria, and in southern Siberia; they are a Mongolian race. The name Tungus comes from the Chinese word "tunghou" or "tungi" which means approximately "barbarians from the east". The name was introduced to Europe in the seventeenth century by the Russians. Some Koreans thus believe that the Tungus were not only their own ancestors but those of the Chinese as well.

Perhaps this explains the strong Chinese influence in Korea. According to the Chinese anthropologist, Pei Wen-Chung, the Mongolian race is descended from the "Homo pekinensis" or Peking Man, who lived 500,000 years ago.

It can be deduced from dolmen-like tombs that Korea was already inhabited in Neolithic times (i. e. 6,000 years ago, in the third epoch of human history). Written documentary evidence goes back as far as the 2nd millenium B. C., thus covering 4,000 years of history. Koreans can therefore prove that they are one of the most ancient cultures on earth.

Anthropologically speaking – that is, from a purely biological point of view – the Koreans belong to a sub-group of the **brachycephalic peoples** of Central Asia (brachycephaly, from the Greek meaning short-headedness). So Koreans were among the short-headed tribes that migrated from Central Asia to the Korean peninsula at different periods.

According to statistics quoted by Kim Kisu, professor at the University of Usok, Koreans have an average height of 161–169 cm (i. e., less than 5'6"). The colour of their hair is generally black to dark brown and grows in thick, separate strands. Like all Mongolian peoples, Koreans have the characteristic epicanthic fold of skin over the inner angle of the eye and have relatively small, dark irises. There is no dominant type of nose.

The Koreans' posture is graceful on the whole, and harmonious. Unlike Europeans, their limbs are shorter and their torso longer. Women are somewhat smaller than men. North Korean women are on the whole somewhat taller than South Korean females. There is a Korean saying that the south produces strong men and the north, beautiful women.

For Koreans, behaviour and speech are closely linked. Assuming that he speaks Korean, the outsider can immediately recognize the kind of relationship that exists between two people. The type of relationship can, of course, change from a familiar one to something much more formal if, for example, the attitude of the socially superior to the subordinate partner is disturbed or hurt by improper conduct on the part of the latter. If the superior and the subordinate adopt a formal tone again, it is clear to the outsider that a closer relationship used to exist but has been spoiled.

Probably the most important aspect of social behaviour for Koreans is **"kibun"**. There is no adequate translation of this very comprehensive concept. Let us describe it as "harmonious understanding". If there is "kibun" you feel like a millionaire; if "kibun" has been destroyed, you feel like someone who has to eat worms – to quote a

Korean proverb. "Kibun" is what holds body and soul together. It is responsible for a good network of social relationships, and allows people to be treated with respect and not contempt. The aim of "kibun" is peace, harmony and security. The odd white lie is often necessary in order to achieve "kibun", and even as children, Koreans are taught to strive for "kibun" and behave accordingly.

This pattern of behaviour has ancient roots. Its source is the longing for peace and harmony. This is why a Korean asks when he meets you, "Are you at peace with yourself?" And when he says goodbye, he often says, "Go in peace". The biggest mistake you can make in Korea is to show off in a group, give yourself airs, or insist that you know better than the others. You ruin the "kibun" and people will avoid you.

In a rural society like Korea's – a society which tends to be patriarchal and even partly feudal still – there is a clear hierarchical structure. The upper classes are said to have more "kibun" than the lower. If, however, a foreigner behaves like a Korean aristocrat, he will be treated with contempt and not respect, and he might even meet with hostility. Here "kibun" is judged by a double standard; and so it is important to avoid arrogant and haughty behaviour.

"Kibun" can also be spoiled if a meal or celebration is not opulent enough. Koreans often get themselves into debt in order to treat

Perfect Harmony – Not Showing the Flag?

Some flags flap in the wind and behave altogether in a rather warlike way; their emblem is often the eagle with his watchful eyes, frightening beak and grasping claws, its whole posture announcing that it is not easy to get on with the people who live under this banner. Other flags, however, appear quite charming, with soft, matching colours. A third group have the rays of a rising sun to remind one of successful wars of liberation from the colonial yoke, or of some other significant historical event. And so on. In the opinion of psychologists, every nation gathers under the flag that represents in symbols the deep-seated fears and hopes of its people.

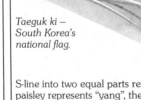

Taeguk ki – South Korea's national flag.

If that is the case, then you may stand under the Korean flag in a rather perplexed state of mind – in harmonious perplexity, however. For "taeguk ki", as the round national emblem on a white background (symbol of peace) with the odd lines in the corners is called, is not meant to remind you of anything heroic. Nor is it meant to warn off potential aggressors – nor to express fears or hopes. Taeguk ki is no more than the symbol of perfect balance, of harmony. Much Asian philosophy is woven into this flag, in its own sign language. If you can draw conclusions about the national character from it, then the Koreans come off well. Whether they would choose this symbol anew after the ruthless industrialization of the last fifteen years is perhaps doubtful, however.

The middle of the white flag is filled by a circle divided by an S-line into two equal parts resembling paisley patterns. The upper red paisley represents "yang", the lower blue one, "ŭm" ("yin") – ancient, originally Chinese symbols for the harmony of the universe. The two different colours represent the dualism of opposing principles or forces in the cosmos or in the absolute: fire and water, day and night, feminine and masculine. The circle that encloses these two opposites expresses the continuous movement in the eternal – no one extreme dominates over an other; what is above today is tomorrow below. Here is one example: rice needs water to grow, whereas a drought causes the plants to dry up; so rain is positive, drought negative. But too much rain can cause floods which destroy the rice plants just as a drought does. A balance between rain and drought is therefore necessary in order to achieve ideal growth.

The three lines in each of the four corners around the circle symbolize this philosophy too. The three solid bars in the top left corner represent heaven, the opposite broken lines in the bottom right hand corner stand for earth. The bars in the bottom left corner symbolize fire, the upper-right bars, water. These signs (trigrams) are based on ancient Pakwa characters which also express the idea of opposing principles.

This circular symbol also appears as decoration on temple gates and on the fan officially designed for the 1988 Olympic Games, but is divided into three parts by two S-lines instead of the two sections we have just mentioned. The very first Korean flag was like this, for Koreans believe that uneven numbers are more perfect than even ones, and so this symbol is nearer the idea of universal perfection.

When Korea was a kingdom, "yang" and "ŭm" symbols were already considered to be the national emblems. However, the royal colours were red and gold, the coat-of-arms plum blossom and dragon. Unlike the five-clawed Chinese dragon on which it was modelled, the Korean dragon was only allowed to display four claws – a further expression of harmony with the much mightier neighbour.   *(Rumpf)*

guests lavishly on special occasions such as birthdays, weddings or funerals. If social conventions or rules of etiquette are not adhered to, "kibun" suffers.

Korean society has a vertical rather than horizontal structure. This fact must be kept in mind at all times. One's "superiors" are treated according to their higher social position in every situation. The old Confucian social framework as regards relations between king and subject, head of family and eldest son, brother and sister, older friend and younger friend, etc. still plays a decisive role in modern Korea. Whoever does not adhere to the rules and conventions of society is considered a non-person, an outcast, a **"sang-nom".** Being a "sangnom" in Korea means living outside the system of relationships which make up human society. Beggars, criminals, butchers (because of the bloody nature of their work) – and foreigners who do not keep to the accepted social conventions – are thought of as "sang-nom". Hierarchy exists everywhere, even among the social outcasts. Thus it is interesting to note that a slaughterer of cattle is considered higher than a pig butcher, and both are better than a dog butcher.

The maintenance of good relationships within society is absolutely essential. If a person has made an enemy of someone, not only the individual concerned suffers, but the whole family. In some families a particular feud is passed on from generation to generation. The western idea of fair play or of giving someone another chance after he has made a mistake or failed is not widespread in Korea. Therefore beware of making enemies in Korea! Koreans themselves try hard to avoid making enemies for they know it will be a fight to the death. Politeness and the cultivation of "positive" relations with people are therefore the principal rules of conduct for every Korean.

The smallest social unit in Korea is, as everywhere in East Asia, the **family.** This is organized on the Confucian model. Respect must always be shown to one's elders. When an older person is present, one may start eating, drinking or smoking only when he has begun to do so. If an older person joins a group of younger people, cigarettes are discreetly put out. In restaurants you will often see a younger man handing a glass to an older person without looking at him directly, but with lowered eyes. It is considered rude to keep on your glasses when talking to an older person, and quite reprehensible if they are sunglasses. At prayers in a Buddhist temple or any other place of worship it is usual to take off your spectacles.

To put elderly people into an old people's home would be considered a very serious offence in Korea, if not a crime. The older members of the family have the best room in the house. The sixtieth birthday, the day the famous cycle of sixty years closes, is celebrated with particular pomp. From this point on it is the duty of the eldest son to provide for his father and/or mother.

The **role of women** is laid down by tradition. In the old days a wife hardly left the house. If she did not bear her husband a son she could be declared a "non-person" or even cast off altogether. Concubinage has now been officially abolished in Korea. Koreans do not speak of family affairs, and especially not of intimate relationships outside the family circle. It has only recently become common for young couples to show affection in public. But kissing or embracing in public are still frowned upon.

In the old days, boys and girls were separated at the age of seven. Nowadays, however, there is coeducation in Korea. Nevertheless, you usually see separate groups of men or women in Korea. This separation of the sexes (the latter are also subdivided into different age groups) is very striking. As Koreans like travelling in groups, you often see the men striding ahead and the ladies following at a respectful distance. Women are treated with respect in Korean society. It is extremely rare for a woman to be harassed in any way in public. Foreign women too can walk everywhere alone without hesitation and feel perfectly safe.

Over 60% of **marriages** are still arranged in Korea, and this costs a lot of money. Professional marriage brokers show huge albums full of photographs of the ladies who are looking for a marriage partner. Very often, complicated horoscope calculations with the personal data of the two people concerned have to be carried out before a meeting is even arranged. It is a geomancer or fortune-teller who decides for or against a marriage in most cases. It is well known that girls improve their chances of marrying by following a course of higher education.

Not until the contract between the two families has been drawn up can young people who want to marry be seen together in public. There is a little ceremony to mark the signing of the contract where the girl appears in pink national dress accompanied by her financé who also wears the traditional "hanbok". As is often the case, the bride's family has to provide a complete dowry, which is probably one reason why daugh-

ters are not so popular in families as sons. A bevy of young daughters who want to get married can cost a pater familias a fortune. In order to achieve "kibun" here too, a family sometimes accrues immense debts.

According to an old belief, a young woman will bear daughters if she smiles on her wedding day. As boys are preferred, the bride is usually seen on her big day with a calm, serious expression. Childless wives suffer a hard fate. They often take their problems to the shaman or the temple and pray for children.

Bridal couple dressed in traditional clothing, or "hanbok".

In Korea a woman's sexual appeal is not judged by breasts or lovely legs – both are covered. Instead, a bare neck and the big toe are considered to have erotic appeal. Girls are supposed to behave in a shy, reserved way or they are treated as "non-persons". Young people who adopt Western manners and customs often become social outcasts. There is, however, a trend towards the adoption of Western habits in Korea now, and it is spreading from the Seoul area over more and more of the country.

Unmarried women – apart from nuns – are often treated as "big babies" by the rest of Korean womanhood, are rarely taken seriously, and are hard to integrate in any group of women. Widows rarely remarry.

Physical contact, especially in public, is considered vulgar. Even shaking hands, as a foreign habit, has been adopted only recently. When you meet someone, you both simply bow and utter a few polite phrases.

A Korean hands over a present with both hands, and it is appreciated when a foreigner does the same. When you enter a room full of people, then make way for yourself by gently pushing the people aside with your right arm, but in a bowing posture. When you do this your left hand should grasp the lower right arm.

All kinds of physical movement are carried out by Koreans in a lei-surely way. They hate rushing or hurrying. This is why they are often unpunctual, which takes foreigners aback. This unpunctuality does not apply to public transport, however. Buses and tourist coaches leave and arrive on the dot. (On the express services all the buses are equipped with televisions and videos. A bus guide welcomes the passengers with a deep bow, announces the film programme, serves drinks and takes the utmost trouble with every passenger.)

One taboo to keep in mind if ever you are with Koreans is blowing your nose in public. They find it extremely rude to do this in the presence of another. A Korean never puts a handkerchief in his pocket.

It is a great advantage if you have visiting cards printed which you can hand over personally when you are introduced in Korea. The foreign visitor should also learn a few Korean phrases and the 24 signs of the han'gŭl alphabet which make it possible to read almost everything, even if you do not understand what you read. Korean titles such as the respectful way of addressing a man (= "nim"), a doctor (= "sa"), a teacher (= "saeng"), a woman (= "ssi"), come after the surname. Men are addressed first, then ladies.

When you enter a Korean house you must always remove your shoes. Slippers are laid out for the guests at the entrance – but not always in European or American sizes!

Koreans never introduce themselves. In a little ceremony you are introduced by friends and acquaintances. When your name is mentioned, the older person says, "It's the first time I've met you". The younger person then says the same. Both bow, and that is the end of the formal introduction. If you are a guest in a Korean home, servants or employees will not be introduced.

It is unusual for Koreans to drop names in a conversation to show that one is acquainted with this or that person. In Korea a name has a certain aura. Titles, the name of the occupation or formal forms of address are used instead. The foreign guest should therefore avoid mentioning the name of the Korean to whom he is talking too frequently in the course of a conversation; it is considered impolite. What then do you say in a conversation when your opposite number has to be addressed directly? Koreans usually use the word "yŏbo", which means roughly "you see".

If ever you are fortunate enough to be invited by the President you must address him as **"kakha"** (Your Excellency). A high government official is addressed as **"yŏnggam"** (=honourable gentleman). Yangban was originally a member of the aristocracy. This is still the name used for a superior when one talks of him in his absence. Scholars, doctors or academics in general are addressed as **"paksa"**, while **"sonsaeng"** (=the elder, firstborn) is the general form of address in

everyday dealings with Korean men. A teacher calls his students **"kun"**, children are addressed as **"yae"**.

Many foreigners get confused by the fact that wives have a different surname from their husbands. In Korea women keep their maiden names. Moreover, foreigners find it hard to tell if a Miss, Mr. or Mrs. is being talked about, for all three have the title **"ssi"**. The surname in Korea always comes before the personal name.

The wife talks of her husband as **"uri chip chuin"** = the master of the house, whereas the husband calls his wife **"yobo"** which means "darling" or "dear".

When name and title are used, exact differences are made depending upon whom one is talking to, what rank or position he or she has, and what kind of relationship exists between the speakers. It is not easy for foreigners to choose the correct form here. On the other hand, many a Western lady with grey streaks in her hair is addressed by the Koreans as "grandmother". For Koreans this is not an insult; they are merely showing their respect for grey hair and age.

The foreign guest must be careful not to eat all the food set before him at a meal; that would destroy "kibun". The host would be dismayed for he would think he had not prepared enough, and he would thus lose face. All leftovers will be used up so you need not worry about things being thrown away – Koreans are very economical and very good at finding a use for things.

At a Korean meal you should do your best to avoid touching anything with your fingers: chopsticks, spoons and little sticks like toothpicks are always laid out for use. It is considered very impolite to touch food. Koreans regard it as very selfish and vulgar too if you refill your own glass. All liquids, such as sauces and drinks, are served by your neighbour and vice versa.

Formerly there was not much conversation at table. A **business lunch** in our sense was looked down upon by the Koreans. But this form of "negotiation" is becoming more fashionable nowadays. The meal is usually followed by entertainment. At bigger functions it is customary for guests to sing a song, tell a story or contribute to the general entertainment in some other way. The Koreans love singing, and they expect their foreign guests to sing or recite poetry too. If you refuse, you are going against the group "kibun". The party will then leave the room with very mixed feelings. Business may also be discussed over a "kisaeng" party (see chapter on "kisaeng"). Here too a certain code of behaviour must be followed.

In Korea the old Roman principle of "do ut des", i. e. "I give so that you give", prevails. If you receive a **present** – of any kind whatever – the Koreans always expect a return gift. This can be a material present or some kind of favour. This principle must be respected. Sometimes you have to be very careful, as the boundary between a simple friendly gesture and an attempt at bribery is fluid. Foreigners especially should be aware of this custom and think it over carefully before accepting or refusing any largish present. If it is not possible to make a return gift, then to accept is not only extremely impolite, but downright insulting and a cause of loss of face. In order to get out of a delicate situation when it is a question of an expensive, official present and where it is quite clear that a similar gift cannot be given in return, you can announce that you will pass it on to some charity or other.

It is equally important to know the rules about giving birthday, wedding and funeral presents. Birthday presents are wrapped in red, the others often in white. At weddings the guest usually hands over an envelope with money which is opened when he enters the house. As in old China, the sum of money is shown on a board for all to see. At funerals too the person paying a visit of condolence hands over a gift of money. It is considered rude to hand over a cheque, for it causes more trouble cashing a cheque, and you do not want to cause the people concerned more trouble than necessary under the circumstances. For foreigners it is important to know that presents are not to be unwrapped in front of the guest; the value of the gift, if

Travelling Folk

If Koreans had not always been very attached to nature, you would have to assume that they had just developed a particular need for nature in these times of great industrial progress. For nowhere in Asia do you meet as many people hiking as in Korea. Young people especially are choosing to explore their country in this way. Armed with rucksacks, and resplendent in anoraks, hiking boots and breeches, they form large and small groups of keen backpackers. And their respect for the environment is exemplary: there are no signs of an affluent society in the form of litter or refuse left lying along the way.

The month of May in particular seems to carry the Koreans' wander-lust to extremes. Paths leading to temples in the forests are crowded with people who have not, however, been driven to these holy places by any religious impulse. They camp in clearings and thoroughly enjoy their pic-nics, dancing gaily on the paths. Older women dressed in "chima-cho-gori", the colourful national dress, are particularly noticeable. They are usually slightly tipsy, and sometimes quite drunk; and they often ask strangers to join in the dancing. The children will have paid for the mothers' outing, and they are allowed to really let themselves go on this occasion, but *only* on this occasion. At home it is quite a different story altogether.

It is particularly astonishing to see whole classes of schoolchildren trav-elling everywhere in May: the whole of Korea seems to be one big school. The younger and older pupils march along on their outings in well-behaved rows of two or three. The teachers walk at the head and the end of the procession and they can be sure that no-one will break away to do his own thing. When the pupils used to wear school uniform it smacked of regimented leisure. But a glance at the children's faces quickly set the outsider right.

Koreans hike through their country; it is, without a doubt, surely one of the loveliest and most intensive ways of getting to know the land.

(Rumpf)

inappropriate, could spoil the "kibun".

Koreans are very self-confident people. Unfortunately, however, they often overrate their own abilities. There is danger in this false assess-ment of oneself, which can lead to what a German friend who has lived in Korea for many years now calls the "90% syndrome". By this he means that many things are started but not carried through to the end. There is frequently the problem of saving face when someone claims to be an expert, and it turns out that he is not. Not until everything is ruined and beyond repair does the "expert" read the instructions. In many fields of activity Koreans are possessed of an unbelievable daring – we might in fact call it recklessness!

We had a very telling experience in our friend's house in Seoul. The house was empty on one particular day and someone broke in. In such cases Koreans give a discreet little cough to tell the burglar it is time he disappeared. The owner of the house has no right at all to chase the burglar off his premises with a stick, or to attack him physically. If a burglar, caught red-handed, threatens an inhabitant and the latter shoots him, this is not regarded as self-defence but as murder. To leave a house in Korea empty and unattended is practically to invite theft. After all, a burglar has to live too. Even if someone breaks into your house and you shout for help, the neighbours will not hurry to your aid. There is only one solution in this case: if you shout "Fire! Fire!" loudly, you can be sure of your neighbour's help.

Our friend has found another solution: during the day he leaves the radio on loud, and this gives the impression that someone is at home. Another gesture is a little notice on the door which says, "Dear burglar,

there is nothing to steal in our house. If you come nevertheless, let us know in advance and you can be our guest at dinner." – For ten months now burglars have steered clear of the house.

We can observe what is to us a most unusual way of dealing with a given situation if we happen to see a traffic accident in Korea. If a driver is involved in a serious accident where people are injured, he must expect to be put in prison immediately to calm the "public consciousness", no matter who caused the accident. So if you drive yourself in Korea, beware!

Acts of helpfulness outside the circle of the extended family, in the public interest as it were, are rare in this country. According to the traditional Korean view of things, whoever helps another disinterestedly does it to appease his own conscience or to atone for past sins.

In business dealings, Koreans attach great importance to patience and perseverance. Business is never discussed immediately or directly. The central point of the discussion is approached gradually and in a very roundabout way. The Korean business partner will move from apparently trivial subjects to flattery and to **"nunch'i"**, the careful observation of the other. He adopts a more wait-and-see attitude, politely reserved and on the alert. He is a tactician par excellence, flexible and firm, like bamboo, as watchful as a tiger, and as cunning and persevering as a fox. Koreans are brilliant diplomats – this applies to their dealings in the world of business too.

In Korea it is considered wise not to display one's true financial circumstances, and not to show off what one has. It is more important to know that what is aimed at is the building up of personal relationships, and especially the inclusion of other family members in business. Koreans do not feel duty-bound to any institution, ideology, or government, to justice, honour or any other ethical or moral principle. But they do feel an obligation and close attachment to other members of their family or clan, their teachers, their political patrons or their boss.

(Thiele)

The Role of Women

In Korea family relationships are defined according to Confucian philosophy. The keystone of all relations is the respect of children for their parents and their absolute obedience to them. This is a perfectly natural duty for two reasons:
1. The parents have engendered the children and given them birth.
2. The parents bring up and educate the children.

Stepchildren have the same obligations to their parents as natural children.

Respect for the parents is carried on even after death. Ancestor worship is eloquent proof of this.

In a wider sense, respect must be shown to all older people, other relatives and friends.

The position of women in the Korean family was, and frequently still is, subordinate to that of the men. It is true that the role of women and their standing in society have changed in recent times because they often work, because Western cultures have influenced Korean life,

and because Koreans now often live in smaller flats where there is only room for the nuclear family. But there are nevertheless many marriages that are still hierarchical in structure, a consequence of Confucianist teaching. According to this philosophy, a wife is considered to be her husband's servant, and she must do all the heavy housework without complaint or protest. Like the women in Islamic countries, she lives an extremely secluded life, and to strangers she is almost invisible in the house.

Confucianism listed seven deadly sins that a women had to avoid, namely: being disobedient to her parents-in-law; not bearing a son; committing adultery; being jealous; bringing hereditary illness into the marriage; thieving; and finally, being a gossip.

These rules, drawn up here as **"ch'ilgo chiak"** for Korean women in general, were set out for "yangban" ladies – that is, for the female members of the aristocracy – in a book of etiquette, Queen Sokye's **"Naehun"**. According to this book, ladies had to behave morally, dress correctly, pay attention to their accent, and run their household prudently. Noble ladies were confined to a life at home in just the same way as their bourgeois counterparts. Hardly any lady would dare show herself in public, in parks or on river banks, except in the company of her husband or her brother. The penalty for doing so would have been a hundred lashes of the whip – this was a law in the Kyongguk taejon (1485).

Even today you rarely see Korean women in men's company. This is something tourists notice immediately. Women often walk separately from their husbands. Women of the same age often appear in groups in public. And in restaurants groups of men usually eat together.

Korean women are extremely hard-working and very competent. You see them carrying heavy loads; as well as having their babies on their backs they are usually laden with various bags and baskets.

In the old days (i. e., at the end of the nineteenth century) the lot of women in Korea must have been really pitiful. Ernst von Hesse-Wartegg (1851–1918), a travel writer born in Vienna who recorded his experiences all over the world in a number of works, described it in his book "Korea" (published 1895): "You can see that men never show women signs of tenderness or even respect. Otherwise the women would pay more attention to their appearance. But why should they? For a very short period only are they the toys of their husbands, then they become their slaves. When they are children they are given a name to distinguish them from their sisters, and they keep it till they are married. But only their parents and relations know this name…"

It is a fact that even today married women in Korea keep their maiden name; so they have a different surname from their husband. This shows too the position of the wife outside the husband's family.

In the old days the sexes were separated at the age of eight or ten. Up to this time boys and girls could play together quite freely. Later, however, the sons lived in the men's quarters, and the girls in the part of the house reserved for the women. Just as there is still a man's and a woman's section in the traditional round tent (yurta) of Mongolian nomads, there was, and sometimes still is, a similar division in Korean houses in the country. In the old days too girls were taught not to let themselves be seen by men, and the boys learned that it was improper to go around with girls or women. There are still traces of this old attitude, although there have been many changes in recent years.

One result of this code of conduct stemming from Confucian philosophy was that there was no family life as we know it – at least for about a thousand years. Marriage was a relationship with the sole purpose of extending the family tree. This is why it was so important for the wife to bear a son. Even nowadays the desire for a male child is particularly strong, for it is the duty of the eldest son to look after his parents in their old age. The family had to be held together and defended, but there was never a close relationship between husband and wife.

The position of women in Korea has definitely improved, especially because of external influences. They have more freedom, and nowadays they at least have the chance of choosing their own partner, although 60% of Korean marriages are still arranged by a marriage broker. Urban life especially has brought a kind of liberalisation to women's lives. Now that the family lives crowded together in a tiny town flat, and now that the women often contribute to the family budget and are full members of urban society, they do tend to be partners in the marriage, and they have a say in family decisions.

Korean family life is assuming Western traits, and the Confucian code of conduct seems to be followed less strictly. At a price, however, which we should not underrate: in the old days divorce was extremely rare, whereas nowadays the number of divorces is rising steadily.   *(Thiele)*

Seesawing is popular among Korean girls and women. Perhaps the game gives them the chance – for once – to "jump out" of the narrow family circle.

Education

The Korean system of education dates back to the year 373 A.D., when the institution of **T'achak** was founded where young upper-class Koreans were taught **Chinese literature, history and philosophy.**

The Shilla period saw the foundation of a parallel institution with the romantic name of **Hwarangdo** or "Flower Youth Movement". The latter, however, laid emphasis on **military skills** rather than on the traditional ideals of education as taken over from China. The ideals of Hwarangdo were loyalty, filial piety, honesty, courage and fairness. The **Kukhak** School, which was then fouded in Unified Shilla (682 A.D.) combined to a certain extent both these trends, offering its students a Confucian education and military training before they left to take over important positions of state.

During the Koryŏ dynasty (918–1392), Buddhist ideals of education were added to the above and taught, especially at the **Kukchagam School,** which was founded in 992 A.D. All these centres of learning were situated in the capital.

Parallel to the schools for the upper classes there were those of other social groups known collectively as **Hyanggyo.** The same subjects were taught there as at the schools of the ruling classes. They were open to anyone who could afford the fees.

In 1272, reflecting the rise and spread of Neo-Confucianism, the "East-West School", **Tongsŏhaktang,** was established to teach exclusively Confucian philosophy. The name East-West was derived from the fact that the school buildings were situated in the east and west of the city. The highest educational institution remained the Kukchagam School which, however, was given the new name of **Sŏnggyungwan** in 1398. It could be compared to present-day Seoul National University. As well as this state institution there were **private schools (Sodang** or **Sowon)** where scholars from the state university often gave classes.

At the end of the Yi dynasty there was a gradual movement away from Chu Hsi's Neo-Confucian philosophy of education, and especially from a hierarchical system whereby only certain social classes had a right to education. By 1882 pupils from all classes could enrol in state schools and universities. This development was due in part to the influence of Western missionaries.

Nowadays attendance at **primary school** for six years is free of charge, and compulsory for all children over six years of age. Since 1969 every child has had the **right to attend middle school** (junior high) regardless of performance; there is an entrance examination for senior high school.

After senior high school, pupils can move on to university, i. e. to **colleges modelled on those in America.** The entrance examinations are difficult, especially for Seoul National University (SNU), which is considered an élite institution.

As well as this university and many other state institutions, there are very many private colleges and universities which have very varied standards. University education usually lasts four years; at colleges of technology the duration of a course of study is usually five years. After that, intensive courses of study are offered – again on the American model – leading to a doctorate.

If Koreans study abroad they usually do so in the USA or in West Germany. A small number of students go to France, Canada, Taiwan or Japan.

Vocational training is not yet highly developed in Korea, because in most trades the skills of the fathers are passed on directly to the sons. Systematic training as part of an apprenticeship has not yet been introduced everywhere in Korea. The first steps to encourage people to acquire formal qualifications were taken in 1967 in the Vocational Training Plan. This made it possible for apprentices or trainees to receive vocational education at special institutes or training centres.   *(Thiele)*

Language and Writing

It was a great and decisive step towards the education of the masses when, on the 25th December 1443, King Sejong of the Yi dynasty presented his court with a new script in the form of 11 vowels and 17 consonants. This script was **"han'gŭl".** Sejong, who was 47 years old at the time and at the peak of his political career as fourth ruler of the new dynasty, foresaw that not only could all classes of traditional Korean society be reached with "han'gŭl", but that the new, simplified system of writing would also enable everyone to write down his own thoughts and ideas on paper. The particular aim of "han'gŭl", however, was to help create an independent, national culture. Sejong turned out to be

right, and "han'gŭl" has kept its undisputed position as Korea's own system of writing up to this very day.

A commission of experts had worked for many years with the learned king on this phonetical alphabet, which had the added advantage that it was easy to learn. In the grounds of Kyŏngbok Palace in Seoul there still stands the pavilion where they all racked their brains over the problem of how to get away from the difficult Chinese characters, which only a small class of privileged scholars could read. The new system was so ingeniously simple that it remained unchanged for 500 years. There was no need for reform until 1933, and even after this, 10 of the vowels and 14 of the consonants remained. From combinations of these 24 basic signs, 140 phonetic signs can be produced. These can be joined to make 230 syllables, with which everything can be exactly written.

It was certainly not very easy to promote "han'gŭl"; the resistance of the majority of the scholars at that period was a major obstacle. Since Chinese characters, among many other things, had been taken over from the great Chinese neighbour 1,500 years before, the privileged classes considered it an act of political disobedience, or at the very least an unfriendly act as far as diplomacy was concerned, to replace Chinese script with "han'gŭl". Many people probably thought it was a passing fad which would only cause problems in education and administration. This is why people had earlier relied upon "idu" ("government script"). This was introduced by the Confucian scholar Sol Ch'ong in 682 (i. e., during the Shilla dynasty); it featured Chinese characters. During the subsequent Koryŏ period the "kugyol" script was developed. It was less complicated than "idu" and was in use up to the end of the nineteenth century.

Sejong, in any case, overcame much resistance. He had Chinese classics printed in "han'gŭl", while poems as well as Buddhist verses were transcribed into the new writing. In the following centuries, however, Confucian scholars managed to raise Chinese in the form of

"kugyŏl" script to a higher level of significance than "han'gŭl". But the first Christian missionaries recognized an opportunity to undermine the power of the China-oriented élite. Realizing that the use of Chinese characters was a reflection of China's influence, the missionaries adopted "han'gŭl". So "han'gŭl" did eventually become a written language – and the greatest cultural achievement of the Korean people.

It is true, however, that there is still no standardized transcription of "han'gŭl" into any other world languages. The Americans have four systems of transcription alone, and these differ greatly in parts. This is why the spelling of Korean place names – to give but one example – is not uniform.

In addition, Chinese has not completely disappeared. It remains as the script of scholarly and educated people, and in most Korean newspapers it is printed side by side with "han'gŭl". In the same way, Chinese characters have been kept in Korean family names alongside the Korean ones.

One legend tells of the origin of "han'gŭl" in a more poetical way than all the historical records. In those days, so is told, King Sejong was suffering from an eye complaint and visited a Korean thermal spring. To relieve the pain in his eyes he looked at the different motifs on the wooden lattice-work over the doors and windows. The king's eyes were not only soothed, but the wooden lattice-work provided the graphical foundation for the new letters, which are written from left to right.

The Korean language, which is uniform all over the country, belongs to the Tungusic-Manchurian group of the Ural-Altaic family of languages. Finnish and Hungarian also belong to this group. There have been occasional attempts to establish a connection with Indo-Germanic languages by comparing roots of different words. Apart from grammatical structures there is no similarity to Japanese, nor to Chinese. It is assumed that at the beginning of Korean history at least two different languages existed, both belonging to the Altaic group. According to this theory the Tungusic one was spoken in Manchuria and the northern part of the peninsula, and the other one, from which modern Korean probably developed, in the southern part. Chinese influence on the language is also apparent in the form of loan words.   *(Rumpf)*

Religion

Shamanism

You can recognize a "mudang" by her cap and flowing robes of yellowish dyed hemp; on her head sway colourful cock feathers. She strides up and down excitedly, swinging her magic mirror, fans, sword and rattle. The muttering of magic formulae turns into a dull babble when spirits speak through her lips. Her movements too become ecstatic, escalating to an uncontrollable twitching and jerking, and even to a state of trance. Drugs or the inhalation of juniper vapour before the dance may be responsible for this. The musicians' drums, gongs and flutes are played more and more intensely until they are hammering out the rhythm.

"Kut", the ancient Korean exorcising ceremony, still fascinates young and old today. At the end of the ritual the people present join in the dance and there is loud singing. It was probably just the same 2,000 years ago. The **"mudang",** the female witch doctor, has once more averted evil by establishing contact with the invisible world of the spirits in her trance.

This form of folk religion is called shamanism. It is typical of peoples who impart upon their surroundings – animals, plants, inanimate objects – the quality of a soul. The frequently negative influence of the latter can only be kept under control by a gifted shaman. And it is still typical of Korea today, although the Land of Morning Calm is a country on the threshold of the industrial age. Neither Buddhism and Confucianism nor Christianity have managed to change this state of affairs. The shrine on the Inwangsan near Seoul proves this. In the old days, shamanist altars were set up outside the precincts of the capital because, in the periods when Buddhism and Confucianism flourished, the "mudang", the shaman priestesses, were forbidden to enter the seat of government. But in spite of official prohibition the shamans were summoned to the palaces as soothsayers – for additional protection, as it were, in spite of all the noble ideals of Confucianism. There are no longer kings in Korea, but the "mudang" are still there.

Three religions – shamanism, Buddhism, and Christianity, in that order – have, together with Confucianism influenced the cultural tradition of Korea as far as it is historically documented. While Buddhism, Confucianism and Christianity (the latter did not play a role until the nineteenth century) were each dominant in certain clearly recognizable epochs, shamanism was always present as the true folk religion of Korea. Fluctuations in the numbers of its followers do not disprove this fact. The aristocratic court élite, however, had rejected spirit worship 1,600 years before. Officially at least. But before that they too had appeared in the role of shaman, even those who held high positions of state. Historical evidence from the first century proves that even kings played this role once upon a time. The ruler who guided his people by his contact with the spirits could determine the policy of his country, and the fate of his subjects, laying it down in the form of great oracles uttered in splendid rituals.

There are external signs of Korean shamanism visible in many parts of the country. As well as the exorcising ceremonies of the "mudang" which we just described, the **"changsung" posts** are another feature that the tourist will notice. These are posts of more than two metres (over 6 ft) in height which are set up on the edge of vil-

Chang-
sung
post

lages to repel evil spirits. They are dedicated to the generals ("chang-sung") of the five regions of heaven – north, south, east, west and the zenith – and the top is carved to represent a traditional government official wearing a hat. The posts are renewed every few years, but the old ones are never removed. **"Sŏng-wandang"** is the name given to cairns that mark crossroads or passes in the mountains. Everyone who passes adds a stone to the pile to ward off the local spirits. (This ritual is also common in Central Asia and in the Himalayas.) A tree near the cairn serves as a "sacrificial altar" for strips of paper or pieces of clothing that bring luck. Fertility rites, on the other hand, were usually linked with blocks of granite – some of these can be seen near the National Museum in Kyŏngbok Palace, Seoul; they were excavated when the underground was being built.

Scholars have discovered that a form of **primitive monotheism,** the belief in one supreme being, existed in Korea parallel to this ancient shamanism. In the first century B. C. there must have been an important cult of the **Sun God Palk,** in which he was worshipped as the creator of all life. The Koreans of this period saw them-selves therefore as sons of the sun ("iltja") and made offerings to this god. Between the Sun God and human beings there were divine mediators called **"olkum"**. One of these saviours was Tangun (Tan-kun) who, according to a popu-lar legend, became the founder of

the first Korean state. These "olkum", however, probably soon became male shamans, **"paksu"** (alternatively "pansu" or "pongsa"), as was the case in the shaman rituals of Siberia, the ancestral home of the Koreans.

Thus shamanism gained prece-dence over primitive monotheism. In the course of history the male "paksu" had, however, to give way to the female "mudang", and they became mere assistants ("kidae") at shamanist ceremonies. Men now play the hourglass drums, dance, or sing at such rituals. Only on Cheju Island have they been able to pre-serve their old, dominant role.

Another relic of a shamanist past is, at least in part, the Korean's feel-ing for nature. This is particularly clear in the way mountains are named, the dragon as a symbol of primitive forces often being used. Thus the "Hidden Dragon" is the name given to a dark mountain of-ten hidden in clouds which the vil-lagers have to bring offerings to. In the mountains too lives **Sanshin,** an old man with a beard who rides a tiger. He is worshipped in little shrines – by herb gatherers – and he appears in many paintings.

People believe that the shape of a mountain even affects the char-acter of the people who live near it: wild, barren mountains produce quarrelsome men, while gentle hills ensure a number of lovely women in the neighbourhood. These ideas could, however, be connected with the Chinese belief in geomancy ("feng shui") which was popular in

The Teaching of Lord Buddha

It began 2,500 years ago with the son of a Nepalese prince. He contested the hereditary privileges of the all-powerful Brahmans, especially their monopoly of ritualistic acts as prescribed by the holy scriptures, the Vedas. So he founded a new religion. Gautama, Siddhartha, Tatagatha – all are names of this princely son who taught humanity the philosophy of pain and suffering and how to overcome them. We know him as Lord Buddha.

But there is not just one Buddha. Everyone can and should become a buddha; there have been many and there will be many more. Buddha is the "Enlightened One", the one who has understood and accepted the **"Four Noble Truths of Suffering"**.

Gautama, who was born around 560 B. C. (there are many different opinions as to the exact date of his birth), grew up in the splendour and pomp afforded by his class and station. Then, at the age of 29, when he was out riding his favourite horse one day, he was confronted with suffering and pain – in the shape of an old man, a leper, a rotting corpse and an ascetic – and realised how senseless his life had been up to then. Buddha then understood the principles of existence: everything is suffering because everything is transitory; in this transitoriness is based the illusion of all existence. To be delivered from this painful cycle of repeated birth and rebirth, to attain nirvana, the extinction of self and a state of deathlessness – this was the ultimate goal.

Buddha died at the age of 80. His first sermon to his favourite disciples is considered to contain the fundaments of his philosophy, the legacy he bequethed to his followers. After years of asceticism and further years of meditation, he formulated it in his theory of the "Four Noble Truths":

– that sufferung is universal because of the transitory nature of life;

– that the origin of suffering lies in "craving", the will to live and the passions;

– that pain and suffering cease when this craving ceases;

– that the Noble Eightfold Path leads to the cessation of suffering.

The central concept of Buddhist religion is the law of **"karma",** universal causality. Believers understand by this that every act of life – every deed and every thought – brings on its own inevitable result. Out of all these acts results the "karma" of each person, which he himself can therefore influence negatively or positively. When a person dies, his "karma" is reborn in another shape and form. This can be better or worse than its former embodiment depending on the state of his "karma" when he died. If, from reincarnation to reincarnation, a being improves his "karma" within the realm of the passions (the flat disc of the world belongs to this realm), then deliverance from the painful cycle of repeated rebirth is eventually possible.

Korean Buddhism recognizes **three "realms"** in its cosmology. One is classified as the **"Realm of Passions"** ("kamadhatu"), in which animals, human beings, spirits, gods and demons dwell; they are all subject to the laws of growth and decay. The symbol of these different forms of existence is the wheel. The second region is the **"Realm of Pure Form"** ("rupadhatu"), in which creatures exist who have already found enlightenment themselves, but have not risen into nirvana out of pity for the human beings who are still seeking it. These enlightened beings are called "bodhisattvas". The third realm of the Buddhist world is the **"Realm of Ideas"** or of non-form ("arupadhatu"), which lies beyond all imagination and perception. These three realms are divided into 28 heavens.

But how can **nirvana** be attained? One must realize that suffering is universal (first truth), that desire is the cause of suffering (second truth), and that suffering ceases when all emotions are extinguished (third truth); the path which leads to the extinction of craving (the source of pain) is pointed out finally in the fourth truth. The last part of this path is meditation which brings deliverance: the memory of earlier forms of existence, the acceptance of the law of "karma" and of the "Four Noble Truths". The fourth of these truths does show a way to end suffering – the cycle of repeated birth and death is interrupted, and nirvana, the state of bliss, is attained.

Shortly after Buddha's death different schools of thought developed which varied in dogma and discipline. They are known collectively as **Hinayana Buddhism** (= "Little Vehicle", deliverance of the self) and this is still widespread in, for example, Burma, Thailand and Sri Lanka. At the beginning of the Christian Era the powerful **Mahayana Buddhism** (= "Great Vehicle", without the egoistic goal of one's own salvation) arose, and it was this form of Buddhism that became the real Buddhist world religion, spreading from India to China and from there to Korea; in Japan it is still alive in the form of Zen Buddhism. Another 500 years later **Vajrayana Buddhism** (= "Diamond Vehicle") appeared, and even later the form of Buddhism found in the Himalayas, **Lamaism.**

(Rumpf)

Korea from the tenth century on. According to this philosophy of "wind and water", landscape, the situation of towns and villages, and the position of houses and ancestral graves determined the fate of a person.

Buddhism

Such was the religious situation that confronted the first Buddhist missionaries in about 300. There is historical evidence of the appearance of this religion, which originated in India, from the year 372, when two monasteries were founded in the capital of the northern Koguryŏ kingdom. This Indian faith, which arrived in Korea from China, was to become the decisive religion of the country in the following centuries up to the end of the Koryŏ Dynasty. An important aspect of Buddhism was that it reached the masses, for the monks applied themselves to education and learning. The influence on Korean art and culture was extremely great.

Buddhism, in its **Mahayana** form (see "The Teaching of Lord Buddha" opposite), spread first of all within Koguryŏ, from there to Paekche, and finally to the Kingdom of Shilla. There the monk Maramanta, who could perform miracles, is said to have enjoyed great favour at court. About 150 years later, at the end of the sixth and the beginning of the 7th century, this "philosophy of suffering and the cessation of suffering" experienced its first heyday, when Korean scholars were sent as missionaries to Japan. By the year 527

Buddhism had already advanced to the position of state religion under the rulers of Ancient Shilla. Another 141 years later, in 668, when the Three Kingdoms had been united under the rule of "Unified Shilla", the state encouraged the spread of Buddhism in the whole country. Finally, during the Koryŏ Dynasty, Buddhism reached its peak: monks meditated in more than 80,000 temples, religion became the foundation of art and literature, and the third son of every family entered the "sangha", the Buddhist priesthood. Magnificant temples were built in the Shillan period, as in the epochs before.

With the decline of the Koryŏ dynasty began the decline of Mahayana Buddhism too. Shamanist sects, which Buddhism had tolerated from the very beginning, multiplied, while Confucianist ideas, which had been widespread especially among high government officials even in Buddhism's heyday, found acceptance again. In addition there was the unbelievable extravagance of monks and temples that was ruining the country's finances. It was probably mainly for the latter reason that the Yi Dynasty refused to support Buddhism.

The Buddhist religion was to achieve a new significance with the beginning of the Japanese occupation of Korea in 1910.

A census in 1980 revealed that about a third of the population is registered as being Buddhist; two thirds of these are women. Monasteries and temples are still wealthy and own large estates and valuable forests.

Korean Buddhism was always influenced in its teachings by Chinese schools. Thus the worship of **Amithaba (Amida) Buddha** plays an important role. By the mere invocation of the name of this "Boundless Light" the believer can achieve deliverance from the cycle of reincarnation. The school of meditation founded by the Chinese Buddhist Chan, which has as its model the patriarch Boddidharma who meditated for nine years under a tree, is also significant.

As in other countries, Korean Buddhism soon split up into different sects, two of which still exist more or less in the old form today.

One is the **School of Celibate Monks (Chogye)** the headquarters of which are in Chogye Temple in An'gukdong. 25 main temples and 1,100 subsidiary ones, about 8,000 monks and 6,000 nuns are supported by around 5 million followers.

The second school, where most of the monks are married, is called after the most powerful sect, **T'aego,** and is subdivided into fifteen different schools. 2,500 monks, 300 nuns and 460 smallish temples are administered by T'aego, which is supported by about one and a half million believers.

Both streams of Korean Buddhism (which, incidentally, also runs a university near Namsan in Seoul)

have one thing in common. They were willing to be tolerant of the needs of the village communities for a folk religion. This is why you find small subsidiary shrines dedicated to Sanshin, the Spirit of the Mountain, within many Buddhist temple complexes. He must be placated with offerings to prevent local spirits acting dangerously.

Neo-Confucianism

The teachings of the two Chinese sages, **Kungfu-tse** (Confucius) and **Lao-tse,** who lived in the 5th and 4th centuries B.C., have had a lasting influence on the Koreans. Especially Confucianism, with its system of ethics, had a civilizing effect. However, the mass of the people were not influenced by Confucianism, only the governing classes, the Establishment. The religiosity of Lao-tse's Taoism, on the other hand, which at times leans towards mysticism, led only to the creation of sects which were classified as "hoa-rangi" (charlatans).

The Neo-Confucianism formulated by the Chinese scholar Chu Hsi in the period of conflict with Buddhism was just as decisive for Korea as for China, and it remained valid from the 12th to the 20th century. During the Yi Dynasty, Neo-Confucian ethics rose to become the state religion, for it was the Confucianist government officials that had helped this dynasty to power in the first place. Study centres, "sowon", were set up all over the country, while education, religious rituals and civil administration were all brought into line with Confucian ideals. The climax of this development was the foundation of the Confucianist university in Seoul, Sŏnggyungwan. In addition, shrines called "hangkyo", complete with altars and schools, sprang up everywhere.

The administration has long since been adapted to modern needs and demands, and the old rites, but for a few exceptions, have been forgotten. Neo-Confucianism has, however, lived on in education, and this has resulted in a surprising social stability. For the "Five Great Relationships" of Confucius (ruling the relationships between ruler and subject, husband and wife, father and son, elder and younger brother, and the relationship between friends) can still be traced in everyday life today. There are positive and negative aspects to this. The subordinate role of women is definitely one of the more negative aspects, whereas the respect for learning and old age, as well as ancestor worship, have their positive sides. As the number of Confucianists is not to be found in any statistics, it can only be guessed how many Koreans still consider themselves such. There are said to be about 5 million of them.

Christianity

The first Christian priest who, it is said, landed on Korean soil in 1592 was a Jesuit coming with no peaceful purpose. He had taken part in a Japanese invasion of the Pusan area, and was said to be assisting the soldiers. His spiritual influence no doubt remained insignificant, not only because of this warlike activity. Peter Grammont, another Jesuit, crossed the northern border of the Yi kingdom about 20 years later and performed a few christenings. The first official missionary however, was the **Chinese priest, James Chou.** He lived in Seoul for ten years and during that time tried to spread the teaching of the Bible among the animistic and Confucian Koreans. His success was also slight and it cost him his life: Chou was executed and the foreign religion forbidden. Another 40 years later the cross returned to Korea in the person of Pierre Maubant, a French Catholic. He is said to have disguised himself as a mourner to enter the country, keeping his face covered and allowing no-one to speak to him.

These often daring attempts to missionize Korea did eventually bring success. By about the middle of the 19th century there were said to be about 20,000 Korean Christians. A little later, however, the pendulum swung back to the other side: in 1866 nine out of 12 French missionaries died on the banks of the River Han near the site of the Martyrs' Church (the church was built in memory of that cruel event). Only three of the priests were able to escape to China; the massacre was initiated by the king's son.

When the country was opened to foreigners in 1882, Christianity spread further. Missionaries acted as teachers and doctors. The desire of young Koreans for decisive social reforms was especially favourable to missionizing: people thought change could be effected more easily under Christianity than under the encrusted structures of Confucianism. The call for democracy was an element of this desire for change. During the Japanese occupation of Korea between 1910 and 1945 the church was once more suppressed, but it cooperated with other Korean groups who were suffering under colonial oppression, so that after 1945 there was a real wave of conversions among intellectuals. This brought Christianity in Korea not only prestige, but also great influence. The centre of Christianization lay in that part of the country that is now North Korea, so that there was a mass exodus of Christians to the south at the end of the terrible Korean War.

In 1981 there were more than 7.6 million Protestants, and about 1.5 million Catholics in South Korea. Seoul is quite rightly called a city of churches, for a number of the 23,500 churches to be found in the country as a whole form an integral part of the capital's skyline.

Islam
About 20,000 Koreans believe in the teachings of the Koran. The sacred book of Islam was introduced to the country in 1950 when Turkish troops arrived under the United Nations flag. In 1966 the first mosque, financed partly by foreign contributions, was consecrated in Seoul. Since then Islamic places of worship have been built in Kwangju and Pusan.

Other Religions
The social situation in the last decades of the 19th century had become untenable for the mass of the people. It was not only Christianity which spread swiftly in this climate: many different religious sects were formed and demanded reform too. Many were short-lived, but some still exist today. Ch'oe Chae-u, the son of a country teacher, founded the **Tonghak Movement** in 1862. This was defined as "Eastern Learning" as opposed to the Western learning of Christianity. The founder was executed two years later in Taegu. The movement found many supporters, however, and they started a bloody rebellion in 1894.

The movement was re-named **Ch'ondo-kyo** during the present century, and it now has about 1.5 million followers. The latter see Ch'ondo-kyo primarily as a religious, not a social, movement.

Among all the other religious sects one in particular, **Taejongyo,** came to people's notice because its followers worship the legendary founder of Korea, Tan'gun.

It is, however, the Unity Church of the more than controversial **Reverend Moon** which gets a lot of publicity, especially abroad. This Korean believes he is a re-incarnation of Christ, and has made a lot of money out of this, especially in the United States, ruling over an economic imperium with branches in the USA and in Korea too.

(Rumpf)

Buddhist Temples

The temples of Korea are among the most beautiful and most impressive sights the country has to offer. Many lie off the beaten track, surrounded by sacred forests, and house important relics or holy scriptures. Some of the temples were places chosen for meditation by monks well-known all over the Buddhist world; others were the seats of notable schools of philosophy. Whatever the reason for their renown, one thing is sure: while visiting Korea one should not pass by its Buddhist temples without giving them the attention they so richly deserve.

It is true that Korean Buddhism is very old (see chapter on religion); Korea's Buddhist temples, however, are not. The influence of Buddhism declined with the fall of the Koryŏ dynasty, the subsequent Yi rulers turning to Neo-Confucianism. This sealed the fate of some of the once magnificent temples. The Japanese Shogun, Hideyoshi, dealt with the rest when he marched through the country with his army in the years 1592–1598. He burned and plundered all the way, and did not spare the temples. The latter were made of wood, as they still are today, and so after the Japanese invasion there was not much left of most of them but a pile of ashes. Restoration, if it took place at all, did not start till the seventeenth century. The 300 years which have passed since then represent a long period of time for a wooden building, and the visitor will

notice that there is much in need of repair and restoration now.

Every Mahayana Buddhist temple was built to symbolize the **three realms of existence.** The visitor enters the lowest realm, the "Realm of the Passions", through a gate where the four gigantic figures of the guardian kings of heaven (Sach'onwang) crush the enemies of religion underfoot. These heavenly guardians of the four corners of the universe hold a pagoda, a dragon, a sword and a lyre respectively. There is often a second gateway where the two bodhisattvas, Munsu Posal and Pohyon Posal, stand guard; Munsu rides a tiger, Pohyon, an elephant.

Before the visitor reaches the temple courtyard, which represents the "Realm of Pure Form", he must often pass the study hall of the monks. And finally, he reaches the main hall of the compound, which symbolizes the "Realm of Ideas" or the world beyond form – that is, the highest realm.

The **main hall** is called **Taeung-jon** if a statue of the historical Buddha, Shakyamuni, is worshipped here. If, however, there is an image of Amida, Buddha of Times to Come (or Buddha of the Western Paradise), the main hall is then called **Kuknak-jon.** Both Shakyamuni and Amida are highly venerated in Korea, but an outsider can only tell the difference by the position of the hands ("mudra"). There is also a third Buddha who is important in some temples – Vairocana – and who was worshipped especially in the Shillan period. He at least is easy to recognize for he holds the index finger of his right hand in his left hand.

Buddhas in the main hall are often flanked by two figures: these represent either other Buddhas (in this case it is a triad: Buddha of Past Times, Buddha of the Present, Buddha of Times to Come) or bodhisattvas. You often see Munsu Posal and Pohyon Posal, who guard the gateway, accompanying Shakyamuni; Kwanseum (Kuan yin), Bodhisattva of Mercy and Compassion, and Taesaju Posal stand on either side of Amida Buddha. Kwanseum is the most popular bodhisattva in Korea.

There are, however, other halls besides the main temple building. The **"Hall of Judgement" (Myongbu-jon)** is very important for believers, for here stands a statue of the bodhisattva Chijang Posal. He holds a casket in his hands containing the key to Paradise. Around him stand two servants and ten judges who decide the fate of a person who has died. Paintings remind the viewer of the drastic penalties for all kinds of sins.

The **Yongsan Hall,** called after the sacred mountain of the Buddhists in India (Kailash), houses a figure of Shakyamuni with many disciples (16 to 500), whereas the **Palsang-jon,** another hall, is often dedicated to the Buddha of medicine, Yaksa Yorae. You can recognize him by his "kusul", a bottle of medicine in his left hand.

Aspects of ancient Korean **shamanism** soon found their way into Buddhism, which had been taken over from China. That is why there are subsidiary shrines erected to shamanist spirits in many temple precincts. The most important spirits are called collectively Samsong (Three Spirits), the Spirit of the Mountain being especially venerated. He is called Sanshin, and is represented as an old man with a tiger. He guards the temple, the monks and the faithful from malevolent spirits who might cause them harm.

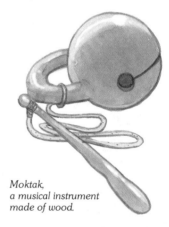

Moktak,
a musical instrument
made of wood.

The living quarters of the grey-robed monks and nuns surround the temple buildings but are usually situated outside the temple walls.

Five traditional musical instruments are used in religious services, when offerings are made or meditation carried out. You cannot miss the large drum; the bronze gong is not quite so conspicuous. A bulbous wooden instrument usually

Light in the Darkness

Long rows of lanterns dangle on ropes strung across the large courtyard in front of the main temple building. Inside some of the temple buildings the faithful have hung up other lanterns. There are especially many on Buddha's Birthday, which is celebrated in May (according to our calendar). These paper lanterns, which are usually made by monks, are a colourful sight in the pale spring sunshine. (And they are very popular with photographers, of course!) But above all they are offerings made by Buddhists. They sell the lanterns as a contribution to temple finances and with this good deed improve their own "karma" too.

Buddhist symbols made of gold and silver paper decorate these offerings. The swastika, the ancient sun symbol of the Aryans, is particularly common (it was of course a slightly-modified version of this ancient symbol which gained notoriety as the emblem of Nazi Germany). Pictures of Buddha and the Chinese symbols of the universe, "yang" and "um", appear frequently on the lanterns, too. ("Yang" and "um" also decorate the Korean flag.)

There is something else the visitor notices: attached to almost every lantern is a slip of paper with the name, address and sometimes even the telephone number of the donor. This is in no way meant to guard against loss, but is to make sure that divine recompense, should it come, be awarded to the right person. Even gods could make a mistake....

To celebrate Buddha's Birthday, innumerable lanterns brighten the streets at night as the latter echo with the sound of fireworks and bangers. Buddha, the Enlightened One, is hardly likely to object to a little noise and merriment at the end of his feastday.   *(Rumpf)*

lies ready for use on the altar in front of the statues of Buddha. The monk or priest holds this "moktak" (see illustration) in his left hand beating it with a wooden stick in the rhythm of the monks' recitations and offertories. A wooden fish which is somewhat bigger but also hollow, and usually colourfully painted or lacquered, hangs beside the drum as an additional instrument.

The **bronze temple bell** is, however, the most important. Many of these bells were cast in the Shillan Period and so belong to a long artistic tradition. However, all except three from this period have been lost. All other bronze bells are from a later period, twelve being from the Koryŏ dynasty. In Japanese temples and Shinto shrines there are said to be 50 bells that were cast in this period and even five from Shilla. It was in particular at the end of the sixteenth century after the Japanese invasion, and then again after 1910, that several Korean bells were transferred to Japan as examples of excellent local craftsmanship and artistry.   *(Rumpf)*

Art

Origins

Thanks to the precision now achieved in methods of carbon dating, it has been possible to prove that Neolithic finds made in a settlement in **Amsadong**/Seoul date back to the year 4280 B.C. And so we are justified in talking about **"5,000 years of Korean art".**

As far as the finds in Amsadong are concerned, we are talking, of course, about so-called prehistoric art forms – i. e. the fashioning of tools, swords, spearheads, etc. These early finds show great similarity to Siberian and Central Asian objects. Pottery from a shell mound in **Tongsamdong** near Pusan has also been exactly dated to 3940 B.C. and is very like the Angangxi remains in what used to be called Manchuria.

Comb and herringbone patterns, when they do occur in Korea, differ from the painted fragments of early Chinese pottery. So it can be concluded that there was indeed a connection between early ethnic groups in Korea and Siberia.

Prehistoric Times:
Bronzes and Pottery

From the 2nd century B.C. onwards, crescent and zigzag patterns appeared on pottery, establishing a link with Chinese pieces. Early bronzes in the shape of daggers appeared in northeast Korea in the first millenium B.C. By around 300–200 B.C. there were elaborate bronze rattles with bells. This early bronze culture probably stemmed from the Yemaek Tungus, a south Siberian tribe which had settled in far away Korea.

In Korea the **Bronze Age** is divided into two epochs: the Early Puyo Period from 700–300 B.C., and the Late Puyo Period from 300 B.C. to the birth of Christ. Bronze daggers constitute the main finds made at Puyo, Sŏngguri, Kŏpodong, Pyŏng-yang, Yŏnan and Kumgokdong. Other objects which are considered typical are bronze mirrors, chased axes, and perforated jade pendants.

The Han River, which flows through Seoul, formed a cultural border between North and South Korea at the end of the Bronze Age. The Yemaek tribe which had settled in northern Korea divided into two groups; the group that settled in the south is known as the Koguryŏ or Han tribe. The Han people developed **Hongdo pottery,** fine earthenware with an ochre surface. Pots of this type were presumably used to hold offerings of food or wine in religious ceremonies.

In southern Korea black pottery was developed at the end of the Bronze Age. The colour was achieved by smearing the inner surface with dung when it was burning hot: the carbonized dung and the black smoke penetrated the pores of the pot, dyeing it black.

In Chonjonni, Taegongni, Yong-jondong and Koryŏng in the south-east of the Korean peninsula there are **cave drawings** which are among the earliest of their kind on earth. The "drawings" were cut and scraped out of the rock, and portray fish, deer, tigers, leopards and wolves. From the way these animals are drawn it can be deduced that they had something to do with early fertility rites. There are even said to be connections between these and similar rock pictures in Siberia and in Europe.

Iron and Gold

About 400 B.C. iron and **iron extraction** were introduced from China. Very soon iron was being extracted from its ores in Korea too. The Bronze Age coincides with the Early Iron Age. Because of the replacement of bronze tools by iron ones, bronze objects were soon only made for religious purposes and so were finer, more elaborate, and of a higher quality than before. The artistic form and decoration of bronzes was developed to perfection, the Siberian influence remaining unchanged, especially in the style of representing animals.

The Second Iron Age, which is also called the Kimhae or Shell Mound Period, lasted historically through the Samhan (Three Han States) period, also known as the Won-Samguk period, i. e. for the first three centuries A. D. At this time Korean culture was particularly clearly divided into a northern and a southern area: nomadic tribes were typical of the north, tillers of the soil

were typical of the south. Ever since the Bronze Age, inhabitants of the lower Naktong River had been cros-sing the narrow strait dividing Korea and Kyushu (Japan), leading to the formation here in the south of a Korean-Japanese cultural unit. One element of this was the hard, grey **Kimhae pottery** decorated with mat and crisscross patterns. The new pottery – nowadays found all over Korea and used mainly for household utensils – must have brought a decisive change to Korean life.

The mining of iron ore in south Korea was linked to the mining of gold. **Gold extraction** brought wealth and this led to the foundation of great kingdoms whose rulers had huge tumuli built as tombs from the 4th century on. In these tombs they laid the finest gold products, golden crown pendants, earrings and other jewellery as burial offerings. Such works of art can now be admired in the National Museums of Seoul and Kyŏngju.

The Tumulus Grave as a Reflection of Power

There are tumuli (burial mounds) in Andong, Taegu, Koryŏng, Songju, Changnyang and other places as well as of course in Kyŏngju (Tumuli Park). They all look almost alike from the outside, but the interiors reveal two different types: there are wooden and stone burial chambers. In the Kyŏngju area only wooden ones are to be found. These were reserved exclusively for the royal families and the aristocracy. The different tombs revealed various art objects: precious golden artefacts and other burial gifts were excavated from the wooden burial chambers. The stone chambers on the other hand contained nothing of such value. The tombs of Koguryŏ and Paekche belong in this second category, while the Shilla graves contain extraordinary golden artefacts. The Shilla tombs are very similar to those of the Scythians and Turkish peoples, so that once more a link can be made with the Eurasian cultural group.

Of the fifty tumuli around Kyŏngju, the **Phoenix Tomb** or **Ponghwang Tumulus** is the biggest of its kind (it is 20 m/65 ft high and 80 m/260 ft in diameter).

A very famous double grave was opened in 1973 and 1974/5 respectively. Since then the world knows the name of the **"Tomb of the Flying Horse"** and the **Hwangnam Tomb.** From these graves alone came six crowns of pure gold with tree and antler decorations that point to a shamanist origin in North Asia and South Russia. Almost a thousand earrings with heart-shaped leaf ornamentation in fine filigree work came to light in this double grave too. The necklaces of gold and glass with the comma-shaped jade pendants, "kikok", which have been interpreted as the image of human semen or the crescent moon, are among the loveliest pieces of jewellery in early Korean history. The girdles that were found are made of gold or silver. They too are hung with pendants in the shape of fish, swords or little "kikok".

Glass objects – some of them even cut glass – which were found even before the year 668 ("Unified Shilla") point to a link with the Roman Empire and ancient Persia.

In keeping with the belief in life after death, many fragments of **weapons** were also found (including spearheads, arrowheads and iron axes) showing that the nobleman had to defend himself in the other world too.

The **stoneware** from the fifth and sixth centuries with its ash glaze shows especially animal forms such as ducks, geese and horses. Vessels like these were to provide for the dead person in the imaginary next world.

Korean funeral offerings can therefore be placed in the same category as those of ancient Egypt or of the early empires of China: the potentate took his whole household with him on the journey to the other world. He planned the journey while he was still alive and could therefore check what should be taken with him and what would be superfluous. Thus the power and prestige of a ruler can be deduced from the number and quality of the objects buried with him.

Religious Art – Buddhist Art
With the introduction of Buddhism to the Korean peninsula in 372 A. D. (i. e., in the period of the Three Kingdoms, Koguryŏ. Paekche and Shilla), religious works of art, and especially Buddhist art, were added to the artistic bronzes, iron utensils and

ceramics of the times up till then. A stone monument discovered in Puyo in 1948 and featuring inscriptions thought to date from the year 642 provides evidence that it was the practice at that time for the aristocracy to sponsor the building of pagodas and the creation of other Buddhist works of art. They did this in order to purchase the favour of the clergy; according to Buddhist belief, the latter could ensure a happy life after death. Rich families sponsored the building of whole temple complexes; these were then filled with holy figures, sculptures and ritual implements by other inhabitants of the area: religious art was born.

Korea's close cultural attachment to the T'ang period, which represented the climax of Buddhist art in China, meant that the Chinese example had exerted a strong influence from about 650 A.D. until 900 A.D. Changan in China, Kumsong (= Kyŏngju) in Korea and Nara in Japan became the centres of Buddhist art in East Asia.

Buddhist sculptures are objects of worship. In Korea they are mainly in the form of gilded bronzes or stone statues and represent Buddha himself or his disciples. Bodhisattvas, the helpers of mankind who do not, however, become buddhas, are worshipped too. Whereas statues of Buddha appear either as single figures (seated alone or standing alone) or in triads, bodhisattvas are represented standing or in a position of meditation, as seen in the illustration. In the latter case the statues are usually of the type called **Maitreya** (a disciple of Shakyamuni).

The most famous **stone image** in Korea is from the middle of the 8th century. It is made of granite and represents **Amitabha (Amida) Buddha** sitting on his lotus throne in the **Sŏkkuram Grotto** southeast

Maitreya bodhisattva statue of gilded bronze.

146

of Kyŏngju. The stone bas-reliefs on the walls of this fascinating cave are among the finest examples of Korean sculptured reliefs.

As well as sculptures, **stone pagodas** and **"sarira"** (receptacles for holy relics) can be counted as superb specimens of Buddhist art. There are in all about 1,000 pagodas scattered around the country in different temples. The National Museums house several examples of this type of stone art. The three-storeyed **lion pagoda of Hwaom-sa** (Hwaom Temple, see p. 208), a Buddhist temple built in the middle of the 8th century, is considered to be the most magnificent representative of this art form. The pagoda is 5.5 m (18 ft) high and is National Treasure No. 35.

Of the approximately 100 **bronze bells** which have survived from Shilla and Koryŏ times, the **holy bell of King Songdok,** now in the National Museum of Kyŏngju, is the biggest (3.78 m/over 12 ft high and 2.27 m/over 7 ft in diameter) and probably the most beautiful. It was cast in 771 by Korean bellfounders who with it demonstrated the greatest skill and craftsmanship. Metal inlaid work is a special feature of bronze art in Korea, and this technique can be seen above all in **incense burners.**

Korea – Stronghold of Celadon
While pottery from the period of the Three Kingdoms displayed plain shapes and simple ornamentation, there was a change in the period of Unified Shilla (668–935). There is

no denying the fact that the new forms were influenced by T'ang China. The vessels had a short, round base and the surface was decorated with floral designs. This was the beginning of early celadon ware.

In these very **early celadons,** the brown-green glaze developed a rough craquelure effect – a characteristic found mainly, for obvious reasons, on long-necked bottles, bowls with edges flaring outwards, and on tall cups with curved lips. The early celadon kilns were situated around Inch'ŏn, on the coast west of Seoul. These kilns were built into the hills like tunnels, the central chamber being divided into sections by steps and partitions.

11th century celadon kilns are to be found mainly in the province of Chŏllanam-do, that is, in the southwest. In the kilns of Kangjin especially, superb celadons were fired with the aid of earthenware moulds. The whole process took place under government supervision – the Koreans took China as an example in this too. Technical improvements were introduced mainly through trade with China, for the traders' junks could sail from the mouth of the Yangtze to the Korean peninsula, landing in Chŏllanam-do.

The pots were covered with brown and dark green feldspar glazes and fired at temperatures of 1,300 ° Celsius. The influence of the Chinese Sung period was obvious, especially that of the towns of Yuezhou and Yaozhou. (Even at this time, fine **white porcelain** was also being produced in Sori/Central Korea.)

Celadon design reached its climax in the first half of the 12th century. The famous **Pisaek green** was achieved by a very balanced, carefully-regulated method of firing. In the end Korean celadon outmatched its Chinese models with this **smooth, uncracked Pisaek glaze** and Korea became the centre of this fine form of East Asian ceramic art. Glazes became more transparent, surfaces were decorated with inlaid patterns or designs in relief. Celadons with iron-brown underglazes, those with overglaze decor, and those painted with gold or inlaid with copper are considered among the rarest pieces.

The decline of celadon became apparent in the second half of the 14th century; it was followed by **Punchong pottery.** In these ceramics a scrafitto (hachure) design was impressed on the outer surface of the pot and then given a white coating.

The importance of pottery grew; many refinements were made. It is interesting to note that in the annals of King Sejong (1419–50) a total of 139 porcelain workshops and 186 kilns were registered as existing in Korea at that time. For the Sason-so (the royal kitchens) alone, 380 potters were employed. Not only did they produce goods of a certain quality but they also checked the standard of the pottery from other kilns that was to be used in the royal household.

Punchong ware and white porcelain are the products that are most typical of the Korean Yi dynasty in the 15th and 16th centuries. They differ from the green Koryŏ celadon mainly in the lighter colouring. The town of Kwangju became the centre of royal pottery production and even survived the Japanese invasion of 1592, although many Korean potters were taken to Japan by force to continue production there. Punchong pottery, however, did not survive after 1592. Only white or blue and white porcelain was common in Korea after that. In Kwangju simple porcelain in blue and white was produced, in the shape of bowls, jugs, household dishes and water pots for inkstones. Dragon motifs especially were very popular at the end of the Yi dynasty (1910).

Korean ceramics are superb, original and natural. They lie somewhere between the refined, that is, more sophisticated and some might say almost artificial Japanese pottery and the classical ceramics of China.

The Koryŏ Press and Gutenberg
The popular assumption in many places that Johannes Gutenberg invented printing with movable metal type must be refuted here. The Koreans had designed six metal letter presses and used them for printing two centuries before the German printer. There is a record of this in the writings of the calligraphy scholar **Lee Kyu-bo,** under whose direction the **first book was printed with metal type in 1234.** It was not of course the Bible that was printed (as by Gutenberg later) but

nevertheless moral writings, general ethical rules of behaviour. The Koryŏ printers printed 28 theses from the famous Confucian "Rites of Past and Present" with the new technique.

The Korean metal type of the Koryŏ press is still considered to be one of the outstanding achievements in the field of printing as a whole. The technical and technological pre-conditions existed in East Asia much earlier than in Europe: the Chinese had invented paper a thousand years before; the Koreans were famous for their excellent metalwork (bronze casting, etc.); and in addition, printing ink, the third necessary component, had been used early on for woodblock printing.

At the risk of overstatement, it could almost be said that Korea *had* to invent metal type. China, who had supplied Buddhist monasteries in Korea with sutra texts and other books printed with wooden blocks up to the beginning of the 13th century, was torn by internal conflicts and no longer in a position to supply them. Moreover, supplies of the wood needed to cut the printing blocks were running out in China. Book production in the Middle Kingdom declined rapidly – the customers had to think out other ways of printing books. And so they thought of metal. In spite of this ingenious invention, metal printing remained relatively unknown for about 170 years, for the Korean printers never really took to metal type. Wood could be worked more easily, more

individually and more finely than the cold, hard metal. A real work of art could be created out of wood, in the form of individually carved characters.

In order to prevent this outstanding invention from passing into oblivion, the second Yi king, Taejong, revived the technique of metal printing in 1403. This time too it was Confucian writings, that is, classics, that were printed with metal type and distributed to civil servants as a manual of government for the education of the people.

The Art of Painting
Early forms of Korean painting can be dated back to the 4th century, when the stone walls of royal **burial chambers were decorated in colour** with scenes from the everyday lives of the deceased. Although Chinese influences did play a role, the Koreans developed native forms, subjects and styles. Examples for this from the Kingdom of Paekche can be found on the walls of the tomb of the "Four Guardian Kings of Heaven No. 6" in Songsanni near Kyŏngju, as well as in a **ceiling fresco** in a tomb at Nungsanni near Puyo.

The first **drawings of landscape** in Korea are to be found on **tiles** that were also discovered near Puyo. These 7th century pictures feature mountain and water scenes which are unique in their genre as they have the added dimension of depth and space.

From the ancient Kingdom of Shilla came the first **pictures of**

horses (Tomb No. 155) painted on **birch bark.**

A few Buddhist **paintings on brownish-blue indigo paper** with exclusively religious themes have survived from the period of Unified Shilla. During the Koryŏ period (918–1392) detailed **portrait painting** was developed; dignitaries liked to have their portrait done frequently. In this period there was a great deal of **landscape painting** that reproduced pines, flowers and birds in an extraordinarily realistic way. Scroll paintings such as "The Diamond Mountains", "The Landscape of Chinyang" or "Eight Views of Songdo" had a direct influence on the school of Chong Son (1675–1759). **Ink drawings** of bamboo bushes, plums and orchids on **paper or silk** were also of very high quality in the Koryŏ period.

In the Yi dynasty, as Buddhism gradually lost its influence, Buddhist subjects in painting became less common. The ethical, moralizing ideas of the Neo-Confucian state repressed everything religious and even actively combatted it. King Sejong's reign (1419–1450) was the most important of the four periods of Yi painting. The two great masters of the time, **An Kyon** and **Kang Hui-an,** had considerable influence on later schools of painting. An Kyon distinguished himself especially as a landscape artist who worked with ink and water colours. His four paintings on silk (1418) show landscapes with typical Korean houses, pavilions, waterfalls

Painting and calligraphy – two art forms highly valued in Asia – came to Korea from China.

and oddly shaped mountains like those you can still see in the Sorak Mountains. The delicate, brownish pastel colours lend an atmosphere of sensual dreaminess to the pictures. An Kyon was influenced in his style of painting by a collection of Chinese pictures belonging to the royal family, with whom he was personally acquainted, partly in his function as academic painter.

Unlike An Kyon, Kang Hui-an himself travelled to China where he got to know the Che style of painting. His most representative painting is the "Sage in Deep Meditation at the Foot of a Cliff".

The Middle Yi Period was marked by Hideyoshi's Japanese invasion and the resulting ravages of war: this had a negative effect on painting. Not until the 18th century was there any stabilization, and then Chinese and European influences were dominant.

The painter **Chong Son** (1676–1759) created a new style of landscape painting which was based on the South Chinese school but was in fact purely Korean in the composition, brush technique and colouring.

The influence of European painting, especially painting in oils which was then unknown in East Asia, was first spread by Jesuit priests (Castiglione, Attiret, Sichelbart etc.) at the imperial court at Chienlung, and from there it reached Korea. Although the Chinese as well as the Koreans did not really know how to make use of oils, and although oil

painting was given up pretty soon in China, it did affect rural folk art and various schools of painting in the 19th century.

The **Chusa** and **Haksan** schools were the leading schools of painting at the end of the Yi Dynasty up to 1910. Landscapes and watercolours by the artists **Hong Se-sop** and **Kim Su-chol** must be mentioned here.

The most recent developments in the field of Korean painting show the great influence of European art, particularly in the work of young artists who have studied in the USA and in Europe.

Yi Chung-sop (1916–1956) was very much influenced by French Fauvism, creating, however, with his paintings of oxen and hens, works of art that were definitely Korean. **Nam Kwan,** who also studied in France, is one of the modern Korean Expressionists. **Kim Hwan-ki** (1913–1974) remained true to this tradition. He studied in France and settled in New York, but he took as his subjects typically East Asian motifs such as the moon, landscape and porcelain painting. **Park Su-gun** (1914–65) became famous as a modern genre painter, depicting village scenes and rural life on his canvasses. There are many young, talented artists in Korea whose studios are mainly in Seoul and whom you can also visit there. The "Museum of Modern Art" in Seoul's Toksu Palace shows the visitor the whole range of young, vital and imaginative talent in contemporary Korean painting.   *(Thiele)*

Celadon,
Lovely as Jade

There is still potter's clay of the highest quality in many parts of the Korean peninsula. Kilns used to be in the hands of a few powerful families or under the control of Buddhist temples. The potters themselves did not count for much in traditional Korean society, and were lower in rank than all other artists. There were but few exceptions – artists who climbed up the social ladder with the help of royal patronage.

Nevertheless, what they created achieved worldwide recognition. Nowhere else was better or lovelier celadon produced than in Korea. It was of such superb quality that the Japanese invaders of the 16th century deported whole Korean villages to their own southern island of Kyushu if they knew that famous potters lived and worked there. That is why many a Japanese potter in Kyushu today boasts of his Korean ancestors. And Madame Pompadour is said to have been the very proud owner of a Korean celadon vase.

Ceramics and porcelain represent the crowning glory of Korean art in the opinion of leading art experts: a glory that even occasionally outshines its Chinese models, although the celadons of the Koryŏ dynasty, which are considered to be the most perfect examples of this form of art and typically Korean, have only been known to the world since the first ones were excavated around

1910. It was in Koryŏ times (918–1392) that the formal precepts of the great neighbour in the west were filled out with Korean artistic ideas. The technical skills that were necessary to do this have since been lost. So, although imitations of Koryŏ celadon can be made nowadays, exact copies cannot.

Shilla pottery dominated the first millenium A. D. Innumerable examples have been preserved because they were laid in the tumuli around Kyŏngju as burial offerings, and survived the passage of time unharmed. It was a different case with the products of the Kingdoms of Paekche and Koguryŏ, which were contemporary to Shilla, for wars did not only break up the dynasties: most of the ceramics were destroyed too. The area around Kyŏngju, on the other hand, did not become a battlefield even when the Koryŏ Dynasty replaced "Unified Shilla" in the 10th century.

Even Shilla potters used the technique of firing their stoneware at high temperatures, the colours dark grey to black being predominant. Brown tones were the result of oxidation, and traces of ash can often be seen on the surface. Shamanist symbols were frequently used as decoration.

When, however, Buddhism was raised to the status of a state religion in the seventh century, forms and designs became more subdued, more sedate, losing some of their vital spontaneity. This was probably the result of the strict stylistic standards dictated by the new religion. Fundamentally, however, Chinese models determined the artistic vision of Korean potters at this period too.

This was to change from the tenth century on, but only very gradually. And the new models came again from China. As early as the third century, kilns had been built in what are today the provinces of Jiangsu and Zhejiang; this is where China's earliest celadon was fired. Poets extolled the bluish green of this pottery, calling it the "secret colour" (bise) and linking it poetically to the autumn sky, the colour of distant mountain peaks and even to the feathers of the kingfisher. In the ninth century "classic" on tea ("Ch'a-king") by the poet Lu Yu, the colour of the celadon glaze was compared to jade, the symbol of immortality. These early Chinese Yue ceramics were the prototypes of the Korean celadons from the tenth century on.

Most of the kilns were situated around Hangzhou Bay, near the port of Ningbo. If the weather were favourable ships could sail along the southwest coast of Korea, reaching Kangjin, the centre of Korean celadon production, in only a week. But ideas as well as wares also reached Korea overland.

From a technical point of view, celadon is hard stoneware made from a grey material. When it is fired at no less than 1,200 ° Celsius it becomes watertight. What is important for the eventual colour is the quantity of iron which the potter adds to the colourless feldspar glaze, as well as the amount of oxygen in the kiln. If there is not much of the latter, then the iron becomes greenish to bluish; if there is a lot of oxygen, the pottery becomes reddish-brown.

There are, therefore, Korean celadons of varying shades of colour, but the best pieces are usually greyish-green and are supposed to remind you of the colour of the kingfisher, as mentioned above. It is also interesting to note that the glaze is finer than Chinese celadon. The kilns around the capital of the Koryŏ dynasty, Songdo (present-day Kaesong in North Korea), and those on Kanghwa Island were famous, but did not attain the leading position of the coastal area around Puan and south of Kangjin in southwest Korea. The ground in this region still yields hundreds of pottery fragments.

The development of Korean celadon production can be divided into three parts. The first period is characterized by the strong **influence of Sung China,** and it lasted from the late 10th century till the middle of the 12th century. Chinese models were successfully imitated at this time; in any case, Chinese forms were always followed closely. The broad-shouldered, slim-hipped vases were even given the same name: in China they were called "mai ping", in Korean this became "mae byŏng".

It was not till the middle of the 12th century that the vases got that sweep, that more pronounced curve between the shoulder and the base (the latter had become slightly broader) which made them appear lighter than their Chinese models. In this second period, up to the end of the 13th century, there was another independent development: the technique of **inlaid work.** This was used in Korea earlier than in China, and was called "sanggam".

Intricate inlaid work has to be executed in several steps: first the design is engraved or cut in the clay, then this relief design is filled with white or brown slip, and finally the edges are smoothed and the superfluous coloured clay removed. Two firings are necessary: the first when the inlay is finished, and the second at a very high temperature when the glaze has been applied.

The beginning of the use of inlay technique can be relatively precisely dated. The Chinese scholar Xu Jing described Korean celadons in great detail in 1124–5, without however mentioning inlaid work; so it can be assumed that it was invented later or became widespread after this date. Archaeologists have excavated inlaid celadon from the tomb of King Mon, which is dated 1159. So the technique must have been popular and widespread by this time.

The third and final phase of celadon production is linked to the Mongol invasion of 1231. The court fled to Kanghwa Island then, and part of the celadon production was transferred there too. However, the quality of the forms and glazes deteriorated; the peak of artistic development was past in inlaid work too. Baroque designs were preferred and decoration tended to be over-elaborate. The political collapse brought on the artistic one, and at the end of the Mongolian occupation celadon production with its fine bluish-green glazes came to a standstill.

The Koryŏ aristocracy had used and appreciated celadon in all kinds of different forms. Not satisfied with dishes, vases or wine vessels alone, they had many other objects for everyday use, and above all incense burners, made of celadon. Typical of the latter were ones made for the table in filigree style or in the shape of animals. The preference of the nobility for celadon tiles too was very expensive. The large quantities necessary had to be ordered from the state kilns at Puan and Kangjin.

When "Koryŏ-sa", the official chronicle of this dynasty, was published in the following Yi dynasty (1392–1910), there were sections on the widespread use of celadon. Five centuries later, in 1914, archaeologists digging at the sites in Kaesong (now in North Korea) described in this book, brought great quantities of celadon tiles to light – tiles which had once covered the pavilion of Koryŏ's king Uijong (1147–1170).

In the Yi dynasty which followed Koryŏ the main question was no longer about life after death, but about a new social order – Confucianism had superseded Buddhism. **Yi porcelain** reflected this spiritual attitude, replacing the courtly and almost feminine elegance of Koryŏ products with its simple, sometimes rather coarse forms. In fact, it was just these forceful shapes and colours that attracted the Japanese invaders in the 16th century.

The output of Yi porcelain can also be divided into two groups:

white porcelain, and stoneware known as "punchong". One could define the latter as an expression of Korean folk art. And, as the glaze contained iron, it is also considered to be a type of late celadon. The aristocratic version of art expressed itself on the other hand in white porcelain, which was also used for ceremonies. Grey, green, and even blue served as decorating colours.

Cobalt blue was especially esteemed for underglaze designs. And here too the Koreans turned back to Chinese models. At the beginning of the Yi dynasty the basic material had to be purchased in the Middle East and imported via China, and so was relatively rare.

With the discovery of local supplies in the 15th century came hopes of readier availability, but the blue turned out to be too dark. The potters found a way out of the dilemma: instead of cobalt blue they used the brown of iron and the red of copper for the decorating colour. In fact copper becomes green when it is oxidized, but if the firing is kept exactly under control it is possible to achieve a warm red. And so Korean artists turned the lack of cobalt to their own artistic advantage, achieving a perfect red colouring that is now considered to be typically Korean.

Celadons: the crowning glory of Korean art. Although this type of porcelain originated in China, it was in Korea that the loveliest pieces were produced.

155

Once more then, Korea set the tone in ceramics, but it was distant Europe that provided it with a name – by way of a 17th century play, "L'Astrée", which was being played in French theatres. A shepherd appeared in the play wearing a greyish-green costume. His name was Céladon, and this was passed on to the ceramics of the same colour from the Koryŏ dynasty. A modest European contribution to these works of art made of clay, feldspar, iron and oxygen. *(Rumpf)*

Architecture

The very first forms of architecture in Korea are **dolmens.** Consisting of two squared stones in a vertical position with a horizontal slab laid on top, this early type of tomb is over 4,000 years old.

There is not a single wooden building in Korea that is more than 600 years old. Apart from the fact that wood does not usually last as long as stone, wars and fires caused a great deal of destruction time and again.

Wooden architecture in Korea – especially temples and palaces – is without exception modelled on the Chinese style and way of building. Independent Korean developments can be found in the stone bases of such buildings, and in the harmonious balance which is always achieved – the different structures are always adapted to the given landscape or environment. Simple, elegant lines are typical of Korean architectural style. There are none of the big, elaborate superstructures, the almost baroque proportions, that are common to the temples of South China.

The Chinese influence goes back as far as the Sung period. Stone platforms, or a base of squared stones set in a terrace form, are characteristic of this time. Wooden buildings, which mainly take the shape of halls, are constructed on these stone foundations. Supporting elements are wooden pillars and wall panels – that is, not solid walls as in Europe.

Typical too are projecting roofs supported by a complicated system of rafters, crossbeams and longitudinal beams. The roofs themselves are covered with glazed or unglazed, round and semi-circular tiles. Ridge figures which are arranged relatively far apart are typical of Korea; they were originally intended to ward off demons. They are not as detailed or as brightly painted as their Chinese counterparts.

Early Buddhist **temple architecture** reached its peak in the 6th century. The wooden buildings of that period have disappeared, but the stone foundations have survived. In the course of the following centuries new wood structures were repeatedly built on these bases, with slight variations and modifications. Hwangyong, Yŏngmyo, Kiwŏn, Punhwang, Pongdŏk and Pulguk temples are examples of these early sites.

Pulguk-sa ("sa" = temple) is one example of a reconstructed wooden building. It was rebuilt in 1972 in the style of ancient Shilla.

When Neo-Confucianism was introduced to Korea during the Yi dynasty (1392–1910), Buddhist temple architecture, including the building of stupas and pagodas, was neglected in favour of Confucian halls or temples, memorials to famous scholars and palace architecture. Most of these buildings were destroyed too, in the 16th century Japanese invasion.

Modern Korean architecture is greatly influenced by Western styles. There are a great many church buildings, for example – the result of the presence of Christian missionaries.

Myŏngdong Catholic Cathedral in Seoul was built in the Neo-Gothic style. The architect was a French priest called Eugène Jean George Coste. It was built as early as 1887 and modelled on European churches.

The English architect Davidson designed the Sŏkchojŏn building of Toksu Palace in 1908/10 – in a mock Renaissance style. A Russian architect was responsible for the "Independence Gate" in Seoul (1898) which he designed in the style of a Roman triumphal arch.

Modern architecture came into its own in 1953 when the **Hongik College** was established at Seoul National University (SNU), the élite university of Korea. Then high-rise functional buildings, some of them over 30 storeys high, were designed by architects and engineers who had undergone part of their training in the United States and Europe and who now taught at the SNU. The age of the skyscraper had dawned – but also unfortunately the age of dreary apartment blocks providing subsidized housing.

Only gradually did the architects move away from purely functional buildings to an architecture that was also artistic and aesthetic, some examples of which can now be seen around Seoul. Government buildings, most of which were constructed on the little island of Yoi in the River Han, and Seoul's National Museum are examples of the new combination of styles.

The new generation of architects is linked with names like **Kang Myong-su** and **Yi Chong-sung**. **T'ongilchŏn Palace,** completed in 1977, is without doubt a very attractive modern building in Kyŏngju, though it must be said that it is built in the ancient Shillan style.

It does seem that modern architecture, when it is not purely functional, is returning to the roots of Korea's architectural tradition.

(Thiele)

Traditional Music and Dance

Traditional Korean music with its traditional instruments is divided into native forms and forms introduced from abroad. To the latter group belong especially those musical forms taken over from China. Regarding types of music and its function, Koreans distinguish betwen Confucian ritual music, court ceremonial music and folk music. Military music is in a category of its own.

According to the "National Institute of Classical Music", there are sixty different types of instruments in Korea, forty-five of which are still played today. Musical instruments are classified systematically; in ancient China this was done according to the material the instruments were made of. Korean instruments are made of metal, stone, silk, bamboo, calabash, pottery, parchment and wood.

"Pyŏngjong", bronze bells, are hung on a frame in two rows of sixteen bells, and are struck with a stick made of horn. The different sizes and weights of the bells produce different tones. Bronze bells were used in Confucian rites and at court ceremonies.

"Ching", gongs, come in many sizes. They are used here at shamanist rituals, Buddhist ceremonies and in military music. Gongs are almost always used in country dancing (for example, at the Suwŏn Folk Museum) to beat the rhythm of the dance. The player carries the gong in his left hand, beating it with a wooden or felt-covered stick.

"Pyŏngyŏng", stone chimes, are also played in courtly ceremonial music. They are arranged on a frame just like the bronze bells. The varying size of the stones gives a variety of tone.

"Kŏmungo" is a six-stringed zither whose strings are laid over a total of sixteen movable bridges; it is said to be a native Korean instrument dating back to the seventh century. It is tuned with round pegs to which the strings are attached. The "kŏmungo" is plucked with a plectrum held in the right hand; the left hand presses the strings, creating the characteristic lingering, vibrating sound.

Closely related to the "kŏmungo", the twelve-stringed **"kayagŭm"** is a zither with a curved soundboard which can be played as a solo instrument or in an ensemble. As the name indicates, this instrument originated in ancient Kaya, a principality near the Kingdom of Shilla. Although similar in many ways to the "kŏmungo", the strings of the "kayagŭm" are plucked with the bare fingers and thumb, giving a different tone quality altogether. It is such a popular instrument that many families have one. It is played at almost

Top, from left to right: drum (choago), lyre, lute (pipa).
Below these: six-stringed zither (kŏmungo).

all festivals of traditional folk music. The body is often decorated with fine, ivory inlaid work, with the sun and the moon, "yang" and "ŭm", on the upper half.

In Korea there is both a native and a Chinese version of the **"pipa"**, lute. The Chinese lute has four, the Korean lute, five strings; both are played with a plectrum or with a bow.

The two-stringed **"haegŭm"** is the equivalent of the Chinese two-stringed fiddle ("san hsien") the body of which is open at the bottom and

covered with snakeskin at the top. This instrument originally came from Central Asia, where it is still played by the Mongolians.

"Taegŭm" is a bamboo transverse flute that is almost half a metre in length. It is used as an accompanying instrument for singing and dancing. When it is played in an orchestra it often introduces the melody.

The **"tanso"** is a native Korean flute with a slightly notched edge. It is played like a recorder. It is considered to be a delicate solo instrument and is played above all in performances of chamber music.

There are various versions of the oboe, **"piri",** in Korea – of the Chinese type or of the type with a soft tone. "Piris" are made of bamboo and have relatively large reeds.

"Saenghwang" is a type of mouth organ consisting of seventeen bamboo pipes set in a body of calabash (gourd). There are finger holes in the lower part of the pipes and little slits in the upper part. Both these features produce the difference in pitch. The instrument resounds when the player breathes in as well as when he breathes out. It can be played as a solo instrument or in a group. This mouth organ is rather difficult to play; it comes originally from South China.

The most popular Korean instrument is the hourglass-shaped drum called **"changgo",** which is covered and played at both ends. It is used in orchestras, in chamber music or as a solo instrument to accompany dancing. The parchment on the left end of the drum is thicker than on the right end, enabling the player to produce both a sharp-sounding tone and a more muffled one. The tones can also be varied by adjusting little triangles of leather tied to the strings which are attached from end to end of the drum.

"Pak" is a wooden clapper in the shape of a folding fan. It is used in ensemble music and marks the beginning of a piece with one tone, the end with three.

This brief introduction to the musical instruments which the visitor to Korea is most likely to see and hear at performances of traditional music in no way does justice to the wealth of instruments found in Korea. Koreans have always been very keen musicians, singers and dancers. Korean musicians who play Western instruments are recognized as being among the best players in the world.

As with traditional music and musical instruments, **Korean dance** is divided into religious, courtly and folk dance.

"Ilmu", Confucian ritual dance, was introduced to Korea at the end of the Koryŏ period. The more important the ceremony is, the more dancers are used – the largest possible number is sixty-four. Eight dancers then perform in eight rows. Two groups of civil and military officials take part with instruments and insignia that are exactly prescribed. These dances are characterized by a formality of the highest order. The "il" dances are only performed twice or three times a year now, usually in commemoration of the Yi dynasty when Confucianism flourished.

Four types of **Buddhist dance** are still performed today. In the **"nabichum",** the Butterfly Dance, a monk wearing a robe with extra-long sleeves dances in imitation of the flight of the butterfly. In the **"moguchum",** or Idol Dance, two monks dance around a totem pole. The **"parachum",** or Cymbal Dance, features a huge pair of cymbals which are banged, and the

"sŭngmu", or Priest's Dance, represents the symbolical struggle between body and soul. Buddhist monks' dances were originally intended to make the soul's journey to the other world after death as pleasant as possible. In order to achieve this, Buddha's assistance was invoked in dance.

Shamanist dances are still performed today at almost every ritual ("kut"), usually by a "mudang" or shaman priestess. They are accompanied by drum, oboe and flute and are intended to drive out demons and all evil. The shaman priestesses dance when they are healing the sick or soothsaying too. Many elements of shamanist dance have been taken over from other religions. The dances often last for several hours.

It is interesting to note that shamanism has experienced a surprising renaissance in the last few years.

There are two forms of **court dance:** native Korean **"hyangak" dances,** and Chinese **"tangak" dances.** The Sword, Crane and Nightingale Dances were, and still are, accompanied by musical instruments and singing. The movements are always restrained, grand, harmonious and elegant. Court dances are performed by young girls or ladies.

Among the **folk dances** that are popular are first of all pantomime-like dances with a satirical background. Abuses or defects in society are criticized in such dance dramas. Each province has its own dances,

the origins of which can be traced back to specific social conditions there. Masks are worn in these dances.

"Nongak" or **Country Dances** were originally performed to influence the gods who were responsible for good growth and a rich harvest. For almost every event in the rural life cycle there was an occasion to dance. Modified versions of these old peasant dances are now performed at Korea's well-known open-air folk museums. The aim of these museums is not only to give the tourist an insight into the life of traditional Korea, but also to draw the attention of the Koreans themselves to the habits and customs of the past. Music and dance have an important part to play here. *(Thiele)*

Food and Drink

In general people speak of "Korean cooking" and cover with this expression the whole range of culinary delights on offer. But just as there is no one style of Indian, Chinese or French cooking, there is not just one kind of Korean cuisine. It is clear that dishes in any country will vary according to regional peculiarities, which, in turn, depend on the climate and culture found there. In addition, there are a number of Korean specialities which are closely connected with one particular season. We should therefore avoid generalizations. At the same time, however, there are "linking" components in food and drink that are enjoyed by the mass of the people all over the country, and it is on these components that we shall concentrate here.

Korean recipes were collected systematically for the first time in 1913, when Pang Sin-yong's first cookery book appeared. Up to then the secrets of Korean cooking had simply been passed down orally from generation to generation.

Koreans eat three meals a day, including a substantial breakfast with mostly warm dishes.

Pepper sauce, soya bean paste, soya sauce, garlic and leeks are almost always to be found on the table, for Koreans love highly seasoned foods.

As all over East Asia **rice** is the staple food of the Koreans. It is served in the form of rice cake, rice pudding and even as a special kind of noodle after being ground and processed. In any arrangement of food on a table, rice is placed in the centre, surrounded by many pots, dishes and bowls containing the accompaniments. As chopsticks are used in Korea, all these accompaniments are served in small, bite-size pieces. Along with the rice we might find beef, chicken, pork, fish, a great variety of vegetables and, in the months of July and August, tasty dog meat! Unlike the South Chinese, who usually eat dog meat in winter in order to benefit from the healthy fat which the animals develop, Koreans like to eat their "kae" in summer.

"Kimchi" plays a particularly important role in Korean meals. There is probably not a single Korean who does not love this delicious condiment consisting of different kinds of vegetables pickled in brine and spicy sauces. There are many variations of "kimchi". It can be made of normal cabbage, savoy cabbage, Chinese cabbage, carrots, radish, turnip, wild garlic, egg plant, cucumber, green peppers and leeks. It is always made in autumn ("kimjang" is the name given to the making of kimchi), seasoned with ground red pepper and garlic powder, and filled into big brown earthenware jars, essential equipment for every Korean house, farmyard, garden and balcony. There it is left over the whole winter to ferment. To be enjoyed in the most varied forms and flavours, "kimchi" is an essential side dish with every meal. In restaurants second helpings of "kimchi" are served free of charge. In the coastal areas of Korea, fish, shrimps, prawns and oysters are "kimchied" too.

Traditionally, Korean meals are served on a table about 40 cm (less than 16 ins) high. The guests sit cross-legged on cushions around this table, usually in an "ondol" room, i. e. a room with the traditional underfloor heating. The food is placed on the table on plates and in bowls; the table itself is often finely carved. For cutlery Koreans use long chopsticks, usually made of metal, and a spoon with a long handle for soup. The chopsticks are often decorated with the characters for "long life". At a high-class meal the dishes are of precious celadon, but the average Korean eats his food from simple stainless steel bowls. When the meal is over, the chopsticks are laid on the table; if it is merely interrupted, you rest the chopsticks on your rice bowl.

As well as various sauces with their share of sesame, vinegar, rice wine, mustard and always a good strong portion of garlic, a great selection of boiled, steamed, roasted and fried delicacies are served at table. At a festive meal **"kujolpan"**, a large platter of boiled meat, various raw vegetables, and a heap of wafer-like pancakes, is served as hors d'oeuvre. The guest takes one of the pancakes, fills it with pieces of meat and vegetable, rolls it all up and pops it in his mouth. After this

starter, which is the equivalent of an hors d'oeuvre plate, all the other courses are served together – if possible – and each guest can help himself to whatever he prefers.

The size of a meal is measured in **"chup"**. Thus, five, seven or nine "chup" (i. e. dishes or courses) are served. Twelve "chup" was the normal number for royal banquets in times gone by. Nowadays a meal on a festive occasion has at least twelve "chup". The same applies to a "kyoja" (banquet). So it is all on a more lavish scale than the old royal dinners.

As in Chinese cooking, the ingredients of Korean dishes are heated very quickly so as to seal the vegetables and meat and so preserve the vitamins. The essential difference between Korean cuisine and that of the rest of the Chinese mainland is the number and variety of cold, pickled side dishes.

A Korean "Sunday dinner" usually consists of nine "chup": rice ("pap"), soup ("guk"), a dish of shellfish, steamed prawns, a dish of cooked fried peppers, pieces of fried fish, various vegetables on skewers, fried noodles and slices of raw fish or some other seafood titbit. Three or four sauces are served along with these dishes and five different "kimchi" variations to mix with the food and season it. A meal like this lasts for between two and three hours, the bowls being refilled again and again.

As well as the ingredients mentioned above many herbs are used

163

in Korean cookery – Koreans take a healthy diet seriously. And so you still find that nettles, wild asters, lilies, ginseng shoots, campanula, mugwort, thistles and shepherd's purse are added to certain dishes. (Some Koreans living abroad have even found themselves in trouble with the law because they picked certain ferns that were protected species. They wanted to make them into a Korean delicacy!) Very early on in the history of the "Land of Morning Calm", the healing powers of wild herbs were discovered and used to restore sick people to a state of health. Do we actually know how many vitamins and positive ingredients are contained in these plants? Their seemingly limitless healing properties have in any case brought about a revival of interest in many parts of the world in the herbs that were traditionally used for cooking and medicine.

Soup ("guk") is a must with every Korean meal. Here too there is an amazing variety; the most common one is made of fermented soya bean paste, "twaenjang guk", with mussels or clams and leeks in it. Another popular soup is a light broth boiled from dried anchovies with vegetables. Very often a clear soup is served with slices of radish or dried seaweed ("miyok guk"): a broth rendered from dried spinach is also very common. In addition there are soups with rice cakes, taro soup and kelp ash soup. There are, of course, regional differences in the way the soups are made. In the coastal areas the main ingredient is fish, whereas inland it is vegetables which are added to a broth. Soups are not very highly seasoned; the guest must add his own seasoning.

Here is a list of ten typical Korean soups which the foreign visitor is sure to like:
- kogi-guk (beef broth)
- kogi-dubu-guk (beef broth with soya bean curd)
- kogi-kamja-guk (beef broth with potatoes)
- jogae-guk (shellfish soup)
- g'ori-guk (oxtail soup)
- yuk-gae-jang (red pepper and garlic soup)
- wanja-guk (soup with meat balls)
- kalbi-guk (soup with short ribs)
- gom-guk (broth with onions, garlic and chilli peppers)
- t'oran-guk (taro soup: taro is a white root plant which contains a lot of starch).

The dishes the Koreans like most include:

- **pulkogi:** fine slices of meat (beef or pork) marinated in soya sauce, garlic, sesame oil, black pepper and spring onions, and then grilled over a little charcoal stove at table. The meat is then dipped in sauces also composed of the above ingredients and eaten with rice, various vegetables and soup.

- **kalbi:** marinated short ribs which are grilled over a charcoal brazier like pulkogi and eaten with sauces. (In every town in Korea you will find restaurants which specialize in pulkogi and kalbi

- **bibim-bap:** a dish of boiled rice, slices of beef, soya bean sprouts, cucumber, mushrooms, lettuce and fried egg.

— **samkye tang:** chicken cooked in ginseng with boiled root vegetables, chilli peppers, garlic, glutenous rice and chestnuts.

— **gakdugi:** a cold dish consisting of "kimchi" pickles, radish, oysters, mint, onions, garlic and seasonings.

— **sokalbi-koo-ee:** grilled chops with tomatoes, onion rings and green peppers.

— **dark-koo-ee:** grilled chicken breast with radishes, leeks, mushrooms, garlic, sugar, pepper, mint, sesame oil, soya sauce and ginger.

— **saengsun yang yumchang-koo-ee:** grilled fish with sesame, soya sauce, onions, garlic and black pepper.

— **dubu-jorim:** steamed soya bean curd with pepper, soya sauce, garlic and sliced leeks.

— **japch'ae:** a meat and vegetable dish consisting of fine slices of beef, spring onions, garlic, sesame oil, ground sesame, soya sauce and black pepper served with mushrooms, vermicelli, cabbage, carrots and green peppers.

Before the meal is served in a restaurant, the waiter sets a mug or glass of brown liquid on the table. This is **"bori ch'a"** or **"mul"**, a tea made of roasted barley. This barley tea is part of every Korean meal, and it may be served hot or cold. This drink tastes a little strange to foreigners and many do not like it at all. Another related drink, **"bori-sudan"**, is also made of barley, but of the fresh grain. Honey is added to

"bori-sudan" and this gives a sweet-tasting drink. Another traditional, delicious drink that is served at table is **"jindallae hwach'ae"**, a tea brewed from azalea blossoms. Lemon juice ("yujach'a") and a ginger root drink called "saeng-gang ch'a", ginseng root tea ("insam ch'a") and a persimmon drink called "su-jonggwa" are among the non-alcoholic beverages that may be served with a meal.

There are two rival breweries in Korea. Each tourist must decide for himself whether he prefers **OB or Crown beer.** In the beerhalls, which are modelled on typical German-American institutions, beer is served with little side dishes of nuts, peanuts, shredded dried fish or vegetables (leeks, cubes of turnip, slices of radish). In Korea beer is comparatively expensive.

In simple restaurants **"makkolli"**, a milky, freshly fermented rice wine, or **"soju"**, a clear schnapps distilled from rice and barley, are served. Often **"pindae tok"** (a pancake stuffed with vegetables) or **"mae untang"** (a hearty and spicy fish soup) will be served with these drinks.

"Soju" and "makkolli" are drunk in **"suljips"**, typically Korean drinking establishments. "Soju" is cheap and probably the most popular alcoholic drink in Korea. Korean rice wine, which is sold in big bottles and is very similar to Japanese "sake", is called **"chungju"**. It is more expensive than "soju", but is of a much better quality. *(Thiele)*

Restaurants in Seoul

Korean

Eunhasu
Sejong Hotel
Tel. 7 76-18 11

Kumsujang
Ambassador Hotel
Tel. 2 61-11 02

Myongwolkwan
Sheraton Walker Hill Hotel
Tel. 4 45-01 81

Posokjong
Lotte Hotel
Tel. 7 71-10

Flamenco
53-6, 2-ga, Myong-dong, Chung-ku
Tel. 7 76-33 78

Gourmet
39, Insa-dong, Chongro-ku
Tel. 7 24-36 18

Naksanjang
129, Tongsung-dong, Chongro-ku
Tel. 7 63-23 74

Pine Hill
2-88-5, Zo-dong, Chung-ku
Tel. 2 66-44 04

Shinjong
21, 2-ka, Myong-dong, Chung-ku
Tel. 7 76-04 37

Hanilkwan
50-1, 2-ka, Myong-dong, Chung-ku
Tel. 7 76-33 88

Ilokcho
49, Insa-dong, Chongro-ku
Tel. 7 24-16 78

Korea House
80-2, 2-ka, Pil-dong, Chung-ku
Tel. 2 66-91 01

Slightly more elegant:

Byolchonji
179, Kwanchol-dong, Chongro-ku
Tel. 7 25-18 18

Chongpung
99, Igson-dong, Chongro-ku
Tel. 7 65-01 01

Chongwongak
53-26, Chongwun-dong, Chongro-ku
Tel. 7 23-35 51

Choonynaggak
9, Muak-dong, Chongro-ku
Tel. 7 25-24 44

Taeha
56, Igson-dong, Chongro-ku
Tel. 7 65-11 51

Taewongak
323, Songpug-dong, Songpug-ku
Tel. 7 62-01 61

Tasong
85-18, Kyunji-dong, Chongro-ku
Tel. 7 23-79 00

Koryowon
32-43, Songwol-dong, Chongro-ku
Tel. 7 23-72 66

Myongwol
34, Igson-dong, Chongro-ku
Tel. 7 65-39 91

Ohjinam
34-6, Igson-dong, Chongro-ku
Tel. 7 65-43 06

Punglimgak
11-2, Kyobuk-dong, Chongro-ku
Tel. 7 24-66 01

Samchonggak
330-115, Songpug-dong, Songpug-ku
Tel. 7 62-01 51

Sonwoongak
260-6, Wooi-dong, Tobong-ku
Tel. 7 65-31 38

Shinragak
54, Chongwun-dong, Chongro-ku
Tel. 7 25-98 61

Chinese

Chungkukkwan
Sheraton Walker Hill Hotel
Tel. 4 45-01 81

Hongbokak
Ambassador Hotel
Tel. 2 60-44 46

Moon Palace
Chosun Hotel Fl. 20
Tel. 7 71-05

Tao-Yuen
Plaza Hotel Fl. 3
Tel. 7 71-22

Asowon
4-310, Ulchiro, Chung-ku
Tel. 2 66-11 91

Heeraedung
30-19, Hannam-dong, Yongsan-ku
Tel. 7 92-66 33

Kosang
319, Tongbuichon-dong, Yongsan-ku
Tel. 7 94-80 01

Kukildaepanjom
Daewang Bldg.
355, Chungrim-dong, Chung-ku
Tel. 7 77-95 23

Tongbosong
2-50-7, Namsan-dong, Chung-ku
Tel. 28-27 27

Arisan
258-6, Itaewon-dong, Yongsan-ku
Tel. 7 94-00 22

Japanese

Akasaka
Hyatt Hotel
Tel. 7 95-01 41

Kotobuki
Plaza Hotel
7 71-22

Ozashiki
Tokyu Hotel
Tel. 7 53-11 51

Zakuro
Savoy Hotel
Tel. 7 76-26 41

Daebon
66-4, Chungmuro, 2-ka, Chung-ku
Tel. 7 76-99 17

Kilcho
13-2, Namhag-dong, Chung-ku
Tel. 2 67-71 11

Missouri
14-5, Pugchang-dong, Chung-ku
Tel. 7 52-39 66

Oriental

Celadon
Sheraton Walker Hill Hotel
Tel. 4 45-01 81

Elysee
Plaza Hotel
Tel. 7 71-22

King's Buffet
Ambassador Hotel
Tel. 2 61-11 01

Ninth Gate
Chosun Hotel
Tel. 7 71-05

Peinsula
Bando Hotel
Tel. 7 82-80 01

Banjul
12-16, Kwanchol-dong, Chongro-ku
Tel. 7 23-18 00

Mamma Mia
58-4, Socho-dong, Kangnam-ku
Tel. 5 55-80 28

Round Table
Savoy Hotel
Tel. 7 76-26 41

Maxim
1-ka, Chungmu-ro
Lotte Hotel
Tel. 7 71-10 (Ext. 142)

Bear House
Pukak Sky Way
Tel. 7 82-14 48

Bear House
3-ka, Toegye-ro, Chung-ku
Tel. 2 66-16 53

Diplomatic Club
2-26, Namsan-dong, Chung-ku
Tel. 7 52-56 29

Four Seasons
15. Stock, Samku Bldg.
Sogong-dong, Chung-ku
Tel. 7 52-58 81

La Cantina
Samsung Bldg.
1-50, Ulchiro, Chung-ku
Tel. 7 77-25 79

Ristorante Opera
Sejong Cultural Center
Tel. 7 23-78 63

A Few Words of Korean

Greetings

Hello, how are you?	– Ŏ-tŏ-sim-ni-ka? Yo-bo se-yo?
Good morning!	– An-nyŏng ha-sim-ni-ka.
Did you sleep well?	– An-nyŏng-hi chu-mu-syŏt-sŭm-ni-ka?
How is your family?	– Ka-jok-dŭl-ŭn ŏ-tŏ sim-ni-ka?
My family is very well, thank you.	– Tŏk-t'aek-e da chal it-sŭm-ni-da.
I hope to see you soon.	– To man-na poe-op-get-sŭm-ni-da.
See you tonight.	– Chŏ-nyŏk-e poe-op-get-sŭm-ni-da.
All the best! Good luck!	– Pok pa-dŭ-sip-si-o.
Please phone again.	– To o-sip-si-o.
How are you, Mr. Pak?	– Pak-si an-nyŏng-ha-sim-ni-ka.
Very well, and you?	– Ne, an-nyŏng-ha-sim-ni-ka?
I'm pleased to see you.	– Pan-gap-sŭm-ni-da.
How's business?	– Sa-ŏp-ŭn ŏ-tŏt-sŭm-ni-ka?
Thanks, quite good.	– Kŭ-jŏ kwaen-ch'an-sŭm-ni-da.
Goodbye!	– An-nyŏng-hi ka-sip-si-yo.
Thank you very much for your hospitality!	– Chal kwan-dae-ha-yŏ chu-siŏ ko-map-sŭm-ni-da.
Goodnight!	– An-nyŏng-hi chu-mu-sip-si-o.
Thank you!	– Kam-sa-ham-ni-da.

Introductions

My name is …	– Chŏ-ui i-rŭm-un … im-ni-da.
What is your name?	– Tang-sin i-rŭm-ŭn mu-ŏt-sim-ni-ka? Sŏng-ham-i nu-gu si-ji-yo?
How old are you?	– Na-i-nŭn yŏt-ch'i-sim-ni-ka?

Conversation

Do you know …?	– Tang-sinŭn? A-sim-ni-ka?
Is/are there …?	– It-sŭm-ni-ka …?
Yes, there are … Yes, I have …	– Ne (ye), it-sŭm-ni-da …
No, there isn't/aren't. No, I haven't.	– Anio, ŏp-sŭm-ni-da.
Where?	– Ŏ-di?
Where is it?	– Ŏ-di it-sŭm-ni-ka?
Here it is. Here they are.	– Yŏ-gi it-sŭm-ni-da.
Can you/we/he/she?	– Hal su it-sŭm-ni-ka?
I/you/he/she/it/we/they cannot …	– Hal su ŏp-sŭm-ni-da
Can you/we do that?	– Tan-sin-ŭn kŭ-gŏt-sŭl hal su it-sŭm-ni-ka?
Please give me …	– … chu-sip-si-o.
Please bring me …	– … ka-jyŏ o-sip-si-o.
Please bring me the newspaper.	– Sin-mun-ŭl ka-jyŏ o-sip-si-o.

I like that.	– Na·nǔn kǔ·gǒt·sǔl cho·a ham·ni·da.
What is that?	– Chǒ·gǒt·sǔn mu·ǒt·sim·ni·ka?
What is that called in Korean?	– I·gǒt·sǔn Han·guk·mal·ro um·ǒt si·ra·go ham·ni·ka?

Shopping

How much does that cost?	– Ǒl·ma im·ni·ka?
Do you have…? Have you got…?	– …i is·sum·ni·ka?
Please show me something else.	– Ta·run·go·sul pǒyo chu·sip·si·yo.
I'd like to buy that.	– I·go·sul sa·get·sum·ni·da.
Thank you very much!	– Kam·sa·ham·ni·da.

In a taxi

Please take me to the Hyatt Hotel.	– Hyatt Hotel ro kap·si·da.
How long does it take from here?	– Ǒl·ma·na ko kol·im·ni·ka?
Stop!	– Se·wo chu·sip·si·yo!
How much is that?	– Ǒl·ma im·ni·ka?

Eating

The meal is ready.	– Chǒ·nyǒk chun·bi·ga toe·ǒt·sǔm·ni·da.
Please come and sit down.	– Ǒ·sǒ wa·sǒ an·jǔ sip·si·o.
I hope you like Korean food.	– Han·guk ǔm·sik·ǔl cho·a ha·sil nǔn·ji·yo.
That is hot (highly·seasoned)!	– Ma·ep sǔm·ni·da!
That tastes delicious!	– A·ju ma·si sǔm·ni·da!
I'd like a cup of coffee, please.	– Cof·fe·rul chu·sip·si·yo.
Could I have a bottle of beer, please.	– Maek·ju han·byǒng chu·sip·si·yo.
Can I have the bill/check, please.	– Ke·san·so·rul chu·sip·si·yo.

Other useful phrases

Yes, sir. Yes, madam.	– Ye
No, sir. No, madam.	– Anio
Thank you very much.	– Kam·sa ham·ni·da.
You're welcome.	– Chon·man·ne mal·sǔm im·ni·da.
Excuse me.	– Sil·re ham·ni·da.
I'm sorry.	– Mi·an ham·ni·da.
That's good. That's bad.	– Jo·sǔm·ni·da. Na·pǔm·ni·da.
That's right. That's wrong.	– Ol·sǔm·ni·da. Tǔl·yot sǔm·ni·da.
Do you speak English?	– Yǒng·ǒ hal·su is·sǔm·ni·ka?
Can you understand me?	– I·hae·ha·se·yo?
Please say that again.	– Ta·si mal·sǔm·hae chu se·yo.
Could you come here, please.	– I·ri o·sip·si·yo.

Regional Section

Regions, towns and cities	Page
Kyŏnggi-do	172
Suwŏn	173
Seoul	175
Kangwŏn-do	184
Ch'ungch'ŏngpuk-do	187
Ch'ungch'ŏngnam-do	189
Taejŏn	189
Kyŏngsangpuk-do	192
Taegu	193
Kyŏngju	195
Kyŏngsangnam-do	200
Pusan	203
Chŏllapuk-do	206
Chŏllanam-do	208
Cheju-do	209

(do = Province)

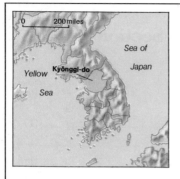

Kyŏnggi-do

As in other countries, the Koreans attribute certain characteristics to the inhabitants of the various provinces. The people from the province of Kyŏnggi are said to be extremely thrifty and have the reputation of haggling over every trifle. They are also compared to a "beautiful woman who is always looking at herself in the mirror". Whether or not this characterization can be applied to the people who live there today is something foreigners can hardly judge!

The most interesting places in the province can be visited in day trips from the Korean capital, Seoul.

Inch'ŏn

This port city on the west coast of Korea, on the Yellow Sea, forms the gateway to the Korean capital. Inch'ŏn lies just 35 km (22 miles) west of Seoul and can be reached in 30 minutes by underground.

It was at the place where Inch'ŏn is now situated (it was formerly known as "Chemŭlpo") that the first Europeans to come by the sea route landed in Korea. That was at the end of the 19th century. In 1866, in the course of the persecution of Catholics, nine French priests were executed here. In 1904, during the Russian-Japanese War, enemy warships fought out artillery duels off Inch'ŏn. And in 1950, the Korean War having broken out, the American General MacArthur ordered UN troops to land here to come to the aid of South Korea. Because of tidal amplitude (almost 10 m/33 ft), the amphibian vehicles had to be landed in a matter of seconds. A monument to General MacArthur stands on a little hill in Chayu Park and commemorates this event.

Inch'ŏn is now Korea's fourth largest port and a large industrial centre. Glass and plywood are the main products.

For fish connoisseurs, there is a great variety of mussel soups, prawns and other seafood in **Yonan,** on the coast south of the town.

The popular resort of **Songdo** is also situated south of Inch'ŏn and can be reached by taxi in 20 minutes. In the hot summer months the beaches are often overcrowded. In that case it is a good idea to take a ferry boat to the islands which lie off the coast. A narrow-gauge railway still operates between Songdo and Suwŏn. It is worthwhile having a ride in the oldtimer carriages through the open countryside.

A sail from Inch'ŏn to the island of **Kanghwa** is something you should not miss. You can see megalithic tombs here dating from the Neolithic period, indicating a very early settlement of Korea. In 1259, during the Mongol invasion, the king and his court sought refuge here. And it was on this island that monks cut the over 80,000 wooden blocks of the Tripitaka Koreana (see history chapter and section on Haein Temple, p. 200). Kanghwa played a decisive role as an important strategic point guarding the entry to the Han River which led to Seoul; the fortifications on the island bear witness to this.

About 55 km (34 miles) north of Seoul lies **Panmunjom.** Here, in 1953, the truce marking the end of the Korean War was signed by representatives of the UN, North Korea and China after 575 sessions. You can only visit the demilitarized zone on organized tours. These are offered by hotels in Seoul.

You can make another day trip from Seoul to the **Sanjong-hosu,** an idyllic "Mountain Spring Lake" northeast of the capital. It lies in a landscape of oddly-shaped rocks. There are pines and other conifers along the shores, and this makes the visitor feel as if he were in a typically Korean landscape painting.

If you travel southeast from Seoul via Inch'ŏn (60 km/37 miles s. e. of the capital) you come to the **Yong-nung,** tomb of the most famous ruler of the Yi dynasty, King Sejong. He is called the "father of the Korean alphabet, han'gŭl" and he was the founder of several scholarly institutions. You can cross the Han River further east to get to the **Silluk Temple,** one of the biggest in the vicinity of the capital. Some of the stone lanterns, memorial tablets and pagodas count as national cultural treasures.

West of Seoul, at the confluence of the Pukhan-gang (= northern Han River) and the Namhan-gang (= southern Han River), the **P'aldang Dam** has been built, and a large recreational area established nearby (P'aldang Resort). Like Suwŏn, the **Namhan Castle** between Seoul and P'aldang served as a place of refuge for the royal family during the Yi dynasty.

The area along the **Pukhan-gang,** the northern branch of the Han River, which rises in the Diamond Mountains of North Korea and flows through landscape which has hardly been changed at all by man, is not as touristically developed. For visitors to Korea who are staying for a longer period, this is an excellent area for hiking and holidays away from it all.

Suwŏn

About 60 km (37 miles) south of Seoul lies Suwŏn, administrative capital of Kyŏnggi Province. This historic city can be reached from Seoul Central Station by suburban train or bus. One of the sights of Suwŏn is the city wall which was built in 1796 and is still well preserved, and its **Bugmun** or **North Gate.** As one of the five Korean fortresses or fortified towns, Suwŏn was an alternative refuge for the royal family when they had to flee

Mask of a young Shaman priestess. Masks are worn mainly for traditional dances.

from Seoul. Nowadays, Suwŏn owes much of its importance to the agricultural faculty of the Seoul National University, which worked out the overall plans for the Saemaul Movement (see "Saemaul Undong, Korea's Green Revolution"). Many experimental farms and fields lie within the vicinity.

The **Folk Village** outside Suwŏn attracts many visitors, both Korean and foreign. A visit is to be strongly recommended, for in the village you can get a good impression of life in a Korean rural community. Resplendent in national costume and wearing false beards, huge palace guards of Mongolian appearance flank the entrance gate. In 68 buildings inside the village a number of craftsmen can be seen at work; agricultural equipment and items used in religious ceremonies are demonstrated and explained. On a visit to the village you first of all pass through some restaurants where, after a thorough tour, you can eat a traditional meal. Then you see the big "changsungs" or roadside gods which stand in pairs and were originally set up as a kind of totem pole outside each village to ward off diseases and other evils. Finally you come to the craftsmen's workshops where pottery is still made in the traditional way, blacksmith's work done, cloth woven and grain ground.

A **Yangban House** may also be visited. From April to October visitors are shown traditional wedding ceremonies (all costumes are originals). There are daily performances of dance and music with traditional instruments and costumes true to style. (Performances commence at 3 p.m.) At weekends many young Koreans stroll through the narrow lanes in their wide, airy "hanbok" clothes; fortune-tellers even reveal a bit of the future to foreigners. Games of dice, seesaws and swings fascinate the Koreans more than the foreigners, for these are traditional forms of leisure. The variety of colours, costumes and people who come here from the provinces could not be greater. It is definitely worthwhile taking a whole day for a visit to Suwŏn.

Seoul

At the end of the Koryǒ dynasty and the beginning of the Yi, or Chosǒn, period in 1392, the town of Seoul grew out of the little place called Hanyang. Seoul is an old city compared to the modern world, but compared to other East Asian capitals it is a relatively young metropolis. The origin of the name is still disputed. Korean historians believe that the word "Seoul" is derived from "Sorabol", which means "capital". It is a purely Korean word for which no Chinese characters exist.

Seoul was originally surrounded by a town wall 16 km (almost 10 miles) long; only a few remains of this wall can be seen today. Only four of the original nine city gates allowing access to Seoul are still standing, the others having been demolished over the years.

Today Seoul covers an area of 627 sq. km (242 sq. miles) and has a population of around 10 million. The city centre lies between the **Samgaksan** (Three Peak Mountain) in the north and **Namsan** (South Mountain) in the south. The visitor's first impression of Seoul is that it was built on several different hills like Rome. So, some parts of the town lie hidden in gentle valleys.

The visitor to Seoul can collect information material from the main office of the Korean National Tourist Corporation (KNTC): 10, Ta-dong, Chung-gu, C. P. P. Box 903, Tel. 7 57-60 30, 60 40. There he will find a whole series of brochures, not just about Seoul itself but also about other towns and provinces of the country.

There are daily guided tours of the city. Hotel receptionists can give you details of prices and times of departure. But you can also get to know the city on your own. A combination of walking and taking taxis (they represent a relatively cheap means of transport) can be recommended for this. The streets of Seoul are very safe, and local people are always very pleased to help you. Even after dark you do not need to worry about walking around the city.

Seoul has a great many sights to offer – old palaces, museums, city gates, temples, galleries, concert halls, recreation parks and the Olympic grounds in the southeast of the city.

A tour of the city should start at the **City Hall**. It is situated on the corner of Ulchiro and T'aep'yongro (ro = street). Diagonally across from it stands the **Toksugung** or Toksu ("Palace of Virtuous Longevity"). This was once a royal villa which King Kojong used as his residence in the last phase of the Yi dynasty up to his abdication in 1907. The palace is an example of traditional Korean architecture – combined, however, with buildings in the European style of the turn of the century. The old palace, which was built 500 years ago when almost all royal residences had been destroyed by Hideyoshi's troops, was the setting for many sad scenes in the history of the Yi dynasty. After another Japanese invasion the last Korean king had to agree here to the annexation of Korea by Japan. Kojong, however, was allowed to use the building as his private residence till his death on 21st January, 1919. The room where he died, known as Hamnyong-jon, can be visited. This old palace and its grounds now house the **Museum of Modern Art.**

If we continue walking south along T'aep'yong Street, we come to the **Namdaemun** or **South Gate** which, along with the East Gate, is National Treasure No. 1 for the Koreans, and the pride of the people of Seoul especially. From the skyscrapers in the area there is a fascinating view of the whole Namdaemun area; the gate itself looks like a doll's house when seen from high up. The inscription on it says: "Gate of Noble Ceremony". It was built from 1394 to 1398 and then reconstructed in 1447, surviving all the troubles of history. Nowadays the city traffic races and roars around it.

From here the tourist should definitely visit the little market streets near the gate where traditional and modern Korea meet. An unbelievable crowd of people mill around the market stalls where everything the average person could desire is offered for sale, from the most delicious fruits to electric bulbs, textiles, household goods, shoes, watches and ginseng. The colourfulness of this overwhelming variety of goods is, moreover, an oasis for the photographer. When you let yourself be swept through the **Namdaemun**

Market, there is the atmosphere of an Oriental bazaar: pedlars with lap dogs pass by, others sell scissors or fruit from the country; some corners look like flea markets, secondhand wares are sold here too.

From here we can turn north again and, having passed the monument to the legendary Admiral Yi, arrive at the spacious grounds of **Kyŏngbok Palace** ("kyŏngbok" means shining happiness). Situated at the end of Sejong Street, this palace, which includes the **National Museum** and the **Folklore Museum,** is a must on every tour. Kyŏngbokkung ("kung" = palace) was built in 1394 in the reign of King Taejo, the founder of the Yi dynasty, but it was destroyed by fire during the Japanese invasion in 1592. It was not reconstructed until 1868 when it served as the royal residence of the 25th king of this same dynasty. Many of the original 200 buildings were demolished by the Japanese and the grounds ornamented with pagodas and other stone monuments. The presence of such buildings eventually led to the establishment of the National Museum in the grounds of the palace in 1972. The museum is situated behind the Capitol. The building was designed along the lines of existing Korean "masterpieces". The pagoda in the centre is a copy of the five-storey Palsang-jon in Pŏpchu Temple (see p. 187). The other parts of the building are modelled on Kumsan and Hwaom Temples (see pp. 207 and 208). Thus, even in the outer form, considerable importance was attached to traditional architecture and the incorporation of achitectural elements from buildings which were, and remain, amongst the loveliest examples of Korean temple architecture.

The exhibition rooms and the large book stall where you can buy excellent catalogues, posters, slides and replicas of original art objects are on the ground floor opposite the main entrance. The museum houses several national treasures of Korean culture. The 13 exhibition rooms on the ground floor acquaint the visitor with objects of Korean history (sculptures, ceramics, pottery, calligraphy, painting and crafts), the different departments being arranged according to dynasty. The exhibition of Buddhist art is especially fascinating with its large statues of stone, granite, wood and bronze. The way the statues are illuminated gives a sublime, mystical atmosphere to the rooms. The museum is open Tuesday to Sunday from 9 am to 5 pm; it is closed on Mondays.

Not far from the National Museum lies the **Folklore Museum.** This museum is a real mine of information for the visitor who is interested in the traditional way of life in Korea, in the old customs which were influenced by Confucianism and in the material evidence of this culture (clothes, agricultural tools and fishing equipment, household goods, medicine, furniture, etc.). Through very vivid dioramas, authentic settings, diagrams and detailed, explanatory texts in English the visitor can learn all he

wants to know about the traditional culture of Korea in an exemplary fashion. It is a real pleasure to wander through the rooms of this museum. Another point of interest: beside the Folklore Museum is the place where Queen Min was assassinated (see chapter on history).

As well as visiting the museums you should be sure to have a look at the valuable objects of Korean culture which stand in the open air in the spacious grounds of Kyŏngbok Palace. Of these, the **ten-storey marble pagoda** in front of the Academy building deserves special mention. It is from Kyŏngchou Temple where it was chiselled in 1348. The splendidly carved stone reliefs convey an excellent impression of 14th century art.

You can have your photograph taken in traditional Korean court dress (hanbok) in front of the Throne and Audience Hall, **Kŭnjŏngjŏn.** In the old days the king could look from the stone terrace over a courtyard in which the standing positions of those taking part in the royal audience were exactly marked, as at the imperial court of Beijing. The stone tablets show that these positions were all arranged hierarchically. When you leave the palace, the north-south axis of the complex (towards the gates Kwanghwamun and Namdaemun) is blocked by the Capitol Building, the modern seat of government.

Inside the palace grounds, however, the **Kyŏnghweru Pavilion** must still be mentioned. A plain but

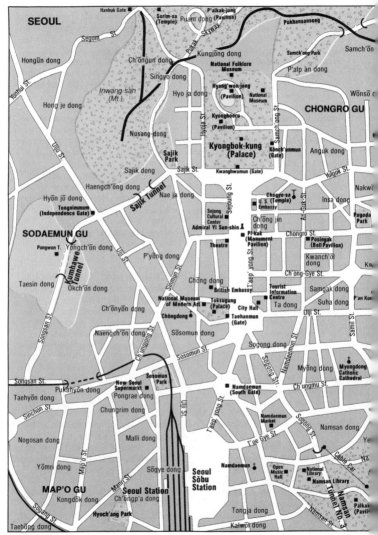

SEOUL

Hanbuk Gate ■
Sorim-sa (Temple) ■
P'alkak-jong
Puam dong (Pavilion)
Pukhansansong
Samch'ŏn

Segom St.
Pukak Skyway
Samch'ang Park

Hongŭn dong
Ch'ŏngun dong
Kungjŏng dong
P'alp'an dong

Yonhui St.
Singyo dong
National Folklore Museum
Wŏnsŏ d

Hong je dong
Hyo ja dong
Nyang'won-jong (Pavilion)
National Museum
CHONGRO GU

Inwang-san (Mt.)
Kyonghoeru (Pavilion)
Samch'ŏng St.

Nusang-dong
Kyongbok-kung (Palace)
Kŏnch'unmun (Gate)
Anguk dong

Sajik Park
Kônch'unmun
Yulgok St.
Nakw

Haengch'ŏng dong
Sajik dong
Sajik St.
Kwanghwamun (Gate)

Hyŏn jō dong
Nae ja dong
Chogye-sa (Temple)
U. S. Embassy
Insa dong

Tongnimmum (Independence Gate) ■
Sajik Tunnel
Sejong Cultural Center
Ch'ŏng jin dong
Pagoda Park

SODAEMUN GU
Admiral Yi Sun-shin ■
Pi'kak (Monument Pavilion)
Chongro St.
Posingak (Bell Pavilion)

Pongwon T. ■
Yŏngch'ŏn dong
Theatre
Kwanch'ŏl dong
Kw

Kumhwawe Tunnel
P'yŏng dong
Ch'ŏng-Gye St.

Taesin dong
Okch'ŏn dong
British Embassy
Tourist Information Centre
Samgak dong
P'an Kor

Ch'ŏnyŏn dong
National Museum of Modern Art
Toksugung (Palace)
Suha dong

Chŏngdong ●
City Hall
Ta dong
Ulji St.

Naengch'ŏn dong
Sōsomun dong
Taehanmun (Gate)

Songsan St.
Sosomun St.
Sogong dong
Samil St.

Pukahyŏn dong
Sosomun Park
Myŏng dong
Myongdong Catholic Cathedral

Songsan St.
New Seoul Supermarkt ■
Namdaemun (South Gate) ■
Ch'ungmu dong

Taehyŏn dong
Pongrae dong
Chungrim dong

Sinchon St.
Namdaemun Market
Namsan dong

Nogosan dong
Malli dong
T'oe Gye St.

Yōmri dong
Sōgye dong
Namdaemun ✝
Open Music Hall ■
National Library
Namsan Library
Cable Car
Na

MAP'O GU
Kongdŏk dong
Seoul Sōbu Station
Tongja dong
Namsan Tunnel No. 3
Palkak (Pavilion)

Taebōng-dong
Sogang St.
Seoul Station
Ch'ŏngp'a dong
Hyoch'ang Park
Kalwōl dong

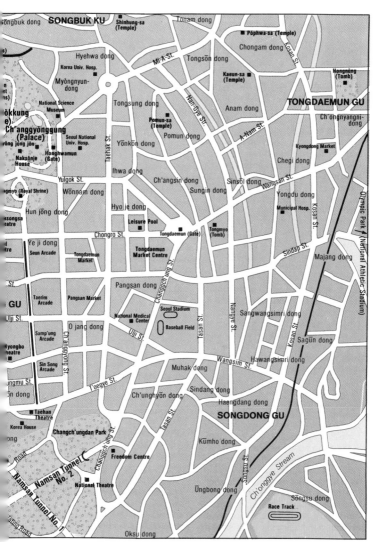

SONGBUK KU
Shinhung-sa (Temple)
Tonam dong
Pŏphwa-sa (Temple)
Hyehwa dong
Chongam dong
Korea Univ. Hosp.
Mi-A-St.
Tongsŏn dong
Kosan St.
Myŏngnyun-dong
Kaeun-sa (Temple)
Hongnŭng (Tomb)
National Science Museum
Tongsung dong
Anam dong
TONGDAEMUN GU
Namgye St.
Ch'ongnyangni-dong
Ch'anggyŏngung (Palace)
Pomun-sa (Temple)
ŏng jŏng jŏn
Pomun dong
A-Nam St.
Seoul National Univ. Hosp.
Honghwamun (Gate)
Taehak St.
Yŏnkŏn dong
Kyongdong Market
Chegi dong
Naksŏnje House
Ihwa dong
Ch'angsin dong
Sinsŏl dong
Wangsan St.
Yongdu dong
Yulgok St.
ngmyo (Royal Shrine)
Wŏnnam dong
Sungin dong
Municipal Hosp.
Kosan St.
Hun jŏng dong
Hyolje dong
Leisure Pool
Tongdaemun (Gate)
Tongmyo (Tomb)
Sindap St.
Chongro St.
Majang dong
Ye ji dong
Tongdaemun Market Centre
Seun Arcade
Tongdaemun Market
Pangsan dong
Changch'ung St.
Namgye St.
Sangwangsimri dong
Taerim Arcade
Pangsan Market
Seoul Stadium
Tasan St.
National Medical Center
Baseball Field
Sagŭn dong
Samp'ung Arcade
Ch'ungmuro St.
O jang dong
Ulji St.
Wangsim St.
Hawangsimri dong
Sin Song Arcade
Muhak dong
Toegye St.
Ch'unghyŏn dong
Sindang dong
Haengdang dong
Taehan Theatre
SONGDONG GU
Korea House
Changch'ungdan Park
Kŭmho dong
Ch'ŏnggye Stream
Namsan Tunnel No. 2
Freedom Centre
Sindang St.
National Theatre
Ŭngbong dong
Songsu dong
Namsan Tunnel No.
Race Track
Oksu dong

179

majestic building, official state banquets and receptions are still held here. The pavilion stands on 48 pillars in the middle of the palace gardens. It is surrounded by a pond which helps to underline the idyllic position of this pillar architecture.

From Kyŏngbokkung we can now turn left and walk eastwards along Yulgok Street to reach **Ch'angdŏkkung.** Built in 1405, this is one of the best-loved palaces in Korea. The **Secret Gardens** are to be found in its grounds. You enter the palace through the **Tonhwamun,** the perfectly-preserved gateway. Ch'angdŏk, once the main residence of the Korean rulers, now houses a small museum which contains personal possessions of the former kings. Some of the furnished rooms can be visited too. Rare portraits of a type that is not typical of Korean painting hang on the corridor walls. There is an added attraction for motorcar fans: the former royal cars, which were among the first in Korea, having been bought by the royal household at the end of the 19th century, are displayed here.

The Secret Gardens, covering 7,800 sq. m. (almost 2 acres), are an example of traditional garden art, influenced by China but developed further in Korea. The gardens were "secret" because the ladies of the court went for walks there and they were not allowed to be seen in public. The gardens are called **"Piwon"** in Korean, and 44 little pavilions are integrated into the landscape, set among the ponds and streams, and inviting the stroller to rest or sit and have a leisurely chat. In the largest of these pavilions, the Yonghwadan ("Hall of the Reflecting Flowers"), the teachers of the academy used to hold the examinations for government service. These were based mainly on knowledge of Confucian philosophy.

South of Ch'angdokkung stands another palace, **Ch'anggyonggung,** a detached residence dating from the Yi period. The beautiful grounds in which the palace stands were until recently the site of the zoo and botanical gardens. Now the zoo has been removed, however, and the palace restored to its original state and opened to the public. At cherry blossom time at the end of April the park attracts thousands of visitors. There is a long tradition of cherry blossom viewing in Korea, as in Japan.

Farther south we find the royal-imperial ancestral shrines in which the family trees of all rulers of the Yi dynasty are kept. These shrines are interesting to visit, especially when official ceremonies are being held (for example, on the first Sunday in May). Descendants of the imperial family have a residence not far from here. This part of the park is called **Naksonjae** and can only be visited if an appointment is made in advance.

After crossing Chong-ro we come to the **Tongdaemun** or **East Gate** of the city. It was almost in ruins in 1869, when it was rebuilt in its present form. Nearby, south of the fifth section of Chong Street, is the **East Gate Market** which is just as fascinating as the one at the South Gate. Here there are also several little antique shops in secluded lanes which have relatively reasonable prices compared to those on Itaewon Street. Spare parts of all kinds, surplus army stocks, various kinds of equipment and all sorts of ironware are on sale here, too. The atmosphere is that of a flea market – and you can indeed get a few fleas into the bargain if you buy the second-hand clothes! Nevertheless, the throng of stalls, booths, carts, troughs and laden market women is really amazing. Groaning, sweating, ringing bells, calling and spitting, sellers and buyers pass through narrow alleys or along the extensive halls of the cemented market buildings.

Tongnimmun, Independence Gate, was built in 1896 in the style of the Arc de Triomphe. Originally constructed on the spot where the West Gate used to stand, it had to be moved a few years ago because a new road was built. It now leads a shadowy existence – perhaps reminiscent of the reform movements it was originally built to honour?

Sajik Park is situated northeast of Tongnimmun. It is historic ground, for every year the kings had to make offerings here in spring and in autumn – as at the Temple of Heaven in Beijing in the old days. These seedtime and harvest offerings were always accompanied by elaborate ceremonies, and were intended to persuade the gods to provide a rich harvest. Within an agricultural society like Korea's, and especially in the capital of the country, these offerings were an important element of state religion. The offerings were laid here on large square blocks of stone. The square symbolized the earth. After 1910 these ceremonies were no longer held in Korea; today the park is a public recreation area with a swimming pool and an archery stand.

North of the 2nd and 3rd sections of Chong-ro is the little **Pagoda Park,** on the spot where the Korean Declaration of Independence was made on the 1st March 1919 – at a time when Korea was still under Japanese colonial rule. There are memorial tablets and statues in this park to commemorate the brave Koreans who dared to rebel against Japanese rule and were killed for it.

Originally the 13-storey Wongaksa Pagoda of marble and granite was supposed to be set up here. It had been part of Wongak Temple, which had been built in 1464 and destroyed in 1512 by Neo-Confucians during the anti-Buddhist campaigns. There is obviously a clear connection between the aims of the two campaigns. The park itself was laid out in 1900 by Sir John MacLeavy-Brown, an Englishman who was a member of the customs service in Seoul at that period.

From the Pagoda Park it is a good idea to walk along the famous antique dealers' street, **Insadong,** in a northwesterly direction to get to Chogye Temple. Insadong Street has a great variety of shops, some of them with very old Korean art objects: various masks, celadon, antique furniture such as chests and tables, wooden candlesticks and mother-of-pearl inlaid work in all forms. But the real "specialities" of the Insadong are Korean paintbrushes, painting equipment, cloth for mounting pictures, seals and inkstones. There is a unique atmosphere in Insadong Street. The sales assistants are very friendly, patient, forthcoming, and always helpful.

At the northern end of Insadong Street we turn westwards, cross Anguk Street, and, after walking along a small, inconspicuous street, we reach the temple precinct of Chogye-sa.

Chogye Temple, which was not built till 1910, is the only Buddhist temple in the city centre. As well as offering a welcome oasis of peace and rest after a tiring shopping session in Insadong Street (!), Chogye puts the visitor in the right frame of mind for similar temples in the provinces. It is built in traditional style and has all the characteristic elements of Buddhist architecture.

In the eastern part of the city, opposite Sejong University, is the **Grand Children's Park** or **Nung-dong** (not shown on the city plan). There is a children's zoo here where youngsters can play with animals. There is also a small botanical garden for older children, a kind of educational garden. There is a little theatre for theatrical performances,

and a shell-shaped arena for concerts. The park is also rather like a funfair with its roundabouts, big dippers and abundance of sweet stalls. Especially at weekends you'll find this place absolutely teems with children – they often come here from other parts of Seoul.

Moving back towards the centre of the city, **Namsan** or **South Mountain** dominates the Chungku district. It's here that we find the exclusive residential areas where wealthy Seoulites and foreigners live. A relatively large number of foreign embassies and other official missions have premises here.

Visitors can take a cable car up the wooded slopes of the mountain to a platform, from which they can walk to the summit. It's also possible to climb Namsan from the very foot of the mountain, however.

Seoul's **Radio and T. V. Tower,** the city's best-known landmark, stands on the summit. Please note that before you take the lift to the viewing platform of the tower you must hand in your cameras, etc. No photographs may be taken from any high building in Seoul. This really is a pity as there is a superb panorama from the top of the tower – of the ever-growing city spreading out into the surrounding countryside, of skyscrapers and tiny traditional houses, of the confused jumble of streets and roads, and of people moving along like ants in the streets below. In good weather you can see as far as the east coast – even part of the port city of Inch'ŏn is visible. As at other television towers, the public platform at Seoul features restaurant facilities, souvenir shops, ice cream, candyfloss... and picture postcards of the view from the tower.

The National Academy of Music, the National Theater and Dongguk University, all seats of classical Korean culture, are situated on the lower eastern slopes of Namsan and within the bounds of Changchung Park.

In order to disentangle the inner city traffic, seven tunnels have been built through Seoul's hills, including three under Namsan alone.

From Namsan we now turn south-west to the **Han River,** cross it by one of the big bridges and reach the artificial island of **Yoi** (Yoido in Korean, "do" meaning island). In the middle of this island is the parade ground, Youido Plaza, which was laid out as a memorial of the military coup of 1961. Large military parades and exercises are still held here.

Incidentally, some information about military exercises in general: on the 15th of each month there is an air-raid alarm exercise in Seoul lasting 40 minutes. You hear the noise of machine guns, planes, and the tumult of battle through loud-speakers on the streets. The streets of the city are evacuated, cars pull up momentarily, but the passengers stay seated. Foreign visitors who are not familiar with such exercises are sure to get a fright and stand still, not knowing what to do. They will be symbolically "saved" by friendly Koreans who will ask them to leave the street and go inside a building. And there is another thing you will no doubt notice: at 11.05 daily there is a sonic bang. This is a reconnaissance plane flying north to the Yalu River. Exactly twenty minutes later – you can almost set your watch by it – there is another bang: the jet has returned from its reconnaissance flight.

But let us return to the island of Yoi. The National Assembly Building stands at the western tip of the island, the KBS building (Korean Broadcasting System) in the south-west. The extensive parade ground was formerly the runway of the city's first airport.

Leaving the island now and returning to the centre of the old town, near the City Hall Square is the **Myŏngdong district** with Seoul's four biggest department stores: Midopa, Shinsegye, Cosmos and Lotte. Foreign visitors can shop here to their heart's content, for prices are fixed. Most counters in the large stores are leased to individual traders, so you almost always deal with separate shopowners.

There is a great variety of small shops in Myŏngdong, where textiles and shoes can be bought at bargain prices. As everywhere in East Asia, you can have clothes of all kinds made for you. Shoes are also made to measure in a very short time.

Myŏngdong has an abundance of "suljips" too (inns where soju is traditionally sold); and there are beer halls, snack bars, and tiny restaurants selling one speciality (noodle dishes, for example, or raw fish, seaweed delicacies, "kimchi" specialities or stuffed meat pastries). Beer halls are sometimes several storeys high and very inviting to the thirsty tourist!

In the midst of this busy district you can visit the oldest Catholic church in Seoul. St. Mary's Cathedral was built of red brick in 1890. During the Korean War (1950–53) it was the only building in the area that was left standing and relatively undamaged. Also in Chung-gu district, but on the other side of City Hall, stands the Anglican church. Built in 1926, the church also serves as the seat of the Korean Anglican bishop. The first bishop of this congregation, Mark Trollope, was buried in the church. His is the only grave within the walls of Seoul, for it was, and still is, forbidden to bury anyone inside the city. The cemeteries of the city are outside its centre. Most of them are situated on hills in the southern part of the town, as in China.

From the Myŏngdong district we now turn southwest towards Seoul Station, which was built by the Japanese at the beginning of our century in European, or to be more exact Victorian, style. It has a domed roof which is (still) visible from a long way off and is therefore useful as a landmark.

(Thiele)

Kangwŏn-do

The people from this province are compared to a Buddha who "sits motionless at the foot of a cliff" and meditates. They are said to be rather inflexible, stubborn and somewhat rigid. Moreover, they are known as "potato eaters" which in Korea amounts to "paupers". The staple food of the Korean just isn't the potato – that is considered a cheap vegetable – but rice.

The capital of this province in the northeast of the republic is **Ch'unch'ŏn.** Also known as the "town of the lakes" because of the many artificial lakes in the vicinity, Ch'unch'ŏn was almost completely destroyed in the Korean War and had to be built anew afterwards. Tourism has developed here only in the last few years. The town and the area around it have become famous for their mulberry trees, the leaves of which are used to feed silkworms and thus form the basis of

184

Ch'unch'ŏn's sericulture industry. The silk produced here is exported all over the world.

The **Sorak Mountains** and the **Sorak-San National Park** constitute the main point of interest in the province. They can be reached from Seoul via the main road linking Seoul – Yangp'yŏng – Hŏngch'ŏn – Inje – Sokch'o, or by taking the new motorway, the Seoul to Kangnŭng Expressway, and then driving north up the east coast road to Sokch'o. The other possibility is to travel by plane.

Sokch'o is the point of departure for excursions into the National Park which is 20 km (just over 12 miles) away. Oddly-shaped rocks and cliffs, waterfalls and deep gorges are characteristic of this nature reserve; the park covers some 344 sq. km (133 sq. miles). The area is divided into Outer and Inner Sorak. The peak after which the park is named, Sorak-san (1,708 m/5,604 ft) is the third-highest mountain in the country after Halla-san on Cheju Island and Chiri-san in Chŏllanam-do. Sorak-san is part of the Diamond Mountains which now lie mainly in North Korea. Inner Sorak has remained more or less untouched by tourism as it is very rugged and almost inaccessible. There are good climbs here, but only for very experienced mountaineers.

The main temple in Outer Sorak is **Shinhungsa,** about ten minutes from the tourist hotels that have sprung up in the last few years in the little mountain village of Sorak-dong. (**Hyang-song Temple** nearby is one of the earliest Buddhist foundations in this region. It was established by the monk Chajang between 632 and 652 A. D. Chajang came from the Kingdom of Shilla to the south seeking solitude for meditation.)

Not all the original temple buildings at Shinhungsa have survived. The paintings inside the halls are mingled with Taoist motifs and themes from folk religion. About 3 km (just under 2 miles) upstream from the temple grounds there is a hermitage, **Kyejoam,** cut out of granite, with religious sculptures from Buddhist mythology inside.

The best time of year to visit the Sorak Mountains is in autumn when the leaves are changing colour and the temples lie in a magnificent sea of colour.

Above Shinhung Temple you can see the **Hundulbawi,** a huge boulder which has become a tourist attraction because it can be moved by a single person (but it is impossible to dislodge it!).

Near the big car park there is a cable railway which takes you up to **Kwongumsong** (1,100 m/3,600 ft) with its ancient fortress. From here you can walk on to a mountain hut set in an idyllic position. At the hut, classical music comes roaring out of loudspeakers to greet you. The walls of the hut are decorated with beautiful photographs of the area. On an old tree stump hang hundreds of slips of paper with the names of visitors from all over the world.

The **Piryŏng** and **Towangsong Waterfalls** are very special points of scenic beauty; their waters turn the sunlight into rainbows of many colours.

The paths to all these places of interest are very well marked everywhere, and exact distances are given, so that if you stay for a few days you can undertake longer hill walks or climbs.

In **Chŏnbuldong Valley** you can see the sharp, needle-like rocks which have time and again been the subject of photographs. These rocks lend the landscape a bizarre, wild appearance. As a result of years of erosion some of them have taken on shapes similar to those of people or animals, and this has given rise to many tales and legends.

If your route from Seoul takes you by way of Inje, then you should first visit **Paektam Temple** in Outer Sorak. The nearby Taesung Waterfall is one of the three highest in Korea.

Sokch'o is the most northerly large town on the east coast, with a population of 71,000. A first-class tourist resort has developed out of the old fishing village in the last few years. A special attraction for the visitors is the long fish-drying frames where thousands of fish are hung up to dry.

The cleanest beach on the whole east coast, **Hwajinp'o Beach,** lies 35 km (22 miles) north of Sokch'o. Although many other spots along the east coast appear ideal for swimming, sunbathing, etc., you cannot just bathe freely wherever you want to in Korea. Many stretches of coast are barred by fences and guarded by soldiers for fear of North Korean attacks from the sea. Western tourists are often disappointed when they come face to face with such security measures, for the beaches on the east coast are not as crowded as those elsewhere and are very beautiful with the mountains in the background.

Approximately 15 km (9 miles) south of Sokch'o we find Yang'yang and the famous temple, **Naksan-sa,** with the 16 m (52 ft) high modern statue of the "Bodhisattva of Mercy and Compassion". The lovely woods and the splendid view over the sea make a walk to this temple compound worthwhile. It was founded in 671 A.D. by the monk Uisang who came from the Kingdom of Shilla. The main hall, Wŏntŏngpojŏn, is linked to the legend of the monk who, having prayed in vain for seven days to see the Bodhisattva, threw himself into the sea. Only then did Kwansumposal (or Kuanyin), the Bodhisattva of Mercy and Compassion, appear to him, hand him a rosary of crystal beads and show him where to pray. The main hall of the monastery was then built on this spot; a statue of the Maitreya Buddha stands in the main hall, the Wŏntŏngpojŏn (see photo 16).

The gate, the pagoda and the bell of the temple are all national treasures of Korea. If at all possible, try to visit this temple and the statue of the Bodhisattva at sunrise. The play of changing colours when the sun appears over the distant horizon of the East Sea will make a lasting impression on you... truly unforgettable.

The motorway linking Seoul with the east coast, the Seoul-Kangnŭng Expressway, was completed relatively recently. **Kangnŭng** is situated on the east coast between Yang'yang and Tonghae and can be reached in about four hours from Seoul. The drive involves crossing the impressive **T'aebaek Mountains** on the way. It is especially the beaches of Kyŏngp'odae and Chumunjin near Kangnŭng that attract visitors.

From Kangnŭng you should visit the **Odae-san National Park.** While here it is definitely worthwhile visiting **Wŏljŏng Temple,** founded by the Shilla monk Chajang. The main attractions of the temple compound are the octagonal, nine-storey pagoda, and a statue of a kneeling Buddha, a very unusual pose in religious sculpture.

Leaving Wŏljŏng Temple, if you follow the course of a river bed at the foot of Mount Odae, you will come to a **"sarira" field** where the ashes of dead Buddhists are kept in rather phallic stone receptacles.

In another temple in the Odae-san National Park, **Sangwon-sa,** you can see the second-largest bronze bell in Korea. Founded in 646 A.D., again by the monk Chajang, Sangwon Temple is situated north of Wŏljŏng-sa. *(Thiele)*

Ch'ungch'ŏngpuk-do

According to the general characterization of the people of this province by the Koreans themselves, they "shine like the moon and are as clear as the wind". They are also considered to have perfect manners.

The greatest attraction in this area is the **Songni-san National Park** (there are other transcriptions of the name, so you may well encounter Sogni-san or even Sogri-san National Park). From Seoul, Songni-san can best be reached via highway No. 1, the Seoul-Pusan Expressway, to Okch'on (south of Taejŏn), where you turn off and head northwards to the park (the drive takes around 3 hours).

Sogni translates roughly as "flee from everyday life", which means in this case that you should retreat to what used to be the biggest temple in Korea, **Pŏpchu-sa** (see photos 5 and 7). As at all important Buddhist

187

temples and monasteries, there are very good hotels and guesthouses for visitors in the vicinity of Pŏpchu-sa. If you are alone and on foot and arrive as a guest in the temple, it is possible to spend the night in a monk's cell.

Pŏpchu Temple is so big that once 30,000 monks were put up here for a Buddhist gathering. An enormous metal pot in the monastery kitchens proves at least that a few thousand people certainly could be fed here!

The temple was founded in 553 A. D. by one of the famous Korean monks of that period, Uisang, who had come from the Kingdom of Shilla. At that time the massif was not yet known as Songni.

There is an interesting legend connected with Pŏpchu. It is said that when Jinpyŏ, a wandering monk from Kumsan Temple (in Chŏllapuk-do), appeared here in the year 784 all the oxen ploughing the fields knelt down to welcome this illustrious Buddhist. The result was that many farmers left their work, had their heads shaved, and entered Pŏpchu Temple as monks. They turned away from all "earthly delights" and served only Buddha from that time on.

Pŏpchu-sa is set in the middle of magnificent cedar forests. Within the confines of the temple stands Korea's **oldest wooden pagoda.** Famous murals inside the pagoda feature scenes from different phases of Buddha's life. Behind the altar in the main hall, the visitor looks into the thousand faces of little seated Buddha figures arranged as on a rising terrace. A colossal bronze statue of Buddha is to be erected in Pŏpchu Temple. Planned for com-

The Maitreya Buddha at Pŏpchu is to be replaced by an even bigger statue.

pletion in 1988, the statue will be approximately 38 m (125 ft) in height – probably the tallest of its kind anywhere. This bronze statue replaces the **Maitreya Buddha** figure which has, since 1964, stood beside the five-storey pagoda.

Other treasures of the temple include a stone lantern supported by a pair of lions (this has survived the ravages of time since 720 A.D.) and a granite vessel in the shape of a lotus blossom. An iron pot, 1.20 m (4 ft) high and 2.70 m (almost 9 ft) in diameter, stands under a curved roof supported by four wooden pillars. I was told by a monk that food was prepared in this pot for the last time in 1592. That was during the Japanese invasion when Korean soldiers were setting out to fight Hideyoshi.

The **Churae-am Rock** is celebrated, and very unusual. A figure of **Amitabha Buddha** has been chiselled out of it. The six Chinese characters for his name have also been cut into the rock. The **Vairocana Buddha** with his incarnation, as well as the **Samboyakaya-Shakyamuni Buddha** in the **Daeungbo Hall** belong to the largest sculptures in the whole country.

Even the iron flagpole to the right of the Maitreya statue is considered to be a treasure not only of this temple, but of the whole of Korea.

The visitor is impressed by the harmonious structure of the whole compound – the many halls, the smaller statues and the living quarters of the monks. You should climb one of the surrounding hills and succumb to the spell of this unforgettable, religious panorama.

(Thiele)

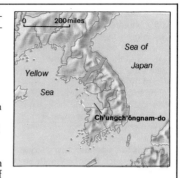

Ch'ungch'ŏngnam-do

The starting point for walks and excursions in this province is Taejŏn.

Taejŏn

Taejŏn is the administrative capital of Ch'ungch'ŏngnam province. Designed by the Japanese in grid squares, it now has a population of 450,000 and is an important communications centre for the south and west of the country. Historically speaking, it is one of the youngest cities in Korea. Taejŏn grew out of the town of Hanbat, which means "extensive field"; it has been called Taejŏn since 1905.

When the Japanese developed this place, they were mainly interested in it as a traffic junction via which they could systematically send rice, their staple food, from the Korean rice fields direct to the coast, and thence to Japan. Even today the town still possesses rice processing plants, as well as branches of the

leather, silk and pottery industries.
At the beginning of the Korean War Taejŏn grew in importance again for a short time, as the South Koreans transferred their government to Taejŏn from the 28th of June to the 14th of July, 1950.

The town itself has no cultural or historical sights, but the vicinity possesses many places of cultural interest – and in particular a number of religious "treasures".

For visitors who are interested in coming here for their health, there is a spa in the suburb of Yusong where rheumatic illnesses are treated.

Again it is a National Park that should be the first destination: in this case the **Kyeryŏng-san National Park,** which you can reach in an hour's bus ride from the capital of the province. In this "Chicken Dragon Mountain" Park (that's the approximate translation of the name) there are temples of various Korean Buddhist sects, shamanist shrines and even holy places of the Korean Christians.

Kap Temple stands on the Chicken Dragon Mountain in the middle of a maple grove. This ancient temple was founded in 420 A.D. by the monk Ado. Ado is said to have been one of the most important Korean missionaries. He studied for many years in North China before systematically spreading the teaching of Buddhism in southwest Korea.

At the temple entrance stands the temple bell from the 16th century with inscriptions in Sanskrit. The main hall of the temple is dedicated to **Shakyamuni Buddha.** Inside a chest almost 9 m (30 ft) high is a painting of Buddha done by 137 Chinese artists in 1649. Once a year, for Buddha's Birthday in May, it is rolled out and hung up.

In the 16th century the monk Yongyu lived in Kap Temple. Yongyu was responsible for gathering firewood, but he also collected gnarled sticks and these were used to beat back the Japanese when they invaded Korea. The Japanese returned with reinforcements, however, and burned down all the wooden buildings in revenge; the present temple dates from the 17th century.

Leaving Kyeryŏng-san Park, we travel on northwards via Kongju to the **Magok Temple.** An old Korean proverb says "Chun magok – Chu kapsa" which basically means "Visit Magok Temple in spring, and Kap Temple in autumn". At these times of year there is a magnificent display of blossom and leaves around both temples. Tourism has had very little effect upon Magok-sa; in fact the west and south west of Korea are altogether unspoilt – and are a very attractive destination, especially for tourists travelling alone who are not tied to a crowded itinerary of "highlights".

Magok-sa was founded by the Shilla monk Chajang in the former Kingdom of Paekche. The story of how Magok-sa got its name is quite interesting: Chajang was in no doubt that many good Buddhist monks would come from this region for he could see that the new faith was growing as well and as quickly as flax. For this reason he called the new monastery he had founded Magok-sa ("Flax Temple"). The pagoda from the Koryŏ Dynasty which is called "Tabotap" is especially interesting. The spire of this religious structure has stylistic elements which are in fact typical of Indian architecture.

From Magok-sa you should return south via Kongju to **Puyŏ**, the ancient capital of the Kingdom of Paekche (18 B. C.–66 A. D.). The surrounding area as well as the town itself are places of ancient history and culture. The inhabitants developed a unique art style here that was relatively little influenced by the Chinese. Certain stylistic features in the fields of pottery, ornamentation, architecture, sculpture and crafts were handed on directly to Japan and had a decisive influence on Japanese culture. Even today this is not a well-known fact, or it can be that it is deliberately suppressed.

If you travel direct from Taejŏn to Puyŏ you will pass the town of **Nonsan.** This is now one of the most important military training areas in Korea. However, not far from Nonsan you will find all the serenity of **Kwanch'ok-sa,** the "Temple of Candlelight" – a fascinating place and one that should not be missed. The tallest stone Buddha in Korea, the majestic **Unjin Mirŭk** – Buddha of the Future – stands here (see photo 10). The plump, cone or gourd-shaped face with its double chin and long ears radiates absolute composure, serenity and peace of

mind. The temple grounds are dotted with pagodas and stone lanterns.

Puyŏ

From Nonsan we travel northwest and come to Puyŏ, ancient capital of the Kingdom of Paekche. The town lies at the foot of Puso-san (Mount Puso) and on the banks of the Kum River. The main point of interest, apart from the ruins of the old castle Puso-sansong in a lovely park on the slopes of Mt. Puso, is the **National Museum.** Puyŏ has the third-largest national museum in Korea, the two largest being in Seoul and Kyŏngju. The Puyŏ Museum is built in the style of ancient Paekche, with majestic yet simple elegance. Some people called it "too Japanese" when they saw it, ignorant of the fact that Paekche had decisively influenced Japanese culture; Shinto shrines in Japan do indeed look very similar.

The architect – obviously an individual, but also someone who knows his history – has, with this beautiful building, created a model example of modern architecture based on traditional forms.

The museum houses a collection of items bearing witness to Paekche culture. Most of the exhibits are objects which have been excavated (arrowheads, bronze clasps, earthenware jug coffins, small bronzes, chamber pots). You are not allowed to take photographs in the museum.

Continuing on from Puyŏ, the route takes us to the west coast and **Taech'ŏn,** one of the oldest seaside resorts in Korea. The long wide sandy beach is the ideal place to relax.

flourishing industrial and commercial centre with oil refineries and many factories. But there are many lovely beaches near P'ohang (Kuryŏngp'o, P'ohang and Chŏngha Beaches). These can also be visited from Kyŏngju and are ideal places for rest and recreation.

On the way from P'ohang to the National Park we pass through the little town of **Yŏngdŏk** which is famous for its selection of seafoods, especially huge crabs, lobsters and crayfish.

Kyŏngsangpuk-do

The people who come from this mountainous province are described by other Koreans as tending to be arrogant, but they are also considered to be independent characters who demand respect. It would probably be very difficult for outsiders, and even more so for foreigners, to be taken into a family here. Marriages usually take place within the community. Kyŏngsang people are also famous for never disregarding or breaking arrangements or contracts. In this they are like the Chinese.

There are three parts of this province that are well worth visiting: the East Coast, Chuwang-san National Park, and the area around Andong. Starting off in P'ohang (on the east coast, northeast of Kyŏngju), we travel northwards along the coast road to the Chuwang-san National Park.

P'ohang was the site of the first iron works in Korea. The town is a

Chuwang-san National Park is a skiing paradise in winter. Many ski resorts have been built at the Taekwallyŏng Pass with lifts and artificial snowmaking machines. Foreigners who visit Korea in winter will find good conditions for winter sports, especially on the Yŏngpyŏng slopes.

The road to **Andong** is a little arduous but worthwhile as here too tourism is not highly developed. There are no sights in Andong itself, but the surroundings more than make up for this.

It takes about ten minutes by bus to get to the **Andong Miruk**, the stone "Buddha of the Future" (Maitreya Buddha in Sanskrit). It is registered as National Treasure No. 115. The artistic design of this stone statue is a masterpiece of Korean sculpture. The serious, majestic face is particularly impressive when seen in evening sunlight.

If you do not mind a rather difficult drive, an excursion to the little village of **Hahoe**, half an hour by bus or car from Andong, can be strongly recommended. Hahoe means "bend in the river". It is a small village on the Naktong River which now functions as a kind of open-air museum, preserving and displaying the traditional rural culture of Korea. Old farmhouses and some "yangban" buildings have been left in their original condition so that you do get a good picture of country life in old Korea – through such genuine examples of peasant culture. The farmers here are also advised to keep their traditional tools for working the land.

Hahoe is, however, famous for another reason: a special kind of masked drama was developed here. There is still a mask maker in the village who can carve the twelve traditional types of wooden mask used in the drama. In the old days they were worn for the **pyŏlsin dances** for which Hahoe was celebrated. Of the ten different styles of masked dance in Korea, the "pyŏlsin" dance dramas are the most ancient.

The masked dances always had, and still have, an element of social criticism. Here the people had the possibility of denunciating abuses perpetrated by the upper classes, the "yangban", as well as certain excesses of the Buddhist clergy. Recently many Koreans have become interested in these masked dances once more, and the tradition of masked drama has experienced a renaissance all over the country.

Taegu
Taegu ("Big Hill"), the third largest city in South Korea with a population of 1.5 million, is capital of Kyŏngsangpuk Province and is situated on the motorway and on the main railway line linking Seoul and Pusan.

The location of the city, surrounded as it is by mountains, calls to mind a rice bowl. This affects the climate: Taegu is said to be both the hottest and the coldest town in the southern part of Korea. It lies on the small rivers Kŭmho and Shinch'ŏn, both of which flow into the River Naktong. Taegu is now the second most important academic centre in

Korea after Seoul. Moreover, it is a centre of trade and a marketing town for the vicinity. Above all, the textile industry and market-gardening are based in the Taegu area. Extensive apple plantations have been laid out in the area over a number of years; one result of this agricultural programme is that 80% of all Korean apples now come from here.

Taegu is one of the oldest towns in Korea. From excavated polished axes and old pottery, especially comb-patterned vessels, it can be deduced that people had already settled here in Neolithic times. Tombs in this area, which look a little like the Kyŏngju tumuli, were found to contain similar objects of the Talgubŏl tribes as well as of the Sorabŭl groups who later founded the Kingdom of Shilla. During the Yi dynasty, Taegu became an important military base. In 1590, shortly before the Hideyoshi invasion, the town was fortified with a city wall and the usual four gates.

A walk round the sights of the town should begin in **Talsŏng Park** where you can see the old castle walls and fortifications as well as Taegu's archaeological sites. This is the original centre of the town. There is now a little zoo in the park. The park is also the site of a martyr's memorial to Ch'oe Che-u, the founder of the religious sect called Chŏndo-Kyo or Tonghak. Beside this memorial, on a granite turtle base, we find the "pisŏk" or funeral stele of the Sŏ clan, one of the ruling families who had taken over the old castle in 1155.

If you walk southeast from Talsŏng Park, you come to the **Kwiam Sŏwon** or Confucian School of Taegu. It is built in traditional style. Like every village and every town in the Yi Dynasty, Taegu had its Confucian School with a shrine where a picture of the great Chinese scholar hung. Bigger schools of this kind are called "sŏdang". The ones which produced a great scholar were called "sŏwon". In a "sŏwon" school there is also a shrine to the founder of the particular school of thought or education. In Taegu this was Sŏ Kojong, in whose honour the shrine in Kwiam Sŏwon was erected. Although the building is relatively young, being built at the turn of the century, it provides the visitor with a good opportunity to see a typical institution of Confucianism, which was so influential throughout the Yi period.

In the old days Taegu, along with P'yŏngyang and Kaesong, was one of the famous "herb towns", for every six months the great hanyak (traditional herbal medicine) markets were held in these three towns. Only Taegu is still famous for this in South Korea today. Namsŏng (South Embankment) Street, also known popularly as "yakchŏn kolmok" (which roughly translates as Medicine Avenue), has many shops of all sizes which stock the greatest selection of herbs in Korea. As well as innumerable herbs and grasses, you can buy dried and pressed centipedes beautifully packed in little boxes, pieces of stag's antlers, dried bear meat and pieces of bear paw, dried fruits, dried and flattened frogs

– all things that can be used in traditional medicine. Do take a look around a shop like this at least once; there is a lovelier smell of grass and herbs than you will experience anywhere else. In the last few years the herbalists have also started to sell electrical machines for cutting up, pulverising and grinding the various animal and plant products.

Kyŏngju

Kyŏngju is situated about 60 km (37 miles) east of Taegu. With a population of approximately 110,000, it is one of the medium-sized towns in Korea. Kyŏngju used, however, to be one of the six greatest towns in the world.

The Golden Age of this former Buddhist metropolis spanned the 7th to the 10th centuries when the local Shilla dynasty succeeded in uniting the Three Kingdoms under its rule. None of the over 100 wooden Buddhist temples which once stood in **Sorabol** (as Kyŏngju was then called) have survived, but a great array of stone sculptures and monuments have, and these are the reason for Kyŏngju's being given the name "Museum without Walls". The adjective "Buddhist" should be added, for the majority of the cultural monuments in this region were moulded by Buddhism. The latter became the state religion in the 6th century and influenced the life of the people then to a very great extent.

As the centre of Shilla culture and capital of "Unified Shilla", Kyŏngju attracted not only wandering monks from China, but also traders from Asia Minor who hoped for good business there. Besides their goods these traders brought knowledge of mathematics, astronomy and technology, from which the Koreans certainly did profit.

When Shillan rule ended in 935, the Korean capital was transferred to Kaesong, and Kyŏngju sank to the level of an average provincial town. It was awakened from its thousand-year-sleep in 1954, when the town and vicinity were proclaimed a national conservation area. Eleven years later tourism began after intensive archaeological research – including excavations and the dating and systematic, scientific cataloguing of all objects that came to light – had been completed. A great deal of what has been achieved in the last few years is not least thanks to the support of UNESCO and its members.

As Kyŏngju and its treasures are scattered over a wide area, you will really need to join an organized tour or hire a car to visit the cultural sites. You must reckon 5–6 hours for a day's tour if you want to visit the sites systematically. Tours leave from the bus station. For the purposes of this guide we shall join one.

Pulguk-sa (Pulguk Temple) is considered the most important Buddhist structure in Korea today. Only the stone foundations of the original buildings have survived. All wooden structures that you see have been reconstructed, old designs and plans having been consulted. Buddha statues, bodhisatva images, bridges, stone lanterns and pagodas are, however, original (i. e., they date from 751 A. D., the year the temple was founded, or the years immediately following).

The most recent renovation was in 1970/7 when an attempt was made to restore the temple according to plans of the original buildings which still exist. Unfortunately, there is only data about a tenth of the buildings in the whole temple precinct.

Six national treasures of Korea are found in this temple. The two ancient granite staircases forming bridges leading to the Amida Buddha hall are National Treasures Nos. 22 and 23 (photograph 2 at the front of the book shows the main entrance stairway to the temple). Since the 1973 restoration tourists are unfortunately not allowed onto these precious bridges. The Sokka Pagoda is National Treasure No. 21, the Tabo Pagoda, No. 20. The latter is considered to be the finest pagoda in Korea. You can find a picture of it on 10-wŏn coins. National Treasures Nos. 26 and 27 are the two bronze statues of Amida Buddha and Vairocana Buddha, both of them 2 m (6.5 ft) high.

Above Pulguk Temple lies **Sŏkkuram Grotto** containing the statue of "Buddha of the Everlasting Light". This grotto is one of the mas-

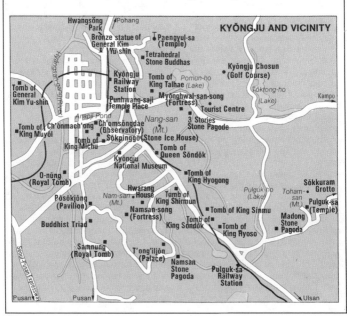

KYŎNGJU AND VICINITY

Hwangsŏng Park
Pohang
Bronze statue of General Kim Yu-shin
Paengyul-sa (Temple)
Tetrahedral Stone Buddhas
Kyŏngju Chosun (Golf Course)
Hwangsŏng-gangnyewy
Kyŏngju Railway Station
Tomb of King Talhae
Pomun-ho (Lake)
Tŏktong-ho (Lake)
Tomb of General Kim Yu-shin
Punhwang-saji Temple Place
Myŏnghwal-san-song (Fortress)
Tourist Centre
Kampo
Anapji Pond
Ch'ŏmsŏngdae (Observatory)
Nang-san (Mt.)
3 Stories Stone Pagode
Tomb of King Muyŏl
Tomb of King Michu
Sŏkpinggo (Stone Ice House)
Tomb of Queen Sŏndŏk
Kyŏngju National Museum
O-nŭng (Royal Tomb)
Tomb of King Hyogong
Sŏkkuram Grotto
Hwarang House
Tomb of King Shirmun
Pulguk-ho (Lake)
Toham-san (Mt.)
Pulguk-sa (Temple)
Pŏsŏkjŏng (Pavilion)
Nam-san (Mt.)
Namsan-song (Fortress)
Tomb of King Sinmu
Madong Stone Pagoda
Buddhist Triad
Tomb of King Sŏndŏk
Tomb of King Ryoso
Samnung (Royal Tomb)
T'ong'iljŏn (Palace)
Namsan Stone Pagoda
Pulguk-sa Railway Station
Seoul Pusan Expressway
Pusan
Pusan
Ulsan

terpieces of Asiatic stone sculpture, and is registered in Korea as National Treasure No. 24. The Buddha figure sits in a majestic pose, facing the east, looking far over the Japan Sea from Mount Toham. When the morning sun rises above the horizon its rays fall on the face of the "Enlightened One". On the inner walls of the grotto bas-relief tablets cut out of granite show the ten disciples of this Buddha in the rotunda. In the middle of the wall behind the Buddha statue is an eleven-headed Kwansum-posal, a goddess of mercy (Guan Yin in Chinese, Kwannon in Japanese). This representation chiselled out of the stone, is considered by many to be the loveliest sculpture in all Korea.

In order to preserve the grotto, visitors are no longer allowed to walk right up to the Buddha statue. After an hour's walk from Pulguk-sa to the Sŏkkuram Grotto, anyone could be forgiven for feeling disappointed to find a glass screen separating the grotto from the narrow pathway set aside for tourists, but the reasons for such a measure are clear. In addition, the cave is supervised at all times, and photography is forbidden.

From Pulguk-sa you should walk to the royal tomb of **Kwaenung.** There are twelve stone slabs set round the tumulus grave; the animals of the East Asian zodiac are represented on these slabs. At the entrance to the tomb stand pairs of military and civilian guards; these figures look rather Persian in appearance. They are said to have been modelled upon servants of King Wŏnsŏng, the 38th ruler of Shilla.

The **Punhwangsa Pagoda,** dating from the middle of the 7th century, is the oldest surviving pagoda of the Kingdom of Shilla. When it was opened during the 1915 restoration a box was found containing needles and sewing things said to have belonged to Queen Sŏndŏk.

In the base section of the pagoda there are four entrances flanked by ferocious-looking guardian figures. Four stone lions lie at the corners of the platform or terrace. Another unusual feature is the building material: at first glance the pagoda appears to be built of bricks, but when you look more closely you realize that it is made of a material that lasts much longer: each brick is a solid, hewn stone! This fact proves the antiquity of the Punhwangsa Pagoda, although only three of supposedly nine storeys have survived to the present day.

The **National Museum of Kyŏngju,** opened in 1975, is the second largest treasure house of Korean culture after the Seoul National Museum. Some of the exhibits have been set up in the extensive grounds around the museum. The heavy, bronze Emille Bell (23 tons), which was cast in 771 A.D., is one of the most beautiful of its type. Its name comes from a legend which tells that a child was thrown into the molten metal when the bell was being cast and screamed for its mother ("emi, emi"). The bell now has a roof over it to protect it.

Inside the museum the exhibits are arranged according to epochs. Swords, pottery, tools and bronzes from the long history of the Kingdom of Shilla are displayed here. The superb gold objects which were excavated from the different tombs in the vicinity date from the pre-Buddhist period.

The pride of the museum is the golden crown from Tomb No. 98 with the "flying horse" motif. The style of the museum building is an imitation of the style of Shillan architecture: a flat, hall-like building resting on pillars, the roof curving slightly outwards.

In 674 A. D., during the rule of the most famous Shilla king, Munmu, **Anap-ji (Anap Pond)** was designed and laid out. The "Lagoon of the Wild Goose" was once part of the fortress Panwŏlsŏng's grounds. Dance performances and other entertainments for the royal family took place here.

When the lake was drained and dredged in 1976, jewellery, hair clasps and a pleasure barge of the king (which had been well preserved in the water because it was sealed off from the air) were discovered in the little pond. These items can now be found in the Kyŏngju museum. The attractive gardens were designed after Chinese models.

The **Panwŏlsŏng** or **Half Moon Fortress** was the site of the palace of the Shilla kings, i. e. the capital grew up around this ancient earthen fortress. The Namchŏn flows past the south side of the grounds, bridged by the remains of the Iljong ("Sun Spirit Bridge") and the Wol-jong ("Moon Spirit Bridge").

One of Kyŏngju's principal attractions is no doubt the presence of over 200 burial mounds in its vicinity. Twenty of these can be visited in the **Tumuli Park**. It is still not known who was buried in most of the tombs. The Tumuli Park was laid out in 1973–75 because a whole group of tombs were situated in close proximity on the site.

Grave No. 155, the "Heavenly Horse Tomb", in the northwest corner of the park is the most famous. The name of the grave comes from a painting on a piece of birch bark which represents a "flying" or galloping horse, a motif that can be found in similar pictures from Central and North Asia. This tomb is itself arranged like a little museum, although most of the 10,000 objects found here are kept in Kyŏngju National Museum.

The bottle-shaped observatory, **Ch'ŏmsŏngdae** ("Moon and Star Tower"), is 9.20 m (30 ft) high and built of large, hewn squared stones. This monument too dates back to the Shilla Period and is now National Treasure No. 31.

It can be assumed that the tower served astronomical purposes. The 12 blocks of the stone foundation, the 30 layers of stones, the 24 stones that jut out, and the 366 stones that were used altogether are significant enough in themselves. This observatory is the most ancient secular building in Korea. It dates from the early 7th century.

The stone water channels are all that remain of the former pleasure pavilion, **Pŏsŏkjŏng.** These channels are built in the form of an abalone which gave rise to the name Pŏsŏkjŏng, which means "Abalone Stone Pavilion". The king and his

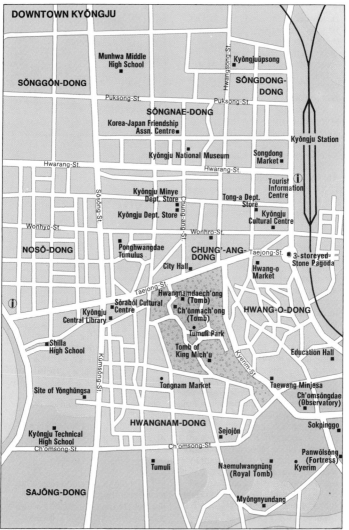

DOWNTOWN KYÖNGJU

SÖNGGÖN-DONG

Munhwa Middle
High School

Kyöngjuŭpsong

SÖNGDONG-
DONG

Hwangsong-St.

Puksong-St.

Puksong-St.

SÖNGNAE-DONG

Korea-Japan Friendship
Assn. Centre

Kyöngju Station

Kyöngju National Museum

Songdong
Market

Hwarang-St.

Hwarang-St.

Tourist
Information
Centre

Kyöngju Minye
Dept. Store

Sosong-St.

Chung-ang-St.

Tong-a Dept.
Store

Kyöngju
Cultural Centre

Kyöngju Dept. Store

Wonhyo-St.

Wonhro-St.

NOSÖ-DONG

Ponghwangdae
Tumulus

CHUNG'-ANG-
DONG

Taejong-St.

3-storeyed-
Stone Pagoda

City Hall

Hwang-o
Market

Taejong-St.

Hwangnamdaech'ong
(Tomb)

HWANG-O-DONG

Söraböl Cultural
Centre

Ch'ŏnmach'ong
(Tomb)

Kyöngju
Central Library

Kümsong-St.

Tumuli Park

Shilla
High School

Tomb of
King Mich'u

Kyerim-St.

Education Hall

Site of Yönghŭngsa

Tongnam Market

Taewang Minjesa

Ch'ŏmsŏngdae
(Observatory)

HWANGNAM-DONG

Sejojŏn

Sokpinggo

Kyöngju Technical
High School

Ch'omsong-St.

Panwŏlsŏng
(Fortress)

Ch'omsong-St.

Tumuli

Naemulwangnŭng
(Royal Tomb)

Kyerim

SAJÖNG-DONG

Myŏngnyundang

courtiers used to enjoy themselves here. In the ancient Chinese manner the king recited the beginning of a poem, setting a cup of wine on the slowly flowing water of the stone channel. Before the floating cup reached the next courtier, the latter had to compose a line to rhyme with it. If he did not manage, he had to empty the cup at one draught. In 926, when a pleasure party like this was under way, rebels from the former Kingdom of Paekche appeared and assassinated King Kyŏnghae. This was the beginning of the fall of Unified Shilla, for seven years after this incident his son, Kyŏngsun, abdicated in favour of the Koryŏ ruler.

About 15 minutes' drive by bus northeast of Kyŏngju city centre lies the newly developed **Pomun Lake Resort.** Since this 300 sq. km (116 sq. mile) recreation area was opened, in 1978, it has grown to become one of the main tourist centres in Korea. The Resort has more than ten luxury hotels, a conference centre, a golf course where international championships can be played, swimming pools, tennis courts, bowling alleys and other sports facilities of the highest quality. A "Swan Boat" sails on the lake; a casino has been opened. Everything a modern tourist could wish for is at his disposal here.

High standards in hotel services are maintained by a Korean school of hotel management which offers training courses for prospective personnel lasting several academic terms. Kyŏngju, the cultural and historical treasure house of Korea, has become a tourist's Eldorado. *(Thiele)*

Kyŏngsangnam-do

As almost everywhere in the Korean provinces, it is above all the Buddhist temples of Kyŏngsangnam-do which attract and fascinate visitors. In Kyŏngsangnam Province we shall first visit **Haein Temple** in the **Kayasan National Park.** Starting out from Taegu, it takes about 1½ hours by bus on the new Olympic Expressway which connects Taegu and Kwangju and is a recent addition to the excellent infrastructure of the country.

Haein-sa was founded in 802 A.D. With its 93 hermitages, cells and subsidiary temples within a radius of 6 km (just under 4 miles) it is one of the biggest and most popular temple compounds in Korea.

The main point of interest, however, lies in two long library buildings where the over 80,000 wooden printing blocks of the **"Tripitaka**

Koreana" are stored. These are Buddhist texts carved in classical Chinese characters on wooden slabs. Monks worked for sixteen years on them on Kanghwa Island in the Yellow Sea, the material on which they worked having been brought from China. It was laid in salt sea water for two years, and then treated to ensure that it would keep for a very long time. The first set of this unique collection was burnt by the Mongols. So the king ordered another set to be made and this was finally finished in 1251.

The first edition was a prayer of supplication to Buddha, for it was hoped through this kind of "offering" to ensure his help against the attacks of the Khitan, predatory tribes from the north who had invaded the country. The second edition had a similar aim: Buddha's assistance was invoked in face of the Mongol invasions. For security reasons the printing blocks were transferred from Kanghwa Island inland to Haein Temple, where they are still kept today in the two library halls. These halls were constructed ingeniously to allow the air to circulate freely, so there is no danger that the wooden blocks will be damaged in the future.

Among the other interesting features of Haein-sa are a stone lantern from the Shilla Period and the pagoda that stands in front of the main temple building (see photo 6).

From the Kayasan National Park we can now travel eastwards on the Expressway No. 9 as far as Taegu and there pick up Expressway 1

down to Pusan. A few minutes after the Onyang-Ulsan Expressway branches off, we turn off to the right in order to visit **Tongdo Temple.** There is a very good road leading to the temple compound.

On leaving the car park you walk through the little village and enter the compound through the big gateway built in the traditional style with wide, curved roofs. Then it is a 15 minutes' walk along a lovely avenue of pines bordered by a little stream until you arrive at the main temple building. On your right you pass the burial grounds that are typical of all Buddhist temples, with large steles resting on stone turtles. The main slab is decorated with Chinese characters which give the dates of birth and death of the dead person, his services to the monks' community and his services as a Buddhist teacher.

Tongdo-sa is Korea's biggest temple precinct. It was founded in 647 A. D. by the Shilla priest Chajang who has already been mentioned several times – in connection with Magok Temple and Hyangsong Temple, for example. The main temple alone has 35 different buildings. If you have time, it is worth taking a few walks in the vicinity of the temple where there are another 13 little hermitages and monks' cells belonging to Tongdo-sa which you can visit.

The temple's name means "Save the World Through Truth". When Chajang returned home after years of study in China, he became a "taeguksa", an "important state priest". It was in this function that he founded Tongdo Temple. It is a Zen Buddhist temple. In the main hall there are no statues because the object of worship is a **"sari", a stone shrine** containing holy relics which Chajang brought back from China. This "sari" has finely chiselled bas-relief slabs and is the most sacred object in Tongdo-sa. There is another complete copy of the "tripitaka koreana" from Haein-sa here in Tongdo Temple. People learned a lesson from the Mongol invasions, and these precious Buddhist scriptures are now kept in different places.

Tongdo-sa is still very important as a Zen monastery. In a little temple nearby lives the most famous Zen monk, Kyŏngbong. It is possible to visit him in Kuknak where he lives.

Another little tip: if you would like to get a good view of the whole complex, climb the hill left of Tongdo-sa.

An excursion to the islands southwest of Pusan can be highly recommended. The archipelago is known as the **Hallyŏsudo National Park.** From the port of Pusan boats sail several times a day through these straits along the coast as far as Yŏsu on the Yŏchon Peninsula. The "Angel Ho", a hydrofoil service for tourists, departs daily at 7.30 a.m., 9 a.m. and 11.30 a.m., calling at Songpo, Ch'ungmu, Samch'ŏnpo and Namhae. You do not necessarily have to travel with this modern jet ship, however; there are other boats which serve the islands but these take longer.

This fascinating seascape with its 115 inhabited and 253 uninhabited islands was declared a nature conservation area on 31st December 1968. But it is not possible to keep a check on every corner of this "Sea Conservation Park". It is only in the particularly beautiful and valuable parts of the nature reserve that people treat nature carefully and with caution; these places are well marked in the local tourist maps. The six water protection areas in this archipelago are Haegumgang, Kojedo, Hansando, Samch'ŏnpo, Odongdo and Namhaedo.

Koje-do, the second largest of Korea's countless islands, has many sites of historical interest, in particular monuments to Admiral Yi Sun-shin who, in his unique turtle ships, fought the Japanese in the waters around the islands off the south coast. On the southeast tip of Koje, on steep cliffs rising from the sea like hedgehogs' spines, stands **Haegumgang.** The long headland with its pine groves and camellia bushes is also a breeding place for many kinds of seabirds. Northeast of Haegumgang there are lovely sandy beaches on the Kujora peninsula which really tempt you just to rest and relax.

The smaller island of **Hansan** lies right next to Koje. Hansan-do became famous after Yi Sun-shin's sea battles, when he employed his ironclad turtle ships against the Japanese fleet in 1592/3. A lighthouse in the shape of one of these ships was erected on Hansan-do in memory of these battles. The island can be reached by ferry boat from

Ch'ungmu. Near the pier on Han-san-do there is a little museum containing objects belonging to famous Korean seamen.

Around **Samch'ŏnpo** ("po" = fishing village) on the mainland there is a bird reserve where you can see many fascinating species, white herons especially. The latter return to Korea from more southerly climes in summer, particularly to **Hak ("Heron") Island.** They stay here for 1–2 months, and then, in October, fly back to their winter home. In the little village of **Noryang** across the bay from Samch'ŏnpo Admiral Yi was fatally wounded by a sniper's bullet.

On **Odong Island** a specially pliable bamboo thrives that Admiral Yi used for his archers' arrows. An old archery stand from that period is evidence of the marine archers' training. In the town of **Yŏsu** (on the peninsula south of Sunch'ŏn), the sail through the Hallyŏ Straits ends.

From the island of **Namhae,** however, you can reach the mainland again by crossing a 650 m long suspension bridge, the Namhae Great Bridge; then take Highway 19 to the Pusan-Sunch'ŏn Expressway, head southwestwards and this will bring you to Chŏlla Province.

Pusan

The second largest city in Korea, with a population of almost 3 million, Pusan lies on the south coast with its many bays, in a valley surrounded by mountains. The transla-

tion of the name Pusan is "Cauldron Mountain" – the main mountain in the vicinity does indeed look like an upside-down cauldron.

As a gateway to Japan and the rest of the world, Pusan is the most important port in Korea. In the long period of isolation during the Yi dynasty, Pusan was the only town with any kind of overseas connections, the most important being those with Japan.

Many ferries leave Pusan for other parts of the South Korean archipelago, e. g. for Cheju, Ch'ungmu, Mokp'o, Yŏsu and Chindo. There are also regular sailings for Shimonoseki and Fukuoka in Japan. Pusan is a port for freighters, tankers and warships alike. Because of the mild climate there are many bathing beaches nearby, of which Haeundae (north of Pusan) and Songdo (south of the city) are the most popular.

It is very interesting to stroll around the city centre and the district near the docks. The **Fish Market** (Chagalch'i) is a great attraction. There is probably no other market of this kind that sells such a variety of fish, seaweed, shellfish and processed sea products. Go into the big market halls where everything is arranged in different departments. On the first floor there are little snack bars where you can eat the most delicious lobster and crab. Visit the section with dried fish where thousands of fish faces hang and stare at you. The seaweed department is also overwhelming for tourists. The

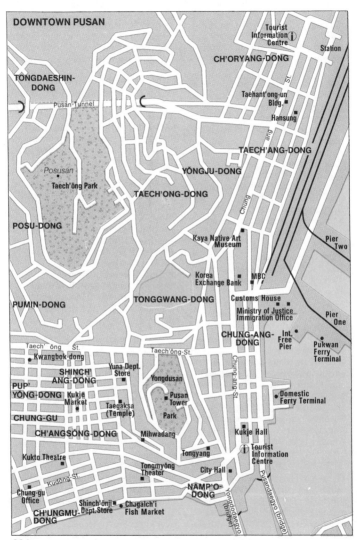

DOWNTOWN PUSAN

Tourist Information Centre

Station

CH'ORYANG-DONG

TŎNGDAESHIN-DONG

Pusan-Tunnel

Taehant'ong-un Bldg.

Hansung

TAECH'ANG-DONG

Posusan

YŎNGJU-DONG

Taech'ŏng Park

TAECH'ONG-DONG

Chung St.

POSU-DONG

Kaya Native Art Museum

Pier Two

Korea Exchange Bank

MBC

PUMIN-DONG

TONGGWANG-DONG

Customs House

Ministry of Justice Immigration Office

Pier One

CHUNG-ANG-DONG

Int. Free Pier

Taech'ŏng St.

Kwangbok-dong

Taech'ŏng-St.

Chung-ang-St.

Pukwan Ferry Terminal

Yuna Dept. Store

SHINCH'ANG-DONG

Yongdusan

PUP'YŎNG-DONG

Kukje Market

Pusan Tower

Domestic Ferry Terminal

CHUNG-GU

Taegaksa (Temple)

Park

CH'ANGSŎNG-DONG

Mihwadang

Kukje Hall

Tourist Information Centre

Kukto Theatre

Tongyang

City Hall

Kudŏng-St.

Tongmyŏng Theater

Pusandaegyo (bridge)

Chung-gu Office

NAMP'O-DONG

Jongdodaegyo (bridge)

Shinch'ŏnji Dept.Store

Chagalch'i Fish Market

CH'UNGMU-DONG

204

smells of the sea and its inhabitants surge over you in all variations. Sample the delicious raw fish with soya sauce, garlic and green horseradish. Fish fans get stuck here as if on a hook, going from stall to stall and tasting all the marine delicacies. A Korean murmured to me in real "Konglish": "Me go to pis malket evely day bo buy flesh pis." Koreans, who often like to laugh at themselves, call their Korean English "Konglish".

At the jetty you can see the catch being heaved on land in big baskets and other containers. As in the market, the heavy work is in the hands of hard-working, hefty fishwives who always like a joke.

From the fish market you can walk towards the town centre along the **Ch'angsŏngdong,** a topsy turvy shopping street where you'll find at least one good example of the typical music cafés. The "Classic Music Coffeeroom" (on the first floor) has about thirty tables standing on a fine tiled floor, and invites you to listen to classical European music. There is always a very nice atmosphere in these cafés. Above the cash-desk hang pictures of Karajan in three different conductor's poses. Against the back wall there is a record bar with 2,000 records of classical music and a disc jockey too! If a guest wishes a certain recording he writes the title on a little piece of paper, and the record is played. When the weather turns cold the usual kerosene stoves heat the room, and in summer the tiles provide the necessary coolness. These cafés have another speciality:

near the door there are two telephone booths where people can phone their boyfriend or girlfriend and invite her or him to a "classical" meeting. It's worth noting that the good tearooms or coffee shops in Korean towns are mostly either in the basement or on the first floor of buildings. This is why foreigners often miss them at first.

After a cup of "Brazil" and the Prisoners' Chorus from Verdi you can stroll on up the **Yongdusan** ("Dragon Head Hill") through the town. From the top of the hill there is a magnificent view over the far-spreading city which climbs up the slopes in a mosaic pattern. At the top of this hill there is a TV Tower with a viewing platform where the whole panorama of Pusan with all the docks is even more impressive and overwhelming. Near the entrance to the TV tower lift there is a very good little aquarium where you can see fish from the Sea of Japan and from the Yellow Sea. In front of it stands a bronze statue of Admiral Yi Sun-shin.

On the way to **Pusan's airport at Suyŏng** you pass the **United Nations Cemetery** where soldiers from 16 different countries who gave their lives in the Korean War 1950–53 have their last resting place. Only the American dead were sent home to be buried in the USA. In a square in the middle of the cemetery, where the flags of the allied nations fly, regular memorial services are held. There is also a small interdenominational chapel for worship.

0   200 miles

Sea of

Japan

Yellow

Sea

Chŏllapuk-do

clearly linked to relations between Korea and Japan over the centuries. Paekche provided the roots from which many aspects of Japanese culture grew (this area is therefore very interesting for the Japanese visitor, probably less so for the European or North American). In search of their own identity, the Japanese inevitably look around this province for the origins of a number of facets of their own culture. But as there is still an attitude of distrust and scepticism towards all things Japanese in modern Korea, this province is treated with reserve by the Koreans themselves.

Chŏllapuk-do

People from Chŏlla are compared to a "slim willow stirring in the spring breeze" by other Koreans. They are farmers who seldom leave their native soil and so are not very interested in what is going on in the world outside.

At the moment the province is not developed for tourism. Broad, fertile plains alternate with low hills. Chŏlla-puk (Northern Chŏlla) is the rice bowl and granary of Korea. There are few touristic sights here, but it is the ideal place for a relaxing holiday – either along the coast with its many bays, or in the smallish, and therefore not so busy, national parks.

This region belonged, historically speaking, to the ancient Kingdom of Paekche, a period of Korean history later neglected to a large degree by historians, political scientists, cultural experts, etc. The reasons for this are

Chŏnju (the administrative capital of this province) is the starting point for excursions and walks; it can be reached by rail (built by the Japanese) as well as via the Taejon-Sunch'ŏn Expressway. This town is famous for paper-making and paper processing. Many Korean fans, writing paper, paper for scroll pictures and oiled paper umbrellas are manufactured here. The Koreans learned paper-making from the Chinese, but they refined the process to such a degree, and Korean paper from this area was eventually so highly thought of by the Chinese and the Japanese, that both in fact bought their paper from Chŏnju.

Particularly in demand as paper for scroll pictures, the paper is perfectly suited to calligraphy. Its surface is so finely textured that excellent characters can be drawn on it with a brush. Many people from Chŏnju and the vicinity still make paper by hand in the traditional way, and dye it too.

The paper factories are often in country houses, and they are easily recognized since big sheets are hung out to dry – like washing! The craftsmen get their raw material from mulberry trees and bamboo. Both basic materials have to be brought here from other parts of the country.

Oh Dong-ho is the name of an old established papermaking family. You will find the Oh Dong-ho factory in the Main Street of Chŏnju, and you may visit it whenever you want. It is amazing how many types of paper are produced here. I got to know about 30 different kinds: everything from coarse wrapping paper made of mulberry bark to seaweed paper and "thousand year paper", which – as its name suggests – is supposed to last particularly long and which is made of "tang" tree bark. Paper, then, for all purposes and functions.

Chŏnju is also famous in Korea for its "bibim-bap" specialities (see "Food and Drink"). In addition, it is here that the biggest number of accompanying dishes are served at meals, no doubt a result of the fertile soil here and the great selection of vegetables in this rural area.

In Mr. Chŏn Jin-han's little private museum you can admire an extensive collection of ancient art objects gathered together here by a private collector. There are especially many objects pertaining to peasant culture on display.

About 30 minutes' bus ride south of Chŏnju lies the **Kumsan-sa,** the "Golden Mountain Temple", on the northern edge of the **Moak-san Provincial Park.**

The Kumsan-sa was named after a temple in a valley of the Upper Yangtze River. It is the most important religious site in Chŏllapuk Province. In 776 A. D. the temple was founded by the priest Chinpyo Yulsa, a Buddhist trained in China, who then dedicated it to the "Buddha of the Future". The Buddha Miruk (Maitreya), flanked by two smaller bodhisattvas, is therefore the main object of worship. The unique design of this statue, its size (11.8 m/ over 38 ft high) and position were reasons for its being registered as National Treasure No. 62. The style of some of the temple buildings here was taken as a model for the National Museum in Seoul. Nowadays about 50 monks and 2 nuns live in the temple precinct.

From Chŏnju we travel south to the twin province of Chŏllanam, (Southern Chŏlla). Chŏllanam-do forms the southwesternmost province of Korea.

Chŏllanam-do

The starting point for excursions in this province is the provincial capital, Kwangju (500,000 inhabitants). From Seoul it can be reached in four hours via the Taejŏn-Sunch'ŏn Expressway; the railway journey takes the same time.

Kwangju was founded in 947 by the very first king of the Koryŏ dynasty. The area is very fertile, being famous for good harvests of rice and cotton, and this was no doubt the reason for Kwangju's foundation. There are also many plantations of mulberry trees here; these are used for sericulture. Cultural points of interest are the Museum of History and the Museum of Korean Art.

The infrastructure of Chŏllanam-do is not as well developed as in other Korean provinces; so it is often difficult to get to places of interest.

The **Chiri-san National Park** lies in the eastern part of the province. Mount Chiri (Chiri-san) is the highest mountain on the South Korean mainland (1,915 m/6,280 ft). The National Park around it is one of the loveliest in Korea, probably because large areas of the terrain have remained unspoiled. It is well worth a visit, especially in autumn when a sea of coloured leaves makes the landscape even more beautiful. The Buddhist temples within the bounds of the park look very picturesque then too. **Hwaom Temple** is the most famous of these temples. Founded in 544 A.D., it is one of the oldest in Korea. The best way to get there is via the Pusan-Sunch'ŏn Expressway; leave the Expressway at Sunch'ŏn, and drive to the temple precinct on highway 17 via the little town of Kurye.

The temple is the headquarters of the Flowery Splendour Sect which was introduced to Korea from China by the monk Uisang. The temple precinct lies in a valley shaped like a boat. Two five-storeyed pagodas symbolize the two masts of the ship. Both are full of symbolism. On the one hand the spreading of Buddhism is compared to boats carrying the faith over the oceans, while, on the other hand, the teachings of this sect came over the Yellow Sea from China.

Three national treasures are kept in the temple: the three-storeyed lion pagoda, which is registered as National Treasure No. 35; the biggest stone lantern made of granite (6.3 m/21 ft), National Treasure

No. 12; and the huge Hall of Judgement built in 1606 (National Treasure No. 67).

From Kwangju we drive in a southeasterly direction via Hwasun to the Chogye-san Provincial Park (centred around Chogye Mountain) where the famous **Songgwang-sa** is situated. This is one of the three most important Buddhist temples in Korea – the other two being Haein-sa (see p. 200) and Tongdo-sa (see p. 201). Songgwang Temple has been a centre of Zen Buddhism since the 12th century and is under the direction of the Chogye Sect, which was developed and fostered by Priest Pojo. This monk appears in a portrait with sixteen other leading priests in a shrine at Songgwang. This portrait has been declared National Treasure No. 56.

From Songgwang-sa we return to Kwang-ju. From here our journey takes us southwest to the port of Mokp'o, our last stop in Chŏllanam Province. **Mokp'o** is especially fascinating because of its fishing port and the fish market, where a great deal of dried fish is sold. This port is the point of departure for sails to the southern archipelago and to Cheju Island (7 hours away).

Cheju-do

Cheju-do is different – this is what people all over Korea say about the island, and it is true. Even the soil of Cheju-do is different; the island has a base of volcanic rock. Lava is used everywhere for building: the black walls of the farmyards, the walls between the fields and the walls of the old fishermen's houses are just a few examples that the tourist will see.

The Koreans describe the island people of their nation, especially the women, as wiry, tenacious, as hard as stone and as strong as the wind. Another saying is that there are plenty of women, wind and rocks on Cheju.

From Seoul you can fly to Cheju Island in an hour. There are also ferries from Mokp'o and Pusan; the crossing takes around 11 hours.

Korea's biggest island covers an area of 1,850 sq. km (715 sq. miles) extending 76 km (47 miles) northeast to southwest, with a breadth of roughly 44 km (27 miles).

The Emerald Isle, or "Island of the Gods" as it is also called, lies in a subtropical region and therefore has a warm, pleasant climate and the corresponding flora and fauna. The highest point on the island is **Mount Halla** (1,950 m/6,400 ft), an extinct volcano which is visible from all corners of the island.

Waterfalls, lava tubes, beautiful sandy beaches and picturesque fishing villages, along with orange groves and fields of rape, are just some of the lovely things this idyllic island has to offer.

The people here live very simply, in a natural, easy-going fashion. They do have to work very hard, but they do this in a leisurely way. The women on Cheju have to work much harder than the men, some-

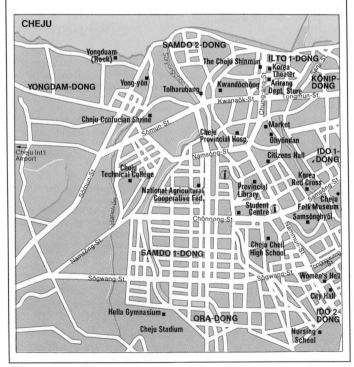

thing which becomes clear when you think of the tiring job the women divers have, for example. They still dive into the sea to gather shellfish, snails, seaweed, cuttlefish and sea urchins. When his wife is diving, the man works in and around the house. Some of the roofs on Cheju are thatched and they have to be firmly secured against the wind. In the old days thick straw ropes were drawn over the roof and weighed down with stones, but now the fishermen use black strips of rubber from old car tyres to lash down the roofing.

You can drive right round the island on a very well built road. From the town of Cheju there are also two parallel roads that cross the island from north to south. There are, in addition smaller roads that are not in such good condition, but which are ideal as hiking paths.

The island was originally thickly wooded. Now it is treeless, partly grazing land. Only in higher altitudes does one experience a varied, subtropical flora. The reason for the deforestation is to be found in the attacks by the Mongols and in the Japanese invasions, when wood was needed for defences, stockades and ships. The ponies and horses which you now see on the island were introduced by the Mongols. They are now bred commercially and exported to other parts of Korea.

The best introduction to the island, its people and its geological structure can be found in the excel-

lent **Cheju Folk Museum** near the KAL Hotel. A visit to this new building will give the visitor a great insight into Cheju life and a very good impression of the island. The museum is didactically well presented, a real mine of information about the island. It is divided into different departments: the person interested in vulcanism, its origins and the specific features on Cheju will find all he wants to know, as will the tourist who is more interested in the flora of the island and its marine fauna.

The visitor also learns about the way of life of the islanders, their shared characteristics, the social structures within the bounds of which they live, the way their houses are built, and about their tools, agricultural products and religious customs. If you really want to get to know the island thoroughly, you must have a good look round this excellent museum.

From the town of Cheju we travel west first of all to the **Yongdu-am (Dragon Head Rock).** This formation of petrified lava is the first place visited by honeymooners on their tour of the island. The Koreans consider Cheju as the ideal "honeymoon island". It looks very picturesque when the brides in red walk over the black lava to be photographed. According to a legend, the dragon descended from the Halla volcano and was turned to stone on this spot.

Outside Cheju's old town is **Shin Cheju,** a new district mainly designed as a tourist centre and holiday area, with big hotels providing all modern leisure amenities. Visitors to the island generally live here, and tours have their point of departure here too.

Economically-minded Koreans hire a taxi for four people and do a tour of the island on their own. You should plan at least two days if you want to see all the sights. From Shin-Cheju we drive further west along the coastal road, past the airport, through Aewol and on to Hallim where we visit the **Hyŏpchae Cave.**

Nearby is **Isidol Farm** (also known as Isidol Ranch or Pasture), founded by an Irish missionary called Isidor and now the main supplier of sheep's wool in Cheju. You can buy hand-knitted pullovers and other garments made of wool there.

Everywhere on the island you will come across **Tol Harubang statues.** These are usually carved out of lava stone. Tol Harubang is called "grandfather", but is actually a sophisticated phallic symbol connected with ancient fertility rites on the island.

In the south of the island, where we travel through mandarin orchards and orange groves, we spend a while at **Chungmun Beach** and visit the nearby **Chŏnjeyŏn Waterfall,** a popular motif for photographers from all over the world but especially for Korean travel groups. West of Chungmun lies the **Sanbang-gul Cave Temple** with a seated

Buddha statue from the Koryŏ Period. From up there you have a heavenly view out to sea. South of the temple, on **Hwasun Beach,** there is a monument in memory of the Dutch sailing ship "Sperber" which was shipwrecked here on the 30th July 1653. The Dutch sailors, together with another Dutchman who had already lived there for 24 years (having landed from an earlier ship), were the first Europeans in Korea. 36 survivors spent 13 years on the island before they could sail on to Japan. The older Dutchman, Hamel, wrote down his experiences on Cheju, and this was the first book on Korea written by a European; it was published in 1668.

Cheju town's counterpart in the south is the town of **Sŏgwip'o** east of Chungmun Resort. There are a number of excellent restaurants here specializing in fishfoods. There are two waterfalls very near the coast that are well worth a visit: the

Chŏngbang Waterfall east of the harbour, and the **Chŏnjiyŏn Waterfall** to the west, not to be confused with the previously mentioned Chŏnjeyŏn waterfall near Chungmun – the similarity of their names means they are often confused!

From Sŏgwip'o, where we spend the night, it is a good idea to cross the island back to the town of Cheju, passing Mount Halla on the way. On our journey we pass **Cheju University** which is in a lovely setting and has many departments including a German one.

Then there is the **Rock Park** on the lower slopes of Halla-san with its collection of bizarre rock formations which could not have been better carved by a sculptor. There are formations in the shape of people, animals and plants to amuse the visitor.

When you return to Cheju, a visit to one of the excellent fish restaurants can be recommended. There, in the privacy of single-tabled rooms, you can eat the most delicious fish dishes, raw, grilled, boiled and fried.

On the north beach at **Hamdŏk** there is also a fish restaurant in an idyllic spot where very good seafoods are served. **Samyang, Kimnyŏng** and **Sehwa** beaches are among the cleanest and loveliest on the island.

Further east you must not miss the famous lava tubes of Manjang and the **"Snake Cave of Kimnyŏng"**. The **Manjang Cave** is the longest volcanic tunnel in the world (7 km/over 4 miles long). It is illuminated, so the visitor can walk a few miles along the petrified lava stream – it is a strange feeling to see the odd lava formations in this dim light and hear the quiet drip of water from the roof. There are guided tours which provide detailed information.

On the eastern tip of the island lies the fishing port of **Sŏngsan** ("Bulwark Harbour"), so called after a volcanic plug that looks like a bulwark. It is one of the total of 360 subsidiary craters of the main volcano (Mount Halla) which can be found on the island. You can climb up to the edge of the crater and enjoy an unforgettable panoramic view if the weather is clear: before you lies the huge crater, and in the distance the outlines of the Japanese island, Kyushu.

A little bay near Sŏngsan is the point of departure for the typical Cheju diving expeditions. When the women divers come on land they sell their fresh catch. These divers, called "haenya" ("water women"), are equipped nowadays with modern diving apparatus, baskets on their backs and the typical white gourds which show their exact diving position on the surface of the sea. Delicacies such as sea urchins, cuttle fish, oysters and mussels are cleaned on the beach and eaten raw, washed down by the famous Korean rice wine, "soju".

(Thiele)

Hotels in Korea

In Korea, the foreign visitor can choose to stay either in a western style room or in a traditional Korean one. Most bigger hotels offer both types of accommodation.

Korean accommodation is called "yŏgwan". This is an ondol-heated room (a room featuring Korea's traditional underfloor heating) where a little matress ("yŏ") is spread on the floor. A quilt ("ibul") is laid on top of this to cover you. The pillow is a headrest stuffed with buckwheat husks, an ideal, flexible support for the back of the neck. The other furniture in a "yŏgwan" is low, so that you have to sit cross-legged or kneel in front of the little dressing table to shave or make up. Bowing to the twentieth century, almost every "yŏgwan" room has a colour TV! In addition, a teapot, tea cups, a candle and matches are laid out for the guest. When you enter the "yŏgwan" you must, of course, remove your shoes.

The service in Korean hotels is excellent. You can order food and drink in your room at more or less any time of the day or night. If there are no restaurants in the hotel, you can ask the hotel staff to bring food and drink from a restaurant outside.

Hotel bills usually include a 10% tax and 10% service charge. In the case of foreign tourists, however, the 10% tax is waived.

There has been an enormous increase in the number of tourists visiting Korea (1967: 84,000; 1982: 1 million; 1985: more than 1.4 million) and hotel capacity has been increasing in line with this. South Korea now has many excellent hotels and a range of other accommodation to offer – everything from luxury class to comfortable, if simple, youth hostels. There are now almost 24,000 hotel beds around the country.

The following list of hotels and youth hostels was compiled from the Korea Hotel Guide 1986, an official publication issued by the Korea National Tourism Corporation. With new hotels being built and existing ones renovated all the time, such a list can never be anything but a representative selection. The KNTC will always have complete and up-to-date information.

The list of hotels is in the following order:
– Seoul
– Pusan
and then the nine provinces:
– Kyŏnggi-do
– Kangwŏn-do
– Ch'ungch'ŏngpuk-do
– Ch'ungch'ŏngnam-do
– Chŏllapuk-do
– Chŏllanam-do
– Kyŏngsangpuk-do
– Kyŏngsangnam-do
– Cheju-do

In each section, the hotels are arranged according to category (de luxe, first class, second class, etc.).

Hotel Address	Number of Rooms	Services	By taxi a) from airport b) from station c) others
Hotels in Seoul			
De luxe Hotels *****			
Ambassador ***** 186-54, 2-ka Changch'ung-dong Chung-ku, <u>Seoul</u> C.P.O. Box 1222 Tel. (02) 275 1101/9 (02) 269 6111/9 Telex K23 269 Cable AMBASSADOR SEOUL	Double 93 Twin 245 Suite 107 Korean 6	Bar, hairdressing and beauty salon, shops, café, cocktail lounge, disco, restaurants.	a) 20 mins. c) 5 mins to city centre.
King Sejong Hotel ***** 61-3, 2-ka Ch'ungmu-ro Chung-ku, <u>Seoul</u> Tel. 776-1811/9 Telex SEJONTE K27 265 Cable HOTESEJONG	Single 46 Double 38 Twin 147 Suite 15 Korean 4	Hairdressing and beauty salon, shops, games room, sauna, health club, café, restaurant, night club, cocktail lounge, secretarial service.	a) 25 mins. b) 5 mins.
Hyatt Regency Seoul***** 747-7, Hannam-dong Yongsan-ku, <u>Seoul</u> C.P.O. Box 3438 Tel. 798 0061/9 Telex K24 136 Cable HYATT SEOUL	Double 232 Twin 330 Suite 39 Korean 3	Tennis, indoor and outdoor pool, sauna, shops, pharmacy, bar, café, nightclub, restaurant, hairdressing and beauty salon, laundry.	a) 25 mins.
Koreana Hotel ***** 61, 1-ka T'aep'yŏng-ro Chung-ku, <u>Seoul</u> Tel. 730 8611/5 730 9911 Telex KOTEL K26 241 Cable HOTELKOREANA	Double 52 Twin 214 Suite 2 Korean 3	Shops, hairdresser's, bar, restaurant, café, cocktail lounge, games room, secretarial service.	a) 30 mins. b) 5 mins.

Hotel Lotte ***** 1, Sokong-dong Chung-ku, <u>Seoul</u> C.P.O. Box 3500 Tel. 771 10 Telex LOTTEHO K2 353 315 Cable HOTELOTTE	Double 437 Twin 470 Suite 64 Korean 4	Indoor pool, indoor golf, sauna, health club, shops, pharmacy, restaurant, theatre restaurant, cocktail lounge, café, night-club, hairdressing and beauty salon.	a) 30 mins.
Seoul Hilton International ***** 395, 5-ka Namdaemun-ro Chung-ku, <u>Seoul</u> Tel. 753 7788 Telex K26 695 KHILTON Cable HILTELS SEOUL	Double 264 Twin 296 Suite 66 Korean 3	Secretarial service, conference room, café, bar, restaurant, night-club, indoor pool, health club, sauna, shops, hairdressing and beauty salon.	a) 25 mins. c) 5 mins. to subway.
Hotel President ***** 188-3, 1-ka Ulchi-ro Chung-ku, <u>Seoul</u> C.P.O. Box 4569 Tel. 753 3131 Telex PRETEL K27 521 Cable HOTEL PRESIDENT	Single 12 Double 44 Twin 223 Suite 16 Korean 8	Hairdressing and beauty salon, secre-tarial service, cocktail lounge, café, bar, restaurants, nightclub, games room, shops, pharmacy.	a) 20 mins.
Hotel Seoul Olympia ***** 108-2 P'yŏngch'ang-dong Chongno-ku, <u>Seoul</u> Tel. 353 5151/7 353 5121/7 Telex SELOLYM K23 171	Single 12 Double 48 Twin 213 Suite 11 Korean 26	Sauna and health club, hairdressing and beauty salon, shops, secretarial service, bar, café, nightclub, restau-rants (incl. Japanese restaurant), garden grill.	a) 25 mins. b) 15 mins.
Seoul Palace Hotel ***** 528, Panp'o-dong Kangnam-ku, <u>Seoul</u> C.P.O. Box 7596 Tel. 523 0101 532 5000 Telex PALACHL K22 657 Cable SELPALACEHTL	Single 8 Double 105 Twin 146 Suite 7 Korean 32	Sauna and health club, shops, games room, hairdresser's, café, restaurant, nightclub, cocktail lounge.	c) 3 mins. from Kang-nam Express Bus Termi-nal.

Seoul Royal Hotel ***** 6, 1-ka Myong-dong Chung-ku, <u>Seoul</u> Tel. 7 71-45 Telex SLROYAL K27 239 Cable ROYALHOTEL	Single 14 Double 135 Twin 123 Suite 23 Korean 14	Café, snack bar, restaurant, nightclub, cocktail lounge, games room, hairdressing and beauty salon.	a) 30 mins. b) 5 mins.
Seoul Plaza Hotel ***** 23, 2-ka T'aep'yǒng-ro Chung-ku, <u>Seoul</u> Tel. 7 71-22 Telex K26 215 Cable PLAZA HL SEOUL	Single 30 Double 273 Twin 213 Suite 24 Korean 2	Hairdressing and beauty salon, shops, secretarial service, café, cocktail lounge, restaurants (Japanese, Chinese, French, Steak House).	a) 30 mins.
Sheraton Walker Hill Hotel ***** San 21 Kwangjang-dong Sǒngdong-ku, <u>Seoul</u> Tel. 453 0121 Tel. 453 0131 Telex WALKHTL K28 517 Cable WALKERHILL SEOUL	Double 153 Twin 539 Suite 67 Korean 11	Indoor and outdoor pool, tennis, golf, casino, games room, sauna and health club, hairdressing and beauty salon, shops, restaurant, theatre restaurant, café, cock-tail lounge, nightclub.	a) 40 mins. c) 20 mins. to city centre.
Hotel Shilla ***** 202, 2-ka Changch'ung-dong Chung-ku, <u>Seoul</u> Tel. 233 3131 Telex SHILLA K28 937 Cable HOTEL SHILLA	Single 2 Double 235 Twin 379 Suite 53 Korean 3	Sauna and health club, indoor and out-door pools, tennis, shops, café, restaurant, nightclub, bar.	a) 30 mins. c) 10 mins. from City Hall.
The Westin Chosun ***** 87, Sokong-dong Chung-ku, <u>Seoul</u> C.P.O. Box 3706 Tel. 7 71 05 Telex K24 256, K28 432 Cable WESTCHOSUN	Double 337 Twin 106 Suite 28	Outdoor pool, sauna and health club, shops, pharmacy, café, restaurant, cocktail lounge, nightclub	a) 30 mins. b) 7 mins.

1st Class Hotels ****			
Crown Tourist Hotel **** 34-69, It'aewŏn-dong Yongsan-ku, <u>Seoul</u> C.P.O. Box 390 Tel. 792 8224/30 Telex CROWNTH K25 951 Cable HOTELCROWN	Double 82 Twin 52 Suite 4 Korean 19	Restaurants (Korean and western), café, sauna and health club, hairdresser's, night-club, cocktail lounge, games room, secretarial service.	a) 20 mins. b) 7 mins. c) 5 mins. from City Hall.
Mammoth Hotel **** 620-69 Chŏnnong-dong Tongdaemun-ku, <u>Seoul</u> Tel. 962 5611/8 Telex K32 482 Cable MAMMOTH SEOUL	Single 15 Double 63 Twin 123 Suite 9 Korean 9	Restaurants, theater restaurant, nightclub, cocktail lounge, sauna, indoor golf, games room, hairdressing and beauty salon.	a) 40 mins.
Hotel Pacific **** 31-1, 2-ka Namsan-dong Chung-ku, <u>Seoul</u> C.P.O. Box 5975 Tel. 777 7811/9 752 5100/9 Telex PACITEL K26 249 Cable HOTEL PACIFIC	Double 26 Twin 70 Suite 2 Korean 5	Restaurants (theater restaurant, Chinese, Japanese, grill), café, nightclub, shops, hairdresser's, sauna, games room.	a) 30 mins. b) 5 mins.
Seokyo Hotel **** 354-5, Sŏkyo-dong Map'o-ku, <u>Seoul</u> Tel. 393 7771 323 0181/7 Telex SEOKYO K26 780 Cable SEOKYO HOTEL	Double 35 Twin 46 Suite 8 Korean 12	Restaurants (Steak House, Korean, Japanese, Chinese), café, nightclub, cocktail lounge, indoor and outdoor pool, sauna, health club, games room, shops, hairdressing and beauty salon.	a) 10 mins. c) 10 mins. from City Hall.

Hamilton Hotel **** 119-25, It'aewŏn-dong, Yongsan-ku, <u>Seoul</u> Tel. 794 0171 Telex KSHAMIL K24 491	Single 7 Double 87 Twin 28 Korean 17	Nightclub, cocktail lounge, shops, hair-dresser's, café, restau-rant, sauna, games room.	a) 30 mins. b) 10 mins.
Hotel Manhattan **** 13-3, Yŏŭido-dong Yŏngdŭngp'o-ku, <u>Seoul</u> Tel. 782 8001/15 Telex K24 767	Double 35 Twin 143 Suite 2 Korean 2	Shops, hairdressing and beauty salon, cocktail lounge, nightclub, health club, restaurant, café, games room.	a) 15 mins. c) 15 mins. from City Hall.
Sam Jung **Tourist Hotel** **** 604-11, Yŏksam-dong, Kangnam-ku, <u>Seoul</u> P.O. Box Yŏngdŏng 196 Tel. 557 1221 Telex K26 680	Single 4 Double 56 Twin 90 Suite 4 Korean 9	Shops, hairdresser's, café, restaurant, sauna, games room, cocktail lounge, nightclub.	a) 40 mins. b) 30 mins.
Tower Hotel **** San 5-5, 2-ka, Changch'ung-dong, Chung-ku, <u>Seoul</u> Tel. 253 9181/9 Telex TOWER K28 246 Cable TOWERTEL	Single 2 Double 29 Twin 122 Suite 29 Korean 23	Outdoor pool, tennis, golf, sauna, health club, hairdresser's, games room, café, restaurant, cocktail lounge, nightclub.	a) 35 mins. b) 15 mins.
Seoulin Hotel **** 149, Sŏrin-dong Chongno-ku, <u>Seoul</u> Tel. 732 0181 Telex SEOULIN K28 510 Cable HOTEL SEOULIN	Single 31 Double 69 Twin 79 Suite 3 Korean 29	Café, grill, Japanese restaurant, cocktail lounge, sauna, shops, games room, secre-tarial service.	a) 30 mins. b) 5 mins.
Kyungnam Tourist **Hotel** **** 366-7, Chang-an-dong, Tongdaemun-gu, <u>Seoul</u> Tel. 2 47 25 00/16 Telex KNHOTEL K 29 389	Double 30 Twin 34 Suite 12 Korean 32	Shops, hairdressing and beauty salon, bowling, games room, sauna, nightclub, café, restaurant.	

Nam Seoul Hotel **** 602-4, Yŏksam-dong, Kangnam-gu. Seoul Tel. 552 7111/9 552 7211/8 Telex NASOTEL K25 019	Double 45 Twin 107 Suite 10 Korean 17	Shops, hairdressing and beauty salon, café, restaurant, theatre restaurant, cocktail lounge, nightclub, games room, sauna, health club.	
2nd Class Hotels			
Bukak Park Tourist Hotel *** 113-1 P'yŏngch'ang-dong Chongno-ku, Seoul Tel. 352 7101/8 Cable SELPARK	Double 39 Twin 30 Suite 6 Korean 52	Nightclub, café, restaurant.	a) 30 mins. c) 15 mins. from City Hall.
Clover Tourist Hotel *** 129-7, Ch'ŏngdam-dong, Kangnam-gu, Seoul Tel. 546 1411/6 546 6311/4	Double 30 Korean 20	Shops, hairdresser's, golf, sauna, health club, games room, café, restaurant, cocktail lounge, nightclub.	
Hotel Green Park *** San 14, Ui-dong, Tobong-ku, Seoul Tel. 993 2171/8	Double 8 Twin 62 Suite 5 Korean 16	Outdoor swimming pool, tennis, café, restaurant, games room.	a) 40 mins. b) 25 mins.
Han Kang Hotel *** 188-2, Kwangjang-dong, Sŏngdong-ku, Seoul Tel. 453 5131 453 5161/5	Single 6 Twin 74 Suite 5 Korean 38	Outdoor swimming pool, shops, café, restaurant, games room, nightclub.	a) 30 mins.
New Kukje Hotel *** 29-2, 1-ga, T'aep'yŏngno, Chung-gu, Seoul Tel. 732 0161/9	Single 43 Double 29 Twin 56 Suite 9 Korean 12	Shops, hairdresser's, café, restaurant, cocktail lounge, sauna, games room.	

Young Dong Hotel *** 6, Nonhyŏn-dong Kangnam-ku, <u>Seoul</u> Tel. 542 0112	Single 5 Double 90 Twin 49 Suite 3 Korean 13	Café, restaurant, theatre restaurant, cocktail lounge, nightclub, sauna, games room.	
Poongjun Hotel *** 73-1, 2-ka Inhyŏn-dong, Chung-ku, <u>Seoul</u> Tel. 266 2151/9 Telex PUNGJUN K25 687	Double 26 Twin 88 Suite 11 Korean 12	Shops, café, restau- rant, cocktail lounge, nightclub.	a) 40 mins.
Savoy Hotel Seoul *** 23-1, 1-ka Ch'ungmu-ro Chung-ku, <u>Seoul</u> C.P.O. Box 291 Tel. 776 2641/50 Telex K23 222 Cable SAVOY HOTEL	Single 19 Double 58 Twin 20 Suite 5 Korean 5	Café, games room, cocktail lounge, bakery.	a) 30 mins. b) 5 mins.
Astoria Hotel *** 13-2, Namhak-dong Chung-ku, <u>Seoul</u> Tel. 267 7111/8	Double 51 Twin 26 Korean 3	Nightclub, cocktail lounge, café, restau- rant, games room, hairdresser's.	a) 40 mins.
Hotel Seoul Rex *** 65, 1-ka Hoehyŏn-dong Chung-ku, <u>Seoul</u> C.P.O. Box 7798 Tel. 752 3191/4 Cable HOTELREX	Single 28 Double 15 Twin 39 Suite 27 Korean 2	Nightclub, café, restaurant, shops, games room.	a) 25 mins. b) 5 mins.
Yoido Hotel *** 1-496, Yŏŭido-dong Yŏngdŭngp'o-ku, <u>Seoul</u> C.P.O. Box 23 Tel. 782 0121 Cable YOIDOHTL	Single 5 Double 75 Twin 26 Suite 1 Korean 9	Cocktail lounge, nightclub, shops, hairdresser's, games room, café, restaurant.	a) 15 mins. b) 10 mins.

Metro Hotel *** 199-33, 2-ka Ŭlchi-ro Chung-ku, <u>Seoul</u> Tel. 776 6781/8 776 8221/7 Telex METROHO K26 486 Cable METROHOTEL SEOUL	Single 24 Double 30 Twin 23 Suite 6	Café, restaurant, shops, games room, hairdresser's.	a) 30 mins. b) 5 mins.
Seoul Tourist Hotel *** 92, Ch'ŏngjin-dong Chongno-ku, <u>Seoul</u> Tel. 735 9001/5 Cable OYANG TEL	Single 14 Double 36 Twin 35 Suite 1 Korean 16	Hairdresser's, cocktail lounge, café, restaurants (Japanese), shops, games room, sauna.	a) 30 mins. b) 10 mins.
Seoul Prince Hotel *** 1-1, 2-ka Namsan-dong Chung-ku, <u>Seoul</u> Tel. 752 7111/9 Telex PRINCE K25 918 Cable HOTEL PRINCE	Single 7 Double 39 Twin 27 Suite 13	Café, restaurants (Japanese, western), cocktail lounge, games room, shops.	a) 30 mins. b) 5 mins. c) 5 mins. from City Hall.
New Oriental Hotel *** 10, 3-ka Hoehyŏn-dong Chung-ku, <u>Seoul</u> Tel. 753 0701/6 Cable NEWORIENTALH	Single 9 Double 26 Twin 39 Suite 6 Korean 4	Café, restaurant, cocktail lounge, games room, shops.	a) 40 mins. b) 5 mins.
3rd Class Hotels **			
Chon Ji Tourist Hotel ** 133-1, 5-ka Ulji-ro Chung-ku, <u>Seoul</u> Tel. 265 61 31/3	Single 4 Double 39 Twin 26 Korean 1	Café, nightclub, games room, shops.	a) 30 mins. c) 10 mins. from City Hall.
New Naija Hotel ** 201-9, Naija-dong, Chongno-ku, <u>Seoul</u> Tel. 737 9011/5	Double 31 Twin 25 Suite 8 Korean 4	Hairdresser's, café, restaurants, games room.	a) 40 mins. c) 5 mins. from City Hall.

Central Hotel ** 227-1, Changsa-dong Chongno-ku, <u>Seoul</u> Tel. 265 4120/9 Cable CENTRAL HOTEL	Single 4 Double 37 Twin 31 Suite 6 Korean 10	Nightclub, sauna, café, restaurants, games room, hairdresser's.	a) 30 mins. c) 5 mins. from City Hall.
Eastern Hotel ** 444-14 Ch'angsin-dong Chongno-ku, <u>Seoul</u> Tel. 764 4101/9	Single 7 Double 17 Twin 11 Suite 4 Korean 12	Cocktail lounge, nightclub, café, restaurant, sauna.	a) 30 mins.
YMCA Tourist Hotel ** 9, 2-ka, Chong-ro Chongno-ku, <u>Seoul</u> Tel. 732 8291/8 Cable HOTEL YMCA	Single 20 Double 18 Twin 41	Games room, restaurant.	
Dae Hwa Hotel ** 18-21, 6-ka Ülchi-ro Chung-ku, <u>Seoul</u> Tel. 265 9181/9	Double 70 Twin 12 Suite 10 Korean 7	Café, restaurant, games room.	a) 40 mins. c) 5 mins. from Kang-nam Express Bus Terminal.
Boolim Tourist Hotel ** 620-27, Chŏnnong 2-dong, Tongdaemun-gu, <u>Seoul</u> Tel. 962 0061/3 962 0021/5	Single 4 Double 51 Korean 5	Café, restaurant, cocktail lounge, nightclub, games room.	

Hotels in Pusan

De luxe Hotels *****

Hotel Commodore ***** 743-80, Yŏngju-dong Chung-ku, <u>Pusan</u> P.O. Box 407 Pusan Tel. 44 91 01/7 Telex COMOTEL K53 717 Cable COMMODORE	Double 193 Twin 106 Suite 10 Korean 16	Café, restaurants (Korean, Japanese, Chinese), cocktail lounge, indoor pool, sauna, health club, games room, hairdresser's.	a) 30 mins. b) 5 mins. c) 5 mins. from Ferry Terminal.

The Westin Chosun Beach ***** 737, Uil-dong Haeundae-ku, <u>Pusan</u> P.O. Box 29 Haeundae Tel. Pusan 72 74 11 Telex CHOSUNB K53 718 Cable WESTCHO	Double 110 Twin 159 Suite 17 Korean 45	Outdoor pool, sauna, health club, shops, hairdressing and beauty salon, café, restaurants (French, Japanese), games room.	a) 35 mins. b) 25 mins. c) 25 mins. from Ferry Terminal.
Hotel Sorabol ***** 37-1, 1-ka Taech'ŏng-dong Chung-ku, <u>Pusan</u> P.O. Box 693 Pusan Tel. 463 3511/9 Telex SOHOTEL K53 827 Cable SORABOL HOTEL	Single 12 Double 44 Twin 74 Suite 10 Korean 12	Shops, hairdresser's, games room, sauna, café, restaurant, cock-tail lounge, nightclub.	a) 40 mins. b) 5 mins.
1st Class Hotels ****			
Hotel Crown **** 830-30, Pŏmil-dong Tong-ku, <u>Pusan</u> Tel. 69 12 41/7 Telex CROWNB K53 422	Double 39 Twin 75 Suite 2 Korean 16	Shops, hairdressing and beauty salon. cocktail lounge, nightclub, sauna, café, restaurants, games room.	a) 30 mins. b) 10 mins. c) 30 mins. from Express Bus Terminal.
Kukje Hotel **** 830-62, Pŏmil-dong Tong-gu, <u>Pusan</u> C.P.O. Box 633 Tel. 642 1330/4 Telex KUKJE K29 096	Single 7 Double 32 Twin 75 Suite 1 Korean 24	Café, restaurant, nightclub, hair-dresser's, sauna, games room.	a) 20 mins. b) 5 mins.
Pusan Tourist Hotel **** 12, 2-ka Tongkwang-dong Chung-ku, <u>Pusan</u> Tel. 23-43 01/9 Telex BSHOTEL K53 657 Cable BUSANHOTEL	Single 6 Double 84 Twin 145 Suite 23 Korean 16	Shops, hairdresser's, cocktail lounge, nightclub, café, restaurant, sauna, games room.	a) 30 mins. b) 7 mins. c) 10 mins. from Ferry Terminal, 15 mins. from Express Bus Terminal.

Haeundae **Kuk Dong Hotel** **** 1124, Chung-dong Haeundae-gu, <u>Pusan</u> Tel. 72-00 81/90 Telex KUKDONG K53 758 Cable HOTEL KUKDONG PUSAN	Double 10 Twin 66 Suite 8 Korean 21	Hairdressing and beauty salon, cocktail lounge, nightclub, café, restaurant, sauna, games room.	a) 40 mins.
Ferry Hotel **** 37-16, 4-ka Chungang-dong Chung-ku, <u>Pusan</u> Tel. 463 0881/90	Double 78 Twin 32 Suite 2 Korean 10	Shops, hairdresser's, cocktail lounge, nightclub, café, restaurant, sauna, games room.	a) 30 mins. b) 5 mins.
Hotel Phoenix **** 8-1, 5-ka Namp'o-dong Chung-ku, <u>Pusan</u> Tel. 22-80 61/9 Telex PNIXTEL K53 704	Double 50 Twin 53 Suite 1 Korean 10	Shops, hairdresser's, café, restaurant, nightclub, sauna, games room.	a) 45 mins. b) 10 mins. c) 10 mins. from Ferry Terminal.
Pusan Royal Hotel **** 2-72, 2-ka Kwangbok-dong Chung-ku- <u>Pusan</u> Tel. 23-10 51/5 Telex BROYAL K53 824 Cable ELEPHANTEL	Single 6 Double 25 Twin 63 Suite 9 Korean 5	Shops, nightclub, café, restaurant, games room.	a) 25 mins. b) 5 mins. c) 5 mins from Ferry Terminal.
2nd Class Hotels ***			
Pusan Plaza Hotel *** 1213-14 Ch'oryang-dong Tong-ku, <u>Pusan</u> P.O. Box Pusan 282 Tel. 463 5011/9 Cable BUSAN PLAZA	Double 38 Twin 61 Suite 2 Korean 15	Hairdresser's, shops, cocktail lounge, café, restaurant.	a) 40 mins.
Moon Hwa Tourist **Hotel** *** 517-65, Pujŏn-dong Pusanjin-ku, <u>Pusan</u> Tel. 806 8001/7	Single 6 Double 19 Twin 18 Suite 5 Korean 32	Shops, hairdresser's, café, restaurant, cocktail lounge, nightclub, games room.	a) 30 mins. b) 20 mins. c) 10 mins. from Express Bus Terminal.

Hotel Tong Yang *** 27, 1-ka Kwangbok-dong Chung-gu, <u>Pusan</u> Tel. 22-12 05/7 Telex TY K3 737 Cable HOTEL TONGYANG	Single 7 Double 32 Twin 12 Suite 3 Korean 10	Café, restaurant, cocktail lounge, games room, shops.	a) 30 mins. b) 5 mins.
Tongnae Tourist Hotel *** 212, Onch'ŏn-dong Tongnae-ku, <u>Pusan</u> Tel. 53-11 21/5	Double 15 Twin 29 Suite 5 Korean 23	Café, restaurant, shops, cocktail lounge, nightclub, hot spring bath.	a) 20 mins. b) 25 mins.
Paradise Beach Hotel *** 1408-5, Chung-dong Haeundae-ku, <u>Pusan</u> Tel. 72-14 61/8 Cable PARA BH K52 145	Double 15 Twin 28 Suite 1 Korean 6	Café, restaurant.	a) 35 mins. c) 25 mins. from Pusan Express Bus Terminal.
3rd Class Hotels **			
Tower Tourist Hotel ** 20, 3-ka Tongkwang-dong Chung-ku, <u>Pusan</u> Tel. 23-51 51/9 Telex KBTOWER K52 046 Cable TOWER HOTEL	Double 85 Twin 9 Suite 4 Korean 10	Café, restaurant, nightclub, games room, shops.	a) 30 mins. b) 5 mins.
Tourist Hotel UN ** 335-5, Amnam-dong Sŏ-ku, <u>Pusan</u> Tel. 26-51 81/4	Single 5 Double 27 Twin 13 Suite 2 Korean 3	Cocktail lounge, nightclub, hairdressing and beauty salon, café, restaurant, games room.	a) 30 mins. b) 15 mins.
Shin Shin Hotel ** 263-11, Pujŏn-dong Pusanjin-ku, <u>Pusan</u> Tel. 88-01 95/8	Single 2 Double 38 Twin 2 Suite 1 Korean 23	Café, restaurant, nightclub, games room, shops.	

Pusan Airang Hotel ** 1204-1, Ch'oryang-dong Tong-ku, <u>Pusan</u> Tel. 463 5001	Single 6 Double 21 Twin 65 Suite 5 Korean 23	Shops, café, restaurants, casino, nightclub.	a) 30 mins. c) 5 mins. from Ferry Terminal 5 mins. from Express Bus Terminal.

Hotels in Kyŏnggi-do

1st Class Hotels ****

New Korea Tourist Hotel **** 674-251, Anyang 1-dong, <u>Anyang</u> Tel. 3-55 21/9 Telex KYCCI K27 949	Single 4 Double 60 Twin 40 Suite 3 Korean 13	Shops, hairdressing and beauty salon, café, restaurant, sauna, nightclub.	

2nd Class Hotels ***

Grand Tourist Hotel *** 199, Üijŏngbu-dong, <u>Üijŏngbu</u> Tel. 42-35 01	Double 24 Twin 7 Korean 3	Cocktail lounge, nightclub, café, restaurant.	

Hotels in Kangwŏn-do

De luxe Hotels *****

Sorak Park Hotel ***** 74-3, Sŏrak-dong <u>Sokch'o</u> Tel. 7-77 11/24 Telex K24 142	Double 10 Twin 54 Suite 21 Korean 36	Casino, hairdressing and beauty salon, shops, games room, café, restaurant, cocktail lounge, nightclub.	a) 15 mins. c) 15 mins. from Express Bus Terminal.
New Sorak Hotel ***** 106-1, Sŏrak-dong <u>Sokch'o</u> Tel. 7-71 31/50 Telex NSHOTEL K24 893 Cable HOTEL NEWSORAK	Double 13 Twin 67 Suite 7 Korean 33	Shops, hairdresser's, cocktail lounge, nightclub, café, restaurant.	a) 15 mins. c) 15 mins. from Express Bus Terminal.

2nd Class Hotels ***			
Ch'unch'ŏn Sejong Hotel *** San 1, Pongŭi-dong <u>Ch'unch'ŏn</u> Tel. Ch'unch'ŏn 52-11 91/5	Double 34 Twin 12 Suite 8 Korean 14	Outdoor swimming pool, café, restaurant, games room, night-club, shops.	c) 2 hrs. from Seoul to Ch'unch'ŏn by bus.
Ch'unch'ŏn Tourist Hotel *** 30-1, Nagwon-dong <u>Ch'unch'ŏn</u> Tel. Ch'unch'ŏn 3-82 85/9	Double 28 Twin 3 Suite 4 Korean 17	Casino, nightclub, cocktail lounge, café, restaurant, shops,	
Wonju Tourist Hotel *** 63, Chung-ang-dong, <u>Wonju</u> Tel. Wonju 43-12 41/50	Single 12 Double 17 Twin 12 Suite 9 Korean 24	Casino, nightclub, games room, hair-dressing and beauty salon, café, restaurant, sauna, shops,	
3rd Class Hotels **			
Dong Hae Hotel ** 274-1 Kangmun-dong <u>Kangnŭng</u> Tel. Kangnŭng 2-21 81/3	Double 18 Twin 27 Suite 12 Korean 26	Indoor pool, tennis, café, restaurant, cock-tail lounge.	c) 4 hrs. from Seoul by Express Bus, hotel 15 mins. from Bus Terminal.
Mt. Sorak Hotel ** 170, Sŏrak-dong <u>Sokch'o</u> Tel. Sokch'o 7-71 01/5	Double 8 Twin 20 Suite 2 Korean 24	Shops, café, restaurant, cocktail lounge.	a) 15 mins. c) 15 mins. from Express Bus Terminal.
Hotel Kyungpo Tourist 255, Kangmun-dong, <u>Kangnŭng</u> Tel. (03 91) 3-22 77/9	Single 2 Double 25 Twin 3 Suite 2 Korean 24	Hairdressing and beauty salon, fishing, hunting, boating, outdoor pool, shops, café, restaurant, theatre restaurant, games room, cocktail lounge, nightclub.	

Hotels in Ch'ungch'ŏngpuk-do and Ch'ungch'ŏngnam-do

1st Class Hotels ****

Songnisan Tourist Hotel ** 198, Sanae-ri Naesongni-myŏn Poŭn-kun Ch'ungch'ŏngpuk-do Tel. Poŭn 20 91/8	Double 30 Twin 51 Suite 11 Korean 53	Casino, golf, tennis, games room, hair-dressing and beauty salon, café, restaurant, nightclub.	c) 2 ½ hrs. from Seoul 1 hr. from Ch'ŏngju 1 hr. from Taejŏn

2nd Class Hotels ***

Eunsung Tourist Hotel * 844, Poktae-dong Ch'ŏngju Ch'ungch'ŏngpuk-do Tel. 64-21 81/5	Double 30 Twin 15 Suite 2 Korean 19	Outdoor pool, tennis, sauna, games room, cocktail lounge, nightclub, café, restaurant.	
Suanbo Tourist Hotel * 205-1, Onch'ŏn-ri Sangmo-myŏn Chungwon-gun Ch'ungch'ŏngpuk-do Tel. 3-23-11	Double 11 Twin 9 Suite 1 Korean 29	Cocktail lounge, nightclub, hot spring bath, sauna, café.	

1st Class Hotels ****

You Soung Hotel ** 480, Pongmyŏng-dong Chung-ku, Taejŏn Ch'ungch'ŏngnam-do P.O. Box Yusŏng 11 Tel. 822-0611/5 822-0711/5	Single 1 Double 8 Twin 59 Suite 12 Korean 74	Outdoor pool, hot spring bath, sauna, shops, café, restaurant, hairdressing and beauty salon.	c) 2 hrs. by train or express bus from Seoul, hotel 15 mins. from Taejŏn.
Jeil Hotel ** 228, 6, Onch'ŏn-dong Onyang-ŭp Ch'ungch'ŏngnam-do Tel. 2-61 11/20	Double 4 Twin 20 Suite 3 Korean 66	Shooting, golf, tennis, outdoor pool, hot spring bath, hair-dressing and beauty salon, shops, cocktail lounge, café, restaurant.	

2nd Class Hotels ***				
Joong Ang Hotel*** 318, Chung-dong Tong-ku, <u>Taejŏn</u> Ch'ungch'ŏngnam-do Tel. 253 8801	Double Twin Suite Korean	26 8 9 16	Cafe, restaurant, nightclub, games room, hairdresser's.	
Dae Jeon Hotel * 20-16, Wŏn-dong Tong-ku, <u>Taejŏn</u> Ch'ungch'ŏngnam-do Tel. Taejŏn 253 8131	Double Twin Suite Korean	23 13 3 13	Café, restaurant, nightclub, games room, hairdresser's.	c) 5 mins. on foot from Taejŏn Railway Station
Mannyonjang Hotel * 478, Pongmyŏng-dong Chung-ku, <u>Taejŏn</u> Ch'ungch'ŏngnam-do Tel. 8 22-00 61	Single Double Twin Suite Korean	3 19 27 1 12	Cocktail lounge, nightclub, hot spring bath, café, restaurant.	c) 2 hrs. from Seoul to Taejŏn by Express Bus, hotel 15 mins. from Express Bus Terminal.
**3rd Class Hotels **				
Onyong Admiral Hotel ** 242-10, Onch'ŏn-dong <u>Onyang</u> Ch'ungch'ŏngnam-do Tel. 2-21 41/7	Twin Suite Korean	18 2 34	Outdoor pool, hot spring bath, cocktail lounge, café, restaurant, games room.	
Hotels in Chŏllapuk-do and Chŏllanam-do				
1st Class Hotels ***				
Nae Jang San Hotel *** 71-14, Naejang-dong <u>Chŏngju</u> Chŏllapuk-do Tel. Chŏngju (06 81) 2-41 31/7	Double Twin Suite Korean	12 55 8 29	Hairdressing and beauty salon, cocktail lounge, nightclub, café, restaurant, sauna, shops.	c) 3 ½ hrs. from Seoul by train or Express Bus, hotel 15 mins from Chŏngju.

2nd Class Hotels •••				
Kun San Tourist Hotel ••• 462-1 Kyŏngjang-dong <u>Kunsan</u> Chŏllapuk-do Tel. 3-41 21/8	Single Double Twin Suite Korean	8 8 83 2 12	Cocktail lounge, nightclub, games room, café, restaurant, hairdresser's.	c) 20 mins. from Iri Railway Station; 3 mins. from Kunsan Express Bus Terminal.
Chŏnju Tourist Hotel ••• 28, 3-ka, Taga-dong <u>Chŏnju</u> Chŏllapuk-do Tel. 83-28 11/5	Double Twin Suite Korean	21 8 3 18	Cocktail lounge, nightclub, café, restaurant, games room.	
3rd Class Hotels ••				
Victory Tourist Hotel •• 21-1 Sinch'ang-dong <u>Kunsan</u> Chŏllapuk-do Tel. 2-61 61/3	Double Twin Suite Korean	45 4 4 10	Hairdresser's, café, restaurant, nightclub, games room.	c) 5 mins. from Express Bus Terminal.
1st Class Hotels ••••				
Shin Yang Park Hotel •••• San 40, Chisan-dong Tong-ku, <u>Kwangju</u> Chŏllanam-do P.O. Box Kwangju 181 Tel. 7-06 71/9 Telex SYPKHTL K735 Cable HOTEL SHIN YANG	Double Twin Suite Korean	8 54 5 26	Golf, sauna, cocktail lounge, nightclub, shops, games room, café, restaurants (Korean, Japanese, Chinese), hairdressing and beauty salon.	b) 10 mins. c) 5 mins. from Express Bus Terminal.
Kwangju Hotel 20, 2-ka, Kŭmnam-ro Tong-ku, <u>Kwangju</u> Chŏllanam-do Tel. 2-62 31/6	Double Twin Suite Korean	19 31 6 9	Shops, cocktail lounge, nightclub, café, restaurant, hairdressing and beauty salon, games room.	a) 20 mins. b) 5 mins. c) 5 mins. from Express Bus Terminal.

Hotels in Kyŏngsangpuk-do and Kyŏngsangnam-do

De luxe Hotels *****			
Kolon Hotel *** 111-1, Ma-dong Kyŏngju Kyŏngsangpuk-do P. O. Box Kyŏngju 21 Seoul 8649 Tel. Kyŏngju 2-90 01/14 Telex K4 469 Cable KOLHTL	Double 6 Twin 204 Suite 7 Korean 23	Tennis, golf, indoor pool, sauna, casino, cocktail lounge, nightclub, café, restaurants, shops.	a) 1 ½ hrs. by bus from Kimhae Airport. b) 40 mins.
Kyŏngju Chosun Hotel *** 410, Sinp'yŏng-dong Kyŏngju Kyŏngsangpuk-do P. O. Box Kyŏngju 35 Tel. 2-96 01/19 Telex CHOSUN K54 467	Double 34 Twin 201 Suite 29 Korean 38	Inddor and outdoor pools, boating, fishing, golf, tennis, bowling, hairdressing and beauty salon, cocktail lounge, nightclub, games room, café, restaurant, theatre restaurant.	b) 10 mins. c) 4 ½ hrs. from Seoul to Kyŏngju by Express Bus.
Kyŏngju Tokyu Hotel *** 410, Shinp'yŏng-dong Kyŏngju Kyŏngsangpuk-do P. O. Box Kyŏngju 6 Tel. 2-99 01/16 Telex KJTOKYU K54 328 Cable KYONGJU TOKYU	Single 8 Double 24 Twin 240 Suite 13 Korean 18	Boating, fishing, outdoor pool, tennis, hairdressing and beauty salon, café, restaurants (view of lake), cocktail lounge, games room.	a) 1 ½ hrs. b) 10 mins. c) 10 mins from Kyŏngju Express Bus Terminal
2nd Class Hotels *			
P'ohang Beach Hotel * 311-2, Songdo-dong P'ohang Kyŏngsangpuk-do Tel. 3-14 01/9 Telex K29 507	Double 22 Twin 8 Suite 18 Korean 8	Boating, fishing shooting, secretarial service, hairdresser's, cocktail lounge, nightclub, games room, café, restaurant.	c) 5 hrs. from Seoul to P'ohang by Express Bus.

Keumosan Hotel* San 24-6 Namt'ong-dong Kumi Kyŏngsangpuk-do Tel. 52-31 51/9	Double Twin Suite Korean	29 35 10 33	Cocktail lounge, nightclub, café, restaurant, games room.	
3rd Class Hotels **				
Pul Guk Sa Hotel ** 648-1, Chinhyŏn-dong Kyŏngju Kyŏngsangpuk-do Tel. 2-19 11/7	Double Twin Suite Korean	5 50 2 24	Hairdresser's, cocktail lounge, nightclub, café, restaurant, tennis, games room.	b) 20 mins. c) 4 ½ hrs. from Seoul to Kyŏngju by Express Bus.
De luxe Hotels ***				
Diamond Hotel *** 283, Chŏnha-dong Ulsan Kyŏngsangnam-do P.O. Box Tongulsan 15 Tel. 32-71 71/9 32-41 51/5	Double Twin Suite Korean	151 93 32 14	Indoor pool, health club, sauna, hair- dressing and beauty salon, café, restaurant.	
1st Class Hotels ***				
Chang Won Hotel *** 99-4, Chungang-dong Ch'angwŏn Kyŏngsangnam-do P.O. Box 30 Ch'angwŏn Tel. Ch'angwŏn 83-55 51/60 Telex CHANGWON CW K52 356	Single Double Twin Suite Korean	2 74 50 4 36	Indoor pool, health club, sauna, shops, hairdressing and beauty salon, cocktail lounge, nightclub, games room, café, restaurants (Korean, Chinese, Japanese).	a) 40 mins. from Kimhae Airport. c) 15 mins. from Masan.
Bugok Hotel *** 326-1, Kŏmun-ri Pugok-myŏn Ch'angnyŏng-kun Kyŏngsangnam-do Tel. Ch'anyŏng 4-51 81/9 Cable BUGOKSPA HOTEL	Double Twin Suite Korean	20 44 1 121	Outdoor pool, tennis, sauna, games room, nightclub, café, restau- rants (Korean, Japa- nese, western).	c) 30 mins. from Taegu. c) 60 mins. from Chinhae.

Lotte Crystal Hotel **** 3-6, 4-ka Changgun-dong <u>Masan</u> Kyŏngsangnam-do Tel. Masan 2-11 12/9 Telex LOTTE CH K53 822 Cable MASAN CRYSTAL	Single 28 Double 37 Twin 34 Suite 8 Korean 14	Hairdresser's, café, restaurants (Korean, Japanese), games room, nightclub, shop.	a) 40 mins. from Kimhae Airport. c) 15 mins. from Chang-wŏn Indus-trial Estate.
Bugok Hawaii Hotel **** 195-7, Kŏmun-ri Pugok-myŏn <u>Ch'angnyŏn-kun</u> Kyŏngsangnam-do Tel. 4-63 31 Ch'angnyŏng	Double 15 Twin 16 Suite 5 Korean 133	Indoor and outdoor pools, café, restaurants (Korean, western, theatre restaurant), games room.	c) 5 ½ hrs. from Seoul to Pugok by Express Bus.
Hotel Chung Mu **** 1, Tonam-dong <u>Ch'ungmu</u> Kyŏngsangnam-do Tel. Ch'ungmu 2-20 91/5 Telex K53 850	Twin 28 Suite 4 Korean 18	Boating, fishing, shooting, outdoor pool, cocktail lounge, nightclub, café, restaurant (Korean, Japanese, western), shops.	c) 10 mins. from Angel Terminal.
Okp'o Tourist Hotel **** 330-4, Okp'o-ri Changsŭngp'o-up <u>Kŏje-kun</u> Kyŏngsangnam-do Tel. Changsŭngp'o 34-37 03/4 Telex DW OKPO K52 482	Double 120 Suite 6 Korean 2	Hairdresser's, shops, secretarial service, cocktail lounge, nightclub, café, restaurant, games room.	c) 1 hr. from Pusan to Chang-sŭngp'o by ferry, c)10 mins. from Chang-sugp'o Ferry Terminal

2nd Class Hotels ***			
Tae Hwa Hotel *** 1406-6, Singjŏng-dong Nam-gu,Ulsan Kyŏngsangnam-do P. O. Box Ulsan 117 Tel. 73-81 91/8 73-33 01/5	Single 54 Double 12 Twin 30 Suite 2 Korean 5	Sauna, cocktail lounge, nightclub, café, restaurant (Japanese), hairdresser's, shops.	a) 2 hrs. from Kimhae Airport. b) 10 mins. c) 5 mins. on foot from Express Bus Terminal.
New Grand Hotel *** 256-20, Sŏngnam-dong Chung-gu, Ulsan Kyŏngsangnam-do Tel. 44-15 01	Double 66 Twin 10 Suite 12 Korean 16	Hairdressing and beauty salon, cocktail lounge, nightclub, games room, sauna, restaurant, shops.	
Ulsan Hotel *** 570-1, Yaŭm-dong Nam-gu, Ulsan Kyŏngsangnam-do Tel. 72-71 46/9	Single 2 Double 7 Twin 25 Suite 2 Korean 14	Shops, hairdresser's, cocktail lounge, nightclub, games room, café, restaurant, sauna.	

Hotels in Cheju-do

De luxe Hotels *****			
Cheju Grand Hotel *** 263-15, Yŏn-dong Cheju, Cheju-do P. O. Box 45, Cheju Tel. Cheju 42-33 21/9 Telex GRANTL K66 712 Cable CHEJUGRANHTL	Double 126 Twin 299 Suite 35 Korean 62	Fishing, golf, outdoor pool, sauna, health club, cocktail lounge, nightclub, shops, hairdressing and beauty salon, café, restaurants (Korean, Japanese, western).	a) 5 mins.
Cheju KAL Hotel *** 1691-9, 2-do, 1-dong Cheju, Cheju-do P. O. Box Cheju 62 Tel. Cheju 53-61 51/69 Telex JKALHTL K66 744 Cable CJUKALHTL	Single 22 Double 124 Twin 124 Suite 11 Korean 29	Outdoor pool, golf, fishing, sauna, games room, cocktail lounge, nightclub, casino, hairdressing and beauty salon, café, restaurants (Korean, western, theatre restaurant).	a) 7 mins.

1st Class Hotels ****			
Cheju Free Port Hotel **** 291-30, Yŏn-dong <u>Cheju</u>, Cheju-do P.O. Box Cheju 99 Tel. 27-41 11/40 Telex SEOHA K66 783 Cable CHEJUHTL SEOHAI	Double 26 Twin 80 Suite 24 Korean 30	Hairdressing and beauty salon, cocktail lounge, nightclub, shooting, games room, shops, sauna, café, restaurant.	a) 5 mins.
2nd Class Hotels *			
Hotel Paradise Cheju * 1315, 1-dong, 2-do <u>Cheju</u>, Cheju-do Tel. 23-01 71/5 Telex PARAHTL K66 728 Cable PARADISE JEJU HTL	Double 18 Twin 27 Suite 4 Korean 8	Hairdressing and beauty salon, café, restaurant, shop.	a) 7 mins.
Sŏgwip'o Park Tourist Hotel * 674-1, Sŏgwi-dong <u>Sŏgwip'o</u>, Cheju-do Tel. 62-21 61/7 Telex PARAHTL K728	Double 16 Twin 32 Suite 2 Korean 16	Hairdresser's, cocktail lounge, café, restaurant, health club, sauna, games room, shops.	a) 1 hr.
Sŏgwip'o Lions Hotel * 803, Sŏgwi-dong <u>Sŏgwip'o</u>, Cheju-do Tel. Sŏgwip'o 62-41 41/4	Double 34 Twin 8 Suite 4 Korean 14	Cocktail lounge, nightclub, café, restaurant, games room, shop.	a) 45 mins.

Youth Hostels in Korea

Academy House San 76, Suyu-dong Tobong-ku, <u>Seoul</u> Tel. 993 6181/5	Double 4 Twin 28 6-bunk Suite 8 Korean 8	Bar, café, restaurant.	a) 40 mins.
Bando **Youth Hostel** 679-3, Yŏksam-dong Kangnam-ku, <u>Seoul</u> Tel. 5 67-31 11/9	4-bunk 18 6-bunk 18 Twin 37 8-bunk Suite 64 Korean 7	Café, restaurant, shop.	a) 20 mins. c) 15 mins. from City Hall.
Aerin **Youth Hostel** 41, 1-ka- Posu-dong Chung-ku, <u>Pusan</u> Tel. 27-22 22/7	Twin 10 6-bunk Suite 22 Korean 11	Café, restaurant, shop, bar.	b) 10 mins. c) 7 mins. from Ferry Terminal.
On Yang Nam San **Youth Hostel** 266-35, Onch'ŏn-ri, Onyang, Ch'ungch'ŏngnam-do Tel. (04 18) 2-57 75/6 (02)2 74-24 90	Double 10 Korean 56	Tennis, hairdresser's, café, restaurant, hot spring bath, shop.	
Kyŏngju **Youth Hostel** 145, 1, Kujŏng-dong <u>Kyŏngju</u> Kyŏngsangpuk-do Tel. Kyŏngju 2-99 91/6	Dorm. 47 Double 6 Twin 3 Suite 2 Korean 22	Café, restaurant, souvenir shop.	b) 15 mins. c) 20 mins. from Express Bus Terminal.

KOREA SOUTH

0   50 miles

Shinhung-sa
(Temple)   ● Sokch'o
Paektam-sa ●   ● Sorak-san
(Temple)   National Park
Ch'unch'ŏn ● Sangwon-sa ● Odae-san National Park
                    (Temple)
                   ● Wŏljŏng-sa
Pukhan   (Temple)
Kanghwa
Island
● Seoul
Inch'ŏn ●
          ● Suwon   ● Yongnung

                         Taebaek
                       ● Mountains

                 Songni-san   ● Andong
                 National Park   Chuwang-san
Magok-sa ● Kyeryong-san Popchu-sa   ● National Park
(Temple)   National Park (Temple)
Taechŏn ●
         ● Puyŏ   ● Taejon
         ● Nonsan
                                            ● P'ohang
                 Kaya-san Haein-sa
                 National Park ● (Temple) ● Taegu ● Kyŏngju
Chŏnju ●
      ● Kumsan-sa
        (Temple)
                 Chiri-san
                 ● National Park
      Hwaom-sa ●
        (Temple) ●
● Kwangju
  Songgwang-sa ● ● Sunch'ŏn
  (Temple)
Mokp'o ●   Namhae
              ● Yŏsu   Hallyŏ   Kojedo
                     Waterway   ● Pusan

Cheju-do   ● Cheju
Halla-san   ● Hwasun
National   Beach
Park   ● Sŏgwip'o

Useful Information

Currency

The standard monetary unit of Korea is the won (W). 1 won = 100 chon. The value of the won is based on the US$, so the rate of exchange varies according to the value of the dollar.

Currency Control

Korean currency is not convertible outside Korea. The import and export of Korean currency over the sum of 500,000 won is forbidden.

As for foreign currency, if more than US$ 5,000 (or an equivalent amount of another currency) is to be brought into the country, this must be registered at customs in a "Foreign Exchange Record".

It's advisable to keep receipts of all foreign exchange transactions. If, on leaving Korea, you have no such certificates of exchange, you may only convert unused won to the value of US$ 100. On production of proof of foreign exchange transactions, you will be able to buy more foreign currency. Such a transaction will be made only once.

Credit Cards, Traveller's Cheques

The following credit cards are accepted in larger hotels, department stores and some shops and restaurants, especially in Seoul: American Express, Diner's Club, VISA, Master Card and Carte Blanche.

Traveller's cheques issued by international banks can be cashed in larger hotels (especially in Seoul) as well as in banks.

Eurocheques will not be accepted by Korean banks.

Entry Formalities

All visitors to Korea (and this includes children under the age of ten) must have a valid passport with a photograph.

Visitors with a confirmed outbound ticket may stay for up to 15 days in Korea without a visa (this applies to U.S., Canadian and Australian citizens). For longer stays, visitors must apply for a visa at a Korean Embassy or Consulate before travelling to Korea (addresses, p. 221).

Citizens of the U.K. may stay for up to 60 days without a visa.

Visitors may not participate in remunerative activities.

Special regulations apply to members of the U.S. Armed Forces. Military personnel should check with their command.

There are two types of visa issued by Korean Embassies or Consulates. The type of visa depends upon the length of stay. A short-term visa is issued for stays of up to 90 days, a long-term visa for periods of longer than 90 days. Applications for the latter require an entry permit from the Ministry of Justice and a residence certificate from the relevant District Immigration Office. For more information, enquire at a Korean Embassy or Consulate.

Foreign visitors to Korea may visit Cheju Island for five days without a visa.

Vaccinations

There are no longer any vaccination requirements made of visitors to Korea. Some doctors do advise a prophylactic typhoid vaccination, however, and cholera innoculation. Ask your own doctor about health measures.

Customs

Most tourists arrive in Korea by plane. In Kimp'o Airport west of Seoul customs clearance is usually unproblematic and not over-strict, especially for tourist groups. When you enter the country you must make an oral declaration of the contents of your hand luggage. A customs declaration on official forms which are available at the customs desk must be filled out in the case of jewellery made of platinum, gold or silver, valuable watches and cameras, tobacco in large quantities, small arms, knives, swords and other weapons. **Duty free** items include all articles for personal use, such as clothes, toiletries or professional equipment. In addition, 400 cigarettes, 50 cigars, 250 g pipe tobacco, 100 g snuff or 100 g plug, and 2 bottles of (760 ccm) spirits may be imported free of tax. Souvenirs and presents may be exported duty free.

Customs duty must be paid on articles such as video cameras, movie cameras, projectors, on hunting weapons, and on cloth in quantities over and above 10 sq. metres.

There is an **import embargo** on all books, magazines, films, records and similar articles which could endanger national security or damage public interests.

Animals and animal products, as well as plants and vegetable products must be declared on arrival at the quarantine office. Quarantine certificates from the land of origin must be produced.

There is an **export ban** on national cultural property – items such as sculptures, paintings and antiques older than a hundred years.

If you want to export antiques you must obtain a certificate from the Cultural Property Preservation Bureau in Seoul. This is usually granted without too many formalities, and will often be procured for you by the antique dealer. Particularly valuable antiques are the exception here, of course.

Protected natural objects such as the eggs of wild birds, stuffed or preserved animals, wild plants and rare seeds of wild plants may not be exported without the permission of the Forestry Office.

The following quantities of **ginseng** may be exported duty free:
1. Red ginseng – root (600 g); slices (1,200 g); extract (900 g).
2. White ginseng – root (600 g).
3. Other ginseng products – powdered extract (450 g); powder (1,200 g); tea (3,000 g); capsules (1,200 g); tablets (1,200 g); liquid mixture (2 l).

Other articles which may be exported only in limited quantities:
cuttlefish – max. 20
ladies' wigs – max. 5
men's wigs – max. 3
false eyelashes – max. 200 pairs.

Health and Medical Care

As a general rule, standards of hygiene in Korea are high. So there is no need to worry about what you eat and drink in tourist hotels, better-class restaurants, etc. More care may be called for in rural areas where it might be as well to drink only bottled water, and avoid ice cream, ice cubes in drinks and unpeeled fruit.

In the case of illness, your hotel will be able to give you the name of a doctor who speaks English. Anyone taking medication on a regular basis should ensure that he has sufficient supplies with him.

In Seoul the following hospitals can be recommended to foreign visitors:
Korea National Medical Center
18–70 Ulchiro, 6-ka
Tel. 2 65–91 31
Seoul Natl. University Hospital
28 Yonkondong, Chongro-ku
Tel. 76 01–01 14
Severance Hospital
15 Sinchon-dong, Sodaemun-ku
Tel. 3 92–01 61
To cover the cost of possible treatment, it is a good idea to take out a travel health insurance.

Transport

Car Hire
For those wishing to go it alone in Korea, there are a number of car hire firms offering competitive rates around the country. For example:
Hertz Korean Rent-a-Car in Seoul
Tel. (02) 5 85-08 01/5
(02) 7 98-08 01/3
(02) 7 24-74 65
Yŏngnam Rent-a-Car in Pusan
Tel. (0 51) 44-50 00
Inch'ŏn Rent-a-Car in Inch'ŏn
Tel. (0 32) 8 83-76 21

Samjin Rent-a-Car in Kyŏngju
Tel. (05 61) 42-33 11
Cheju Rent-a-Car on Cheju Island
Tel. (0 64) 42-33 01/5

For a comprehensive list, apply to any office of the Korean National Tourism Corporation (addresses below).

Rates for a 24-hour period vary between W 38,000 and W 50,000. Prices include a 10% tax and unlimited mileage. Drivers must be over 21 years of age and in possession of a passport and international licence.

If you wish to rent a car with a driver, you should expect to pay between W 49,000 and W 75,000 per day.

Taxis
There are three types of taxi in Korea: regular taxis, call taxis and hotel taxis.

In Seoul there are more than 30 private taxi firms with more than 10,000 regular taxis.

The basic charge in major cities is W 600 for up to 2 kilometres, then W 50 per 400 m. Between midnight and 4 am there is a surcharge of 20%. In Seoul a nominal charge is made for time lost in slow-moving traffic. Taxi stands are to be found at regular intervals in city centres; taxis may also be hailed on the streets.

The approximately 2,000 taxis which are on call in Seoul make a basic charge of W 1,000 for the first 2 kilometres and then W 100 for every 400 m after that. Hotels will have the telephone numbers of call taxis; such taxis can, in addition, be hailed on the street.

The so-called "Hotel Taxis" are higher-class taxis most often found near major hotels. Besides the usual meter system of payment, these taxis can be hired per hour (W 7,000) or per day (W 65,000).

Airport Bus

Two bus lines link Kimp'o Airport with Seoul town centre. One goes from the airport to the Sheraton Walker Hill Hotel, stopping at hotels such as the Seoul Garden, the Koreana and the Plaza on the way. The second line runs between the airport and Chamsil with stops at the Palace Hotel, Express Bus Terminal, Riverside Hotel, Nam Seoul Hotel, Korea Exhibition Centre, and the Seoul Sports Complex. The airport bus leaves Kimp'o Airport every 10 minutes from 5.30 am until 9.30 pm. The fare is W 500.

Airport buses also link Kimhae International Airport in the southeast with Pusan and even with Pomun Lake Resort (via Kyŏngju) and Cheju International Airport with Cheju via Shinjeju (New Cheju).

City Buses

All Korean towns and cities have very good bus services.

Fares are paid either with tokens (available at most shops) or with ready money. The basic fare is W 120 if you pay with tokens, W 130 otherwise. You must buy a new ticket when you change buses. The bus driver usually collects the fare so, if paying with cash, try to have the exact fare ready to drop into the transparent box as you get on.

You'll find that buses are very crowded, especially during the rush hour, and that everything happens very quickly. A taxi is probably a safer bet for anyone who is unsure of his surroundings! In any case, if several people are travelling together, a taxi could well be better value.

Routes and departure times are not posted at individual bus stops. A number system is used to indicate bus routes.

Normal buses are blue and beige. Green and beige buses make fewer stops, guarantee a seat – and are more expensive.

Subway

There are four lines on Seoul's underground railway at the moment. With a total length of over 110 km, the system is the 7th largest in the world and is the main means of transport in the city. The four lines are colour-coded and the stations are marked with numbers and with names in han'gŭl and Latin script. Fares are inexpensive (Zone 1: W 200, Zone 2: W 300); there are ticket machines or windows from which one can buy tickets.

The first line of the Pusan subway is also now in operation.

Electricity

Originally 100 volt, which is sufficient and safe for 110 volt electrical appliances. It is, however, gradually being converted to 220 volt power; that is why you find two different sockets in many hotels, one for 110 volt/60 Hz the other for 220 volt/

60 Hz. It is advisable to carry an adapter.

Photography
It is forbidden to photograph military installations, airports or bridges. In addition, you may not take photographs from the top of high buildings.

Civil Defence Alert Drills
In the cities there are civil defence alert drills lasting a maximum 30 minutes on the 15th of every month, or if this is a Sunday, on the day before or the day after. Notice of them is always given beforehand in the English language newspapers. If you are in a private room at the time, put out the lights and stay there until the third tone of the siren. If you are in the street, the best thing to do is follow the other pedestrians inside a building or into the subway.

Shopping
The tourist will find a great selection of popular souvenirs on sale in Korea. It is difficult to choose between pottery, lacquerware, silk, amethysts, smoky topazes, dolls, embroidery, brass, masks, fans, paper kites and even wigs and false eyelashes (!) – and these are only a few of the many possibilities. One item which is particularly famous and very popular is, of course, ginseng, which is said to have great invigorating properties.

You can also buy other articles, (electrical appliances, antiques, etc.) at reasonable prices in Korea. The latter however – and some other Korean products – come under customs export regulations (see section on customs).

In the cities there are department stores, markets and many small souvenir shops. One of the most popular shopping districts in Seoul is Myong-dong. Itaewon (approx. 20 minutes from the city centre) is famous for its antique shops. Insa-dong in the centre of town also specializes in antiques.

At Seoul's main markets at the East Gate and at the South Gate you can get to know a typical Korean market; and here they like bartering. The markets are open every day except public holidays.

Please note that, in accordance with the Convention on International Trade in Endangered Species of Wild Fauna and Flora (**CITES**), you should not buy any souvenirs that are made of wild animals or parts of them, nor of wild plants. By refraining from buying such "souvenirs", you are making an important contribution to the conservation of endangered species of animals and plants.

Opening Hours

Shops: There are no fixed opening hours, but the big department stores are usually open between 10.30 am and 7.30 pm (also on Sundays, but with one closing day during the week). Smaller shops usually open at 9 am and close at 7 pm or even later. Food shops and markets open very early every day and do not close till late evening.

Banks: Monday to Friday from 9.30 am to 4.30 pm; on Saturday from 9.30 am to 1.30 pm.

Government Offices: 9 am to 5 pm from Monday to Friday.

Post Offices: Monday to Friday from 9 am to 5 pm, Saturday from 9 am to 1 pm.

Foreign Embassies, etc.: Monday to Friday from 9 am to 5 pm.

Tipping

Although there is no tradition of tipping in Korea, the growth of tourism is bringing changes here.

Strictly-speaking, it is not necessary to tip taxi drivers unless they help with luggage, and services in restaurants and hotels are covered by a 10% service charge. The safest bet, however, is to judge the situation for yourself and acknowledge good service with between W 500 and W 1,000; porters receive around W 200 per piece of luggage, taxi drivers about 5% of the fare.

Clothing

Korea is on a line with southern Spain, California…. Spring, from March to May, is warm if breezy; summer, June to August, is hot and humid; in autumn, September to November, conditions are mild and pleasant, and ideal for travelling; in winter Korea is subject to the phenomenal three cold days followed by four warm ones. So, you'll rarely need more than lightweight cotton clothes supplemented by a warmer jacket and pullover.

In some luxury hotels (and for official functions) formal dress will be required of both sexes.

On the (few) bathing beaches of the east and southeast coast, topless bathing and nudism are frowned upon.

Laundries

There are laundries everywhere which also do small repairs. Dry-cleaning takes c. 2 days, ironing or pressing 1 hour. You pay W 4,000 to have a suit cleaned, W 1,000 to have it ironed. Most hotels also have a laundry service.

Postal Services, Telephone

Telegrams can be sent (in English) by telephone; the number to call is 115. Give your own telephone number, the kind of telegram you wish to send (ordinary, urgent or lettergram), the address of the recipient and then the text. Alternatively you can go in person to a Korean International Telecommunications Office (KIT).

For ordinary telegrams, rates per word are as follows: Australia W 660, Canada W 430, U.K. W 610, U.S.A. W 350.

Stamps for **inland mail** can be bought at larger hotels, in some shops and at post offices. **Overseas mail** can only be sent from post offices. A postcard to Europe or North America costs W 350, an airmail letter (max. 10 g) W 440; a postcard to Australia costs W 310, an airmail letter W 400.

Local telephone calls can be made from public telephones; you'll need two 10 won coins to make a three-minute call.

In larger hotels and post offices you'll find yellow telephones from which you can make **long-distance calls;** 10 won and 100 won coins are used here.

For **international calls** you can either dial direct (International Subscriber Dialling) or through the operator. For further details, call 1030 in Seoul, 117 in other cities.

Important Telephone Numbers
Police: 112
Fire Service: 119

Time Difference
Korea is at G.M.T. + 9 hours.

Tourist Information

Apply to any of the information offices of the Korea National Tourism Corporation (KNTC).

KNTC Head Office
10, Ta-dong, Chung-gu
C.P.O. Box 903
Seoul
Korea
Tel. (02)7 57-60 30, 60 40
Telex: KOTOUR K28 555

You will find tourist information offices dotted around the Korean capital – in the railway and bus stations, at the south and east gates, in Myŏngdong district, for example.

Airport Information Offices

Kimp'o Airport:
Airport Terminal Building,
Kimp'o International Airport,
Seoul
Tel. (02) 6 65-00 86/00 88

Kimhae Airport:
218 Taejo, 2-dong, Puk-gu,
Pusan
Tel. (0 51) 98-11 00

Cheju Airport:
2096 Yongdam-dong, 3-do,
Cheju
Tel. (0 64) 42-00 32

Pusan Tourist Information
Railway Station,
Tel. (0 51) 4 63-49 38
Pukway Ferry Terminal,
Tel. (0 51) 4 63 31 61

Kyŏngju Tourist Information
Railway Station,
Tel. (05 61) 2-38 43
Kyŏngju Express Bus Terminal,
Tel. (05 61) 2-92 89
Pulguk Temple,
Tel. (05 61) 2-47 47

If visitors to Korea have any kind of complaint, they should call:
Seoul (02) 7 35-01 01

KNTC Overseas Offices

The KNTC has offices all around the world. For example:

Vogue House, 2nd Floor
1, Hanover Square
London, W1R 9RD
Tel. (01) 4 08 15 91 or 4 09 21 00

230 North Michigan Avenue
Suite 1500
Chicago, Illinois 60601
Tel. (3 12) 3 46 66 60/1

510 West Sixth Street
Suite 323

Los Angeles, Calif. 90014-1395
Tel. (2 13) 6 23 12 26/7

Korea Center Building
460 Park Avenue, Suite 400
New York, N.Y. 10022
Tel. (2 12) 6 88 75 43/4

Suite 2101, Tower Building
Australia Square, George St.
Sydney 2000
Tel. (02) 27 41 32/3

Korean Representation Abroad

In case of enquiries regarding visas,
etc., apply to a Korean Embassy or
Consulate:

Korean Embassy
4 Palace Gate
London W8 5NF
Tel. (01) 5 81-02 47/9 or 5 81-02 50

Korean Embassy
2320 Massachusetts Avenue N.W.
Washington D.C. 20008
Tel. (2 02) 9 39-56 00/2

Korean Embassy
85 Albert Street, 10th Floor
Ottawa, Ontario K1P 6A4
Tel. (6 13) 2 32-17 15, 17 16, 17 17

Korean Embassy
113 Empire Circuit
Yarralumla
Canberra, A.C.T. 2600
Tel. (0 62) 73 30 44 or 73 39 56
or 73 35 86

Korean Embassy
Plimmer City Centre, 12th Floor
Plimmer Steps

Wellington
Tel. 7 39-0 73/4

Diplomatic Representation

Any tourist office or your travel
agent should be able to give you the
address of your embassy or consulate in the country you are visiting.
We would advise you to keep the
address and phone number handy
in case of loss or damage to personal effects, or should you have
any other problems.

Embassy of the U.K.
4, Chóng-dong, Chung-ku
Seoul
Tel. (02) 7 35-73 41/3,
(02) 7 20-45 66

Embassy of the U.S.A.
82, Sejong-ro, Chongno-ku
Seoul
Tel. (02) 7 32-26 01/19

Canadian Embassy
10th Floor, Kolon Building
45 Mugyo-dong, Chung-ku
Seoul
Tel. (02) 7 76-40 62/8 or 89 94

Australian Embassy
5th, 6th and 7th Floors
Salvation Army Building
58-1 I-ka, Sinmun-ro, Chongno-ku
Seoul
Tel. (02) 7 30-64 90/5

New Zealand Embassy
Korean Publishers Building
105-2 Sagan-dong, Chongno-ku
Seoul
Tel. (02) 7 20-42 55 or 7 30-77 94

Further Reading

A Handbook of Korea. Korean Overseas Information Service, Ministry of Culture and Information, Seoul, 1978.

Kim, Yung-chung: Women of Korea. A History from Ancient Times to 1945, Ewha Woman's University Press, Seoul, 1979.

Korea: Its People and Culture. Hawkon-sa Ltd., Seoul, 1970.

Bureau of Cultural Properties, ed.: The Arts of Ancient Korea, Kwang Myong Publishing Co., 1974.

Hall, Basil: Account of a Voyage of Discovery to the West Coast of Corea and the Great Loo-Choo Island, London, John Murray, 1818.

Carpenter, Frances: Tales of a Korean Grandmother, Seoul, Royal Asiatic Society, 1973.

McCann, David R.: An Anthology of Korean Literature, Ithaca, New York: China-Japan Programm Cornell University, 1977

McCune, E.: The Arts of Korea, an Illustrated History, Charles Tuttle Co. Inc., 1962.

Lee, Hye-gu: An Introduction to Korean Music and Dance, Royal Asiatic Society, 1977.

Kim, Che-won and St. Gompertz, G. M.: The Ceramic Art of Korea, Faber and Faber, 1961.

Rees, David: Korea, the Limited War, New York, St. Martin's Press, 1964.

Chee, Sang-su: Annual Customs of Korea, Korea Book Publishing Co., 1960.

Korea Quarterly. Quarterly. Korea Quarterly Publications.

Lee, Peter H., editor: Flowers of Fire – Twentieth-Century Korean Stories, Honolulu, University Press of Hawaii, 1974.

Korea

The following denominations are currently in use:

Notes: 500, 1,000, 5,000 and 10,000 won

Coins: 1, 5, 10, 50, 100 and 500 won

Please note:
Every effort was made to ensure that the information given was correct at the time of publication.

However, as it is not possible for any travel guide to keep abreast of all changes regarding passport formalities, rates of exchange, prices, etc., you are advised to contact the appropriate authorities (embassy, bank, tourist office ...) when planning your holiday.

The publishers would be pleased to hear about any omissions or errors.

Places of Interest

Anap Pond	198	Hwaom Temple	208
Andong	192	Hyang-song Temple	185
Ch'ŏmsŏngdae	198	Hyŏpchae Cave	212
Ch'unch'ŏn	184	Inch'ŏn	172
Ch'angdok Palace	180	Kanghwa	173
Ch'anggyŏnggung	180	Kangnung	187
Cheju	210	Kap Temple	190
Chiri-san National Park	208	Kayasan National Park	200
Chŏngbang Waterfall	213	Kyejoam	185
Chŏngjiyŏn Waterfall	213	Koje-do	202
Chŏnjeyŏn Waterfall	212	Kumsan-sa	207
Chŏnju	206	Kwaenung Tomb	197
Chogye Temple	182	Kwanch'ok-sa	191
Chŏnbuldong Valley	186	Kwangju	208
Chungmun	212	Kyeryŏng-san	190
Churae-am Rock	189	Kyŏngbok Palace	176
Chuwang-san National Park	192	Kyŏngju	61, 195
Haein Temple	200	Magok Temple	190
Haegumgang	202	Maitreya Statue	189
Hahoe	192	Manjang Cave	213
Hak	203	Moak-san Provincial Park	207
Halla-san (Mt.)	210	Mokp'o	209
Hallyŏsudo National Park	202	Myŏngdong	183
Hamdŏk	213	Naksan Temple	186
Hansan	202	Namdaemun (South Gate)	176
Hundulbawi	185	Namhae	203

Namhan Castle _____ 173

Namsan _____ 175

Nonsan _____ 191

Noryang _____ 203

Odae-san National Park ____ 187

Odong _____ 203

Paektam Temple _____ 186

P'aldang Dam _____ 173

Panmunjom _____ 173

Panwŏlsŏng Castle _____ 198

Piryŏng Waterfall _____ 186

Pŏpchu Temple _____ 187

Pŏsŏkjŏng Pavilion _____ 198

P'ohang _____ 192

Pomun Lake Resort _____ 200

Pukhangang _____ 173

Pulguk Temple _____ 195

Punhwangsa Pagoda _____ 197

Pusan _____ 72, 203

Puyŏ _____ 191

Sajik Park _____ 181

Samch'ŏnp'o _____ 203

Samgaksan _____ 175

Sanbang-gul Cave Temple __ 212

Sangwon Temple _____ 187

Sanjong-hosu _____ 173

Seoul _____ 57, 175

Shin Cheju _____ 211

Shinhung Temple _____ 185

Silluk Temple _____ 173

Sŏgwip'o _____ 212

Sŏngsan _____ 213

Sokch'o _____ 186

Sŏkkuram Grotto _____ 64, 196

Songdo _____ 172

Songgwang Temple _____ 209

Songni-san National Park ___ 187

Sorak-san National Park ____ 185

Suwŏn _____ 173

T'aebaek Mountains _____ 187

Taech'on _____ 191

Taegu _____ 193

Taejŏn _____ 189

Talsŏng Park _____ 194

Toksu Palace _____ 175

Tongdaemun (East Gate) ___ 180

Tongdo Temple _____ 201

Tongnimmun _____ 181

Towangsong Waterfall _____ 186

Tumuli Park _____ 198

Wŏljŏng Temple _____ 187

Yŏngdok _____ 192

Yŏsu _____ 203

Yoi-do _____ 183

Yonan _____ 172

Yongdusan _____ 205

Yongnung Tomb _____ 173

Contents

Photographs

Impressions in Pictures 6
Captions 50

Impressions

The Olympic Games – Small
Country with Big Plans 52
☐ Five Rings for the Tiger 54
Where is the King? 56
Seoul – Young Moloch with
an Ancient Face 57
Kyŏngju – The Pearl Still
Shines 61
Race to the Buddha in the
Grotto 64
Butterflies in the Rice Field 67
Spring Breeze Serves Tea –
Kisaeng: More Than Just
Beauty 68
Pusan – Window to Japan 72
The Admiral and the Turtle
Ships 75
Cards are Trumps 77
Shoes off in Korea House 79
And to close, a fairy tale ... 80

Information

History 81
Map: The Early Three
Kingdoms 82
History at a Glance 89
Geography and Regional
Divisions 90
☐ Korea at a Glance 92
Climate 94
Climatic Table 95
Fauna and Flora 96
Hanyak – Traditional Medicine 100
Ginseng – the Anthropo-
morphic Root 102
Industrial Expansion 104

Saemaul Undong – Korea's
Green Revolution 106
Transport 107
On Korea's Expressways 108
The Korean Town 110
The Korean Village 112
Man and Society 114
☐ Perfect Harmony – Not
Showing the Flag? 116
☐ Travelling Folk 123
The Role of Women 125
Education 128
Language and Writing 129
Religion 131
☐ The Teaching of Lord
Buddha 134
Buddhist Temples 140
☐ Light in the Darkness 142
Art 143
Celadon, Lovely as Jade 152
Architecture 156
Traditional Music and Dance 158
Food and Drink 162
Restaurants in Seoul 166
A Few Words of Korean 169

Regional Section

Kyŏnggi-do 172
Seoul 175
City Plan Seoul 178
Kangwŏn-do 184
Ch'ungch'ŏngpuk-do 187
Ch'ungch'ŏngnam-do 189
Kyŏngsangpuk-do 192
Map Kyŏngju and Vicinity 196
City Plan Downtown Kyŏngju 199
Kyŏngsangnam-do 200
City Plan Downtown Pusan 204
Chŏllapuk-do 206
Chŏllanam-do 208
Cheju-do 209
City Plan Cheju 210
City Plan Shincheju 212
General Map Korea (South) 238
Useful Information 239

Hildebrand's Travel Guides

Vol. 1 Sri Lanka (Ceylon)
Professor Manfred Domrös and
Rosemarie Noack

Vol. 3 India, Nepal
Klaus Wolff

Vol. 4 Thailand, Burma
Dr. Dieter Rumpf

Vol. 5 Malaysia, Singapore*
Kurt Goetz Huehn

Vol. 6 Indonesia
Kurt Goetz Huehn

Vol. 7 Philippines*
Dr. Dieter Rumpf
Contributions by Dr. Gerhard Beese
and Wolfgang Freihen

Vol. 9 Taiwan
Professor Peter Thiele

Vol. 10 Australia
Michael Schweizer and
Heinrich von Bristow

Vol. 11 Kenya
Reinhard Künkel and
Nana Claudia Nenzel
Contributions by
Dr. Arnd Wünschmann,
Dr. Angelika Tunis and
Wolfgang Freihen

Vol. 13 Jamaica
Tino Greif and Dieter Jakobs

Vol. 14 Hispaniola (Haiti, Dominican Republic)
Tino Greif and Dr. Gerhard Beese
Contribution by Wolfgang Freihen

Vol. 15 Seychelles
Christine Hedegaard and
Clausjürgen Eicke
Contributions by Wolfgang Debelius

Vol. 16 South Africa
Peter Gerisch and Clausjürgen Eicke
Contributions by Hella Tarara

Vol. 17 Mauritius
Clausjürgen Eicke
Contributions by Peter Gerisch,
Joachim Laux and Frank Siegfried

Vol. 18 China
Manfred Morgenstern

Vol. 19 Japan
Dr. Norbert Hormuth

Vol. 21 Mexico
Matthias von Debschitz and
Dr. Wolfgang Thieme
Contributions by Werner Schmidt,
Rudolf Wicker, Dr. Gerhard Beese,
Hans-Horst Skupy, Ortrun Egelkraut,
Dr. Elizabeth Siefer, Robert Valerio

Vol. 24 Korea
Dr. Dieter Rumpf and
Professor Peter Thiele

Vol. 25 New Zealand
Robert Sowman and
Johannes Schultz-Tesmar

Vol. 26 France*
Uwe Anhäuser
Contribution by Wolfgang Freihen

* in print

Hildebrand's Travel Maps

1. Balearic Islands Majorca
   1:185,000, Minorca,
   Ibiza, Formentera
   1:125,000

2. Tenerife 1:100,000,
   La Palma, Gomera,
   Hierro 1:190,000

3. Canary Islands
   Gran Canaria 1:100,000,
   Fuerteventura, Lanzarote
   1:190,000

4. Spanish Coast I
   Costa Brava, Costa
   Blanca 1:900,000,
   General Map 1:2,500,000

5. Spanish Coast II
   Costa del Sol, Costa
   de la Luz 1:900,000,
   General Map 1:2,500,000

6. Algarve 1:100,000,
   Costa do Estoril
   1:400,000

7. Gulf of Naples
   1:200,000,
   Ischia 1:35,000,
   Capri 1:28,000

8. Sardinia 1:200,000

*9. Sicily 1:200,000
   Lipari (Aeolian) Islands
   1:30,000

11. Yugoslavian Coast I
    Istria – Dalmatia
    1:400,000
    General Map 1:2,000,000

12. Yugoslavian Coast II
    Southern Dalmatia –
    Montenegro 1:400,000
    General Map 1:2,000,000

13. Crete 1:200,000

15. Corsica 1:200,000

16. Cyprus 1:350,000

17. Israel 1:360,000

18. Egypt 1:1,500,000

19. Tunisia 1:900,000

20. Morocco 1:900,000

21. New Zealand
    1:2,000,000

22. Sri Lanka (Ceylon),
    Maldive Islands
    1:750,000

23. Jamaica 1:345,000
    Caribbean 1:4,840,000

24. United States,
    Southern Canada
    1:6,400,000

25. India 1:4,255,000

26. Thailand, Burma,
    Malaysia 1:2,800,000,
    Singapore 1:139,000

27. Western Indonesia
    1:12,700,000,
    Sumatra 1:3,570,000,
    Java 1:1,887,000,
    Bali 1:597,000,
    Celebes 1:3,226,000

28. Hong Kong 1:116,000,
    Macao 1:36,000

29. Taiwan 1:700,000

30. Philippines 1:2,860,000

31. Australia 1:5,315,000

32. South Africa
    1:3,360,000

33. Seychelles General Map
    1:6,000,000,
    Mahé 1:96,000,
    Praslin 1:65,000,
    La Digue 1:52,000,
    Silhouette 1:84,000,
    Frégate 1:25,000

34. Hispaniola (Haiti,
    Dominican Republic)
    1:816,000

35. Soviet Union General
    Map 1:15,700,000,
    Western Soviet Union
    1:9,750,000,
    Black Sea Coast
    1:3,500,000

*37. Madeira

38. Mauritius 1:125,000

39. Malta 1:38,000

40. Majorca 1:125,000,
    Cabrera 1:75,000

41. Turkey 1:1,655,000

42. Cuba 1:1,100,000

43. Mexico 1:3,000,000

44. Korea 1:800,000

45. Japan 1:1,600,000

46. China 1:5,400,000

47. United States
    The West 1:3,500,000

48. United States
    The East 1:3,500,000

49. East Africa 1:2,700,000

50. Greece: Peloponnese,
    Southern Mainland,
    1:400,000

51. Europe 1:2,000,000
    Central Europe
    1:2,000,000
    Southern Europe
    1:2,000,000

52. Portugal 1:500,000

53. Puerto Rico,
    Virgin Islands, St. Croix
    1:294,000

54. The Caribbean
    Guadeloupe 1:165,000
    Martinique 1:125,000
    St. Lucia 1:180,000
    St. Martin 1:105,000
    Barthélemy 1:60,000
    Dominica 1:175,000
    General Map 1:5,000,000

55. Réunion 1:127,000

56. Czechoslovakia
    1:700,000

57. Hungary 1:600,000

59. United States, Southern
    Canada 1:3,500,000

*in print

Personal Notes